WIMBLEDON

100 Years of Men's Singles

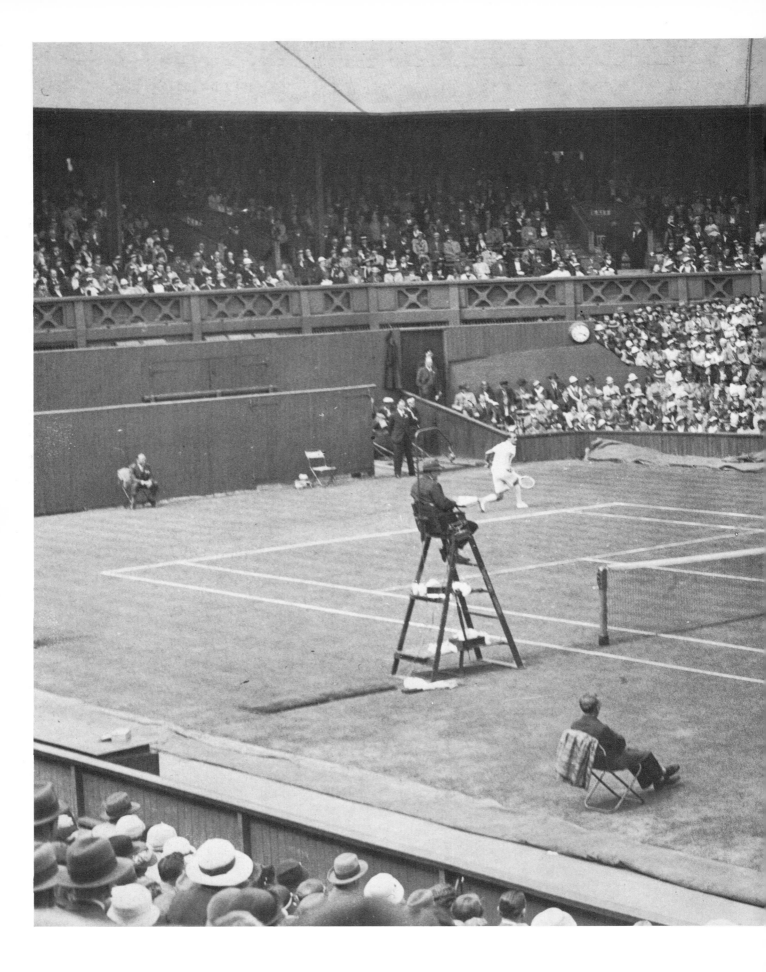

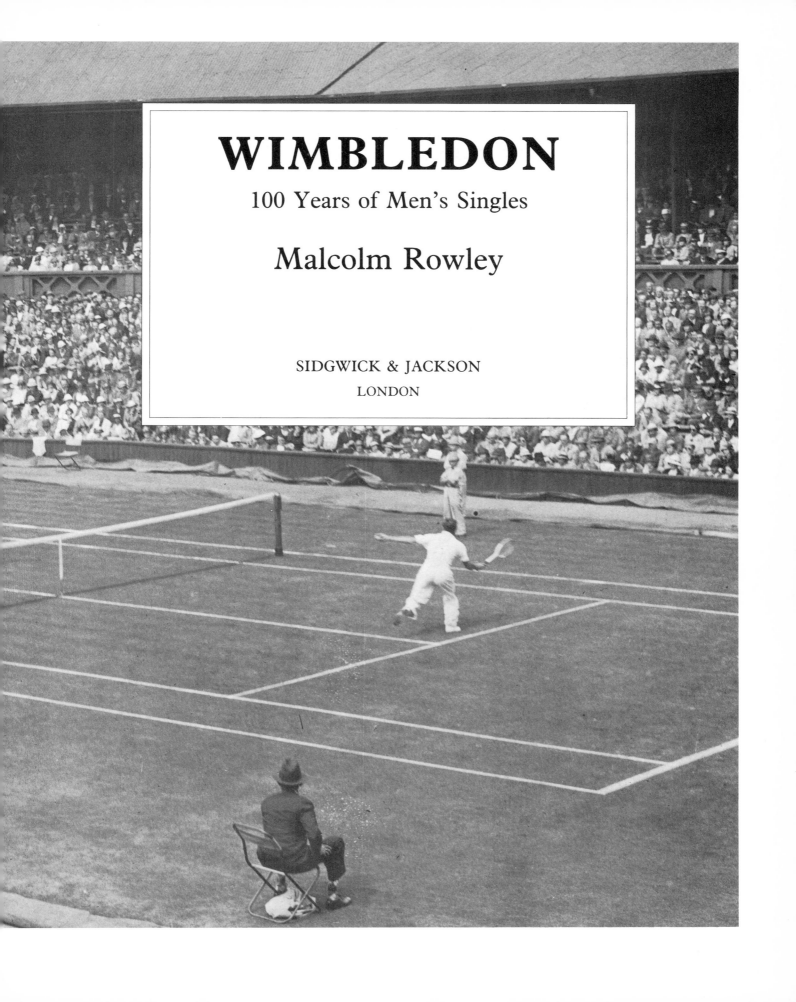

WIMBLEDON

100 Years of Men's Singles

Malcolm Rowley

SIDGWICK & JACKSON

LONDON

First published in Great Britain in 1986 by Sidgwick & Jackson Limited
Text copyright © Malcolm Rowley 1986
Newspaper reports copyright © named newspapers

Designed by Roger Lightfoot

ISBN 0 283 99223 9

Printed in Great Britain by
R J Acford, Industrial Estate, Chichester, Sussex
for Sidgwick and Jackson Limited
1 Tavistock Chambers, Bloomsbury Way
London WC1A 2SG

Picture Acknowledgements

Our grateful thanks to the Wimbledon Museum and to Tommy Hindley for
permission to reproduce the pictures on the following pages:
Wimbledon Museum: pages 2-3, 6, 8, 9, 11 (left and right), 15, 16, 18, 19, 20,
    24, 26, 27, 31, 32, 33, 35, 38, 39, 40, 50, 52, 59, 68, 70, 81, 87
Tommy Hindley: pages 7, 36, 41, 44, 46, 57, 58, 70, 99, 103, 105, 112, 115, 119
    (left and right)

Contents

Acknowledgements

Spencer Gore (above). The first Wimbledon men's singles champion in 1877, Gore's historic victory was watched by a crowd of approximately two hundred

Boris Becker (far right). The winner of the ninety-ninth Wimbledon men's singles final in 1985. An estimated world-wide television audience of 250 million watched him become the youngest-ever men's singles champion

'Lawn tennis will never rank among our great games, and anybody who has played cricket or rackets will soon be choked off by the monotony of the sport.'

This is how Spencer Gore worded his reaction to the sport of lawn tennis shortly after he became the inaugural winner of the Wimbledon men's singles title in 1877. But after ninety-nine men's Championships spanning 108 years the status of the sport has changed so much that the Wimbledon fortnight is now among the most important events in the world's sporting calendar.

From Spencer Gore's victory to Boris Becker's in 1985 there have been fifty-three men's champions. The following pages trace the history of their successes in celebration of the centenary of the Wimbledon men's singles Championship.

The publishers decided that the most interesting way to present a record of the finals would be through newspaper coverage. This obviously provides a large amount of otherwise forgotten detail. In the early years, however, the national press viewed the new tennis tournament in much the same way as Gore did, only printing the bare results. For this reason I have selected reports from *The Field* magazine from 1877 to 1883 – the seven years in which it provided the winner with the 25-guinea Challenge Cup. As well as giving the Championships extensive coverage, as all the national newspapers do now, the weekly publication was also involved in establishing the new sport of lawn tennis and in the organization of the first Wimbledon Championship.

I would like to thank the following (existing) newspapers for permission to reproduce their final match reports and pictures: Brisbane *Courier Mail, Chicago Tribune, Daily Express, Daily Mail, Daily Mirror, The Daily Telegraph, The Field, The Guardian, Melbourne Herald, News of the World, The New York Times, The Observer, The Sporting Life, The Sun, Sunday Express, Sunday Mirror, Sunday People, Sunday Telegraph, The Sunday Times, The Sydney Morning Herald, The Times* and *Washington Post.*

I would also like to thank photographer Tommy Hindley for his meticulous care in making the most of some very old volumes. All the cuttings were researched at the British Newspaper Library in Colindale, North London, and the co-operation of the staff was, as always, very much appreciated.

In addition, the book would not have been possible but for the existence of the Kenneth Ritchie Library at the excellent Wimbledon Museum and, in particular, for the help of the curator Valerie Warren and librarian Alan Little. Their records of the Championships are extensive and include hundreds of books and photographs.

Unfortunately some of the newspaper cuttings are damaged through age and three have had to be reset but I am sure they will prove of interest to any sporting buff.

Major Wingfield. His pioneer efforts in the development of lawn tennis were rewarded when he received £200 and a gold watch from a public collection made in his honour

1 | The Early Years

1877–80

Once the rules of the game of lawn tennis had been drawn up, the Wimbledon Championships soon attracted large crowds. Rev. John Hartley won two of the first four men's singles titles.

The first Wimbledon singles Championship. Only the singles court was marked out when the Championship began in 1877. Doubles were not introduced until 1884

On 26 May 1877, the committee of the All England Croquet and Lawn Tennis Club decided to stage a lawn tennis meeting for amateurs later that summer. The motion was proposed by J.H. Walsh, who was one of the founder members of the All England Club in 1868, and the editor of *The Field* magazine. He persuaded the proprietors of his journal to present a silver Challenge Cup worth 25 guineas, in readiness for the winner of the men's singles event.

On 9 June 1877, a letter (see below) appeared in *The Field* to announce the birth of the Wimbledon men's singles Championship – the first lawn tennis tournament in the world.

Two years earlier Henry Jones, also a member of the All England Club and a writer for *The Field*, had suggested that part of the club's croquet grounds be set aside for the new game of lawn tennis. The four-acre site at Worple Road, Wimbledon, was adjacent to the London and South Western railway, just over a mile from the courts that stage today's Championships. The All England Club agreed to Jones' proposal and allowed him £25 for the purchase of equipment. Within a short time lawn tennis proved to be more popular with members than croquet and, the club being short of money, the suggested lawn tennis Championship was viewed as a potential fund-raiser as well as a new and interesting sporting fixture.

However, before this inaugural event could be held, a sub-committee had to be formed to set out the rules of the new sport. This was comprised of Henry Jones (tournament referee), C.G. Heathcote and Julian Marshall. Jones was an expert on all sports and one of the leading authorities in the country on card games, especially whist. Both Heathcote and Marshall were 'real tennis' enthusiasts.

Lawn tennis had its roots in the ancient game of real tennis. In the sixteenth century Henry VIII had claimed to be the 'tennis champion of England', but its origins go back a further two centuries to a game played by the kings of France. Also known as 'royal' or 'court tennis', it is an indoor racket game played over a net, with the ball also being hit around the walls.

In 1874 Major Walter Clopton Wingfield, a magistrate, patented a game called Sphairistike.

Wingfield, a cavalry major who was keen on all racket and ball sports, described his innovation as a form of real tennis that could be played outdoors on an hourglass-shaped court using a net but no walls. He produced sets to accompany his game of two pear-shaped rackets, one net, twelve balls and a book of rules; these cost 16 guineas. He chose the name 'Sphairistike' – from the Greek words meaning 'sphere' and 'stick' – in the hope that it would impress the wealthy, but it was shortened to 'Spiky' by those who didn't like the game.

Although Sphairistike was not widely pursued, the idea of playing tennis in the open was proving popular and another major – called Harry Gem – put forward some alternative rules. He marked out a tennis court on a lawn at the Manor House Hotel, Leamington Spa, in 1872; a plaque in the grounds claims that the first lawn tennis club in the world was formed there that year. He preferred a rectangular court and, whereas Major Wingfield had used rackets scoring, Major Gem used the real tennis scoring system.

The main difference between the two systems is this: in rackets players can only score a point on their serve and the first to 15 wins the set; in real tennis the players take turns to serve a game of the best of seven points and the first to six games wins the set.

Jones' committee had many subjects to consider and, in an attempt to establish standard rules for lawn tennis, they arranged a meeting with the Marylebone Cricket Club which was the governing body of real tennis and rackets. Following the meeting, however, the MCC decided to keep the sport of lawn tennis flexible and adopt Major Wingfield's hourglass-shaped court (78 ft long, 30 ft wide at the base and 24 ft in the middle). They agreed once again with Major Wingfield's patent to keep the rackets scoring system, but rejected a proposal that the centre net should be raised from a height of 4 ft in the middle to 7 ft! Finally, they stated that all players could alter these guidelines to suit their own abilities!

Obviously the response from the MCC was not positive or precise

---

LAWN TENNIS CHAMPIONSHIP.

The All England Croquet and Lawn Tennis Club, Wimbledon, propose to hold a lawn tennis meeting, open to all amateurs, on Monday, July 9, and following days; entrance £1. 1s. Names and addresses of competitors to be forwarded to the Hon. Sec. A.E.C. and L.T.C., 9, The Cedars, Putney, before Saturday, July 7, or on that day before 2.15 p.m. at the club ground, Wimbledon. Two prizes will be given—one gold champion prize to the winner, one silver to the second player. The value of the prizes will depend on the number of entries, and will be declared before the draw; but in no case will they be less than the amount of the entrance money, and if there are ten and less than sixteen entries, they will be made up to £10. 10s. and £5. 5s. respectively.

Gentlemen on entering and paying their entrance fee will receive a ticket of admission, entitling them to practise on the club ground up to the date of the matches. There are twelve separate lawns; but on Saturday afternoons, and during the croquet championship week, which immediately precedes the date fixed for the lawn tennis championship, only those lawns will be available for practice which are not required by croquet players. Players must provide their own rackets, and must wear shoes without heels. The club will provide balls for the matches. Balls, in all respects similar to those that will be used in the matches, may be obtained for practice by applying personally to the gardener, All England Croquet and Lawn Tennis Club, Wimbledon, at the rate of 12s. per dozen balls.

The draw will take place at the Pavilion, on the club ground, on Saturday, July 7, at 2.15 p.m. punctually. Competitors have a right, by themselves, or deputies to be present. It will be conducted in accordance with the All England Regulations for the Management of Prize Meetings, to be obtained of Horace Cox, 346, Strand; price 6d.

A programme will shortly be issued containing further details and a statement of the rules that will be adopted. The programme will be forwarded on application to the Hon. Sec., 9, The Cedars, Putney, inclosing a stamped directed envelope.

enough to run an open tournament and Messrs Jones, Heathcote and Marshall set about making their own Championship rules. First they established that the court be rectangular, measuring 78 by 27 ft. The net was to be 5 ft high at the posts and 3 ft 3 in. at the centre. A serve that touched the net and dropped into the box was to be allowed (and not called a 'let'), and the service line was to be 26 ft from the net (as opposed to 21 ft now).

The next proposition was to revise the scoring. Jones felt that Major Wingfield's rackets system needed to be made more exciting and he preferred the scoring used in real tennis.

For the 1877 Championships the rules stated (without MCC backing) that each match should consist of five sets. Each set would be won by the first player to win six games, except in the Championship final when two clear games advantage were needed. The players were to take turns to serve a game, which was to be the best of seven points. For his first point a player would score 15, for his second 30, for his third 40, and game for the fourth. (These numbers followed the quarters of a clock face and '40' was only used as an abbreviation for '45'.) Should both players win three points each (40-40) that would be called 'deuce'; two consecutive points would then have to be won for the game.

The terms 'deuce' and 'love' both had French origins. 'Deuce' came from a *deux*, a parity, while 'love' was an Anglicization of *l'oeuf* – a nought being of the same shape as an egg.

Somehow, everything was ready in time for the first Championship. It is remarkable to consider how the foresight of a few men helped make the Wimbledon fortnight one of the major sporting events in the world calendar.

In 1877 the All England Club made a profit of £10 (compare this with a profit of £5¼ million in 1985). This provided much-needed money for a repair to the pony roller that had been donated by Mr Walsh's daughter in 1868. This roller can still be seen in the corner of the centre court, having been used when the new stadium at Church Road was being built in the early 1920s. The exits are too small for it to be moved so, much like the Wimbledon men's singles Championship, it is here to stay.

Henry Jones. He wrote under the name of Cavendish in The Field *and, as referee, was at the centre of the organization of the first Wimbledon Championships*

Major Gem. Along with his friend Augurio Perera he formed the Leamington Lawn Tennis Club in 1872 – the first in the world

A crowd of approximately 200 watched the first final of the men's singles Championship at Wimbledon. It had been put back three days to Thursday, 19 July because of rain. **Spencer Gore** emerged from the twenty-two competitors as the winner; none of the entrants had ever played under the rules of the All England Club and it was Gore who showed the greatest will to win. Unlike the other players, who were content to play rallies from the baseline, Gore would rush into the net at every opportunity and gently tap winning volleys. William Marshall, his opponent in the final, had no answer to this nor to Gore's quick underarm serve, and the match lasted only 48 minutes.

Gore was presented with the silver cup donated by *The Field* and, as champion, automatically qualified for the 1878 final, the Challenge Round. Meanwhile, thirty-four players would be entering the separate All Comers competition and one would win the right to meet the champion. It was not until 1922 that this system was changed and the champion was required to enter the first-round draw with everyone else.

Despite his unique victory in 1877 Gore criticized the sport of lawn tennis: 'The game is a bore,' he said, 'and will never rank among the great sports of cricket and rackets.'

PASTIMES.

LAWN TENNIS CHAMPIONSHIP.

The final tie for the Lawn Tennis Championship was postponed from Monday, on account of the rain, until Thursday. The weather was still far from favourable, and the ground dead and slippery owing to the wet, and therefore not conducive to good play or to long rests. Nevertheless, about two hundred spectators assembled on the ground of the All England Croquet and Lawn Tennis Club.

The result was a more easy victory for Mr Spencer Gore than had been expected. Mr W. Marshall won the toss, and served the first game. Off his service there was a smart little rest, which ended in Mr Gore's favour. Mr Gore also won the next three strokes; one game to love. The second game began like the first, a good rest following Mr Gore's service, decided in Mr Marshall's favour. Mr Gore won the next four strokes, and scored the last game to love, the last stroke being very hardly contested, the rest comprising several fine returns on both sides. In the third game there was only one good rest. Mr Marshall won four strokes to two: one game to two. The next game to two players arrived at deuce without any important struggle; Mr Gore won the next two strokes; three games to one. The fifth game Mr Marshall got 30 to 15, when some very pretty tennis ensued; a good rest from a wonderful backhand return of Mr Gore's off a ball that seemed quite out of reach (40 to 15), and then a great rest, both returning very difficult balls, till at last the sixth game fell to Mr Gore: four games to one. The next game was short, Mr Gore winning four strokes to two: five games to one. The seventh game was a replica of the sixth, except that one excellent rest (decided by Mr Marshall) occurred; but Mr Gore won by four strokes to two, and so secured the first set, by six games to one, after fifteen minutes' play.

The rain now came down in earnest, but held up after a quarter of an hour. Meantime it had done as much mischief as possible, deadening the ground, and consequently spoiling the rests. The first game of the second set was secured by Mr Marshall by four strokes to two. The second and third games were short, Mr Marshall losing the first stroke of the second game by serving two faults, and Mr Gore deciding a short rest in the third game by running up to the net and placing the ball prettily with one of his volleys, at which he is a great adept. Each game had won by four strokes to one: two games to one. The fourth game 30 all was soon reached, when Mr Marshall, with a well-judged and well-placed return, made it 40, and, winning the next stroke, scored game. Two games all. Mr Gore then won a love game; three to two. In the sixth game a well-placed return by Mr Gore decided the first stroke. Mr Marshall then served two faults, but made the game 30 all with a great backhand return that elicited a round of applause. Notwithstanding Mr Marshall's good play, however, Mr Gore got the next two strokes, and the set stood four games to two in his favour. The first service of the seventh game led to a splendid rest, finally decided by Mr Gore by one of his favourite volleys, placed out of his adversary's reach. Mr Marshall won the next stroke, Mr Gore the three following; five games to two. The eighth game commenced with a rattling service by Mr Marshall, which won the stroke. Mr Gore then showed some good head play, winning a stroke with another of his accurately placed volleys, and the next by a soft return, just placed over the net, when Mr Marshall was at the back of the court and could not get up in time. Finally Mr Gore won four strokes to two, and the set by six games to two, after thirteen minutes' play. Two sets to love.

The third set, Mr Gore won the first game by four strokes to two. The next game, a good rest, was decided in favour of Mr Gore. Then Mr Marshall, by some unaccountable accident, served four faults running, and thus lost the second game; a love game. He, however, recovered his form in the next two games, winning the third by four strokes to two, though he had a bit of bad luck in one of his adversary's returns, touching the top of the net and falling impossible; and the fourth game also by four strokes to two. Two games all. The next game deuce was soon reached, when Mr Gore won two strokes; he once, strange to say, in the early part of the game serving two faults. Three games to two. The sixth game Mr Marshall lost two strokes by serving four faults, but nevertheless won one after a fine rest, and the score was soon called deuce. Mr Gore won advantage and game; four games to two. The seventh game Mr Marshall came again, winning the first stroke after a long rest, well played on both sides, and soon arriving at 40 to 15. The last stroke Mr Marshall won by a fine return, heavily cut, the ball shooting rapidly past Mr Gore, who could not return it; three games to four. The eighth game began with a capital rest, decided by Mr Gore; but the score soon reached 40 to 30, Mr Marshall wins, and then, by a crushing service, he made the set four games all, amidst some excitement. In the ninth game Mr Gore returned the compliment of a severe service, and followed it with another, which was well returned; 15 all. The game then reached 30 all, and finally Mr Gore won it; five games to four. The deciding game was not very interesting; both played well, one return of Mr Gore's, which made him 40 to 30, being much applauded. He won the next stroke, and the set, by six games to four, in twenty minutes; three sets love, and the match.

Mr Gore, therefore, becomes Lawn Tennis Champion for 1877, and wins the twelve guinea gold prize, and holds the twenty-five guinea silver challenge cup, presented by the proprietors of *The Field*.

Mr W. Marshall and Mr C. G. Heathcote, having each been beaten only by the champion, tied for second and third prizes, and, as they could not fix another day to play their match, agreed to decide it at once by the best of three sets. After the decision of the principal event a good many of the spectators went away, and so lost an excellent exhibition of lawn tennis. Mr Marshall won two sets, both by six games to four. Mr W. Marshall, therefore, takes the silver prize (value seven guineas), and Mr C. G. Heathcote the third (value three guineas).

1878 Frank Hadow
beat Spencer Gore
7–5 6–1 9–7

Frank Hadow won through the six All Comers rounds and beat Spencer Gore in the Challenge Round final without dropping a set. This was remarkable considering that he had first watched a game of lawn tennis only a month before!

The 23-year-old coffee planter was home on holiday from Ceylon when L. Erskine, a friend of his family, invited him to play a game of lawn tennis. Hadow excelled, and Erskine persuaded him to enter the new All England Club Championship. Both players won through to the All Comers final, then Hadow beat his mentor and qualified to play Gore.

Following Gore's victory a year earlier several players had tried to outlaw his volley tactics but Hadow had his own answer in the development of a new stroke – the lob. Both players were troubled during the final, Hadow from a headache caused by the sun and Gore from a bad wrist. He soon tired of rushing back from the net to play the lobs and stayed on the baseline where he proved no match for Hadow in the long rallies.

After his victory, Hadow returned to Ceylon and was not seen at Wimbledon again until he was persuaded to attend the men's singles Championship's fiftieth anniversary in 1926.

Another name to remember from the 1878 Championship is that of A.T. Myers. Although beaten in the second round he was the first player to serve overarm at Wimbledon.

THE CHAMPIONSHIP

This match was played on Thursday, a day intervening between the final round of the All Comers and the match for the Championship. About 700 spectators found their way to Wimbledon to witness the match. The day was intensely hot, and both players seemed to have had quite enough of it at the end of the third set, although the match might have lasted into five sets, had fortune been more propitious to Mr Gore.

Shortly after four o'clock Mr Gore commenced serving, and scored two strokes, Mr Hadow one. In the rest which followed, Mr Gore commenced his favourite tactics of running up to the net to volley when his adversary is at the back of the court, and has not an easy return. But this plan had not the slightest effect on Mr Hadow, who returns everything within reach, and who continually tossed the ball over Mr Gore's head. This he now did, but Mr Gore jumped up and returned the ball, and Mr Hadow failing at the next toss, Mr Gore won the stroke. Another toss over, Mr Gore ran back and returned, Mr Hadow put the ball in the net and Mr Gore scored the first game. The second game, Mr Gore put two in the net and one out of court, and Mr Hadow won a love game by a toss over Mr Gore's head. One game all. Some short rests brought the third game to 15 all, when another ball tossed over Mr Gore's head, and a failure on his part to return an awkward one, made Mr Hadow 40 to 15. Mr Hadow then put a ball in the net off a difficult service, but in returning the next ball he played it on the net cord, and it dropped impossible to return. Two games to one Mr Hadow wins. In the fourth game a question arose as to the right of a player to hold his racket beyond the net, so as to volley the ball before it was passed. The umpires differed as to the meaning of the rule, until it was finally given that the player is at liberty to hold his racket anywhere he can reach. We do not intend to discuss this question; but are of opinion that the old All England rule had better have been retained, viz., that if a player touches the net he loses a stroke. This rule has the effect of preventing a player from reaching far over the net; and the question whether or not he touches the net is much more easily decided than whether he holds his racket over it. The stroke was given in favour of Mr Gore, who volleyed the ball before it had passed the net; but Mr Hadow won the next four strokes in a canter, the last by a toss. Three games to one Mr Hadow wins. In the fifth game 15 all was soon called when Mr Gore served two two faults. Notwithstanding, he arrived at deuce, but, sending two balls in succession out of court, Mr Hadow won the game. Four games to one. In the sixth game each won a stroke, when a fine volley at the net by Mr Gore, quite in his old style made him 30. He then sent one out of court, failed at a service, and placed one in the net, the last by no means a difficult stroke, and so Mr Hadow won five games to one. The seventh game commenced with a good rest, decided by Mr Gore's running in to the net and volleying. Mr Gore quickly ran up his score to 40-30, when he served two faults. Mr Hadow won advantage, but the score returned to deuce again off a lucky service of Mr Gore's which struck the net cord. A couple of short rests followed, Mr Hadow putting the ball twice in the net, which made the score two games to five in favour of Mr Hadow. The next game was devoid of incident. After 30 all, Mr Hadow put two balls out of court. Three games to five. The ninth game two short rests were decided in Mr Gore's favour. Then a finely judged rest was played; Mr Gore in the end running up to the net to volley, had the ball tossed. This he jumped up at and returned; but a second toss by Mr Hadow won the stroke. A long and well-played rest followed, and another good one, both strokes being decided in Mr Gore's favour. Four games to five. In the tenth game Mr Hadow scored 30 by his service. Then each player won a stroke. The next was decided by a beautifully placed return by Mr Gore, out of his adversary's reach; and a volley at the net, after a difficult return gave Mr Gore this important game. Five games all – a wonderfully good and well-deserved pun-up by Mr Gore, after losing five games running. An advantage set was now compulsory by the match conditions as printed in the programme. In the eleventh game Mr Gore sent two not very easy ones out of court, and, in trying one of his volleys, put the ball in the net. 40 love. Mr Hadow now lost a stroke, and put two awkward ones out of court. Deuce. Mr Gore lost advantage by playing a ball out of court, but recovered his position after a fine rest, by playing one of his favourite volleys on to Mr Hadow's racket, Mr Hadow being near the net in a position to return the volley on the volley. The remainder of the set was all one way. Mr Hadow won the advantage game, and, after three short rests, won a love game, thus gaining the first set by seven games to five.

In the second set the first game produced two good rests, which resulted in a score of 15 all. The play on both sides was for a short time weak, Mr Gore putting two in the net, and then each player one out of court, none of the returns being particularly difficult. One game love, Mr Hadow wins. The first stroke of the second game Mr Gore won prettily with a softly-played twist just over the net. Thirty all being reached, Mr Gore plays a well-cut ball, which must have been a warm one, for it went clean under Mr Hadow's racket. Mr Gore then resorting to the net-volley tactics. Mr Hadow tossed the ball over his head, but it dropped just beyond the base line. Mr Hadow's tosses, as a rule, and many of his returns, were just within the base line – or, as is commonly said "he knew the length of the court." This game was scored to Mr Gore. One game all. The third game commenced with two short rests, both decided by Mr Gore with volleys at the net; and then Mr Hadow, with a return out of reach, scored 15. Each put a ball in the net, and the score being called 40-30 Mr Gore wins a due rest ensued. After a variety of returns Mr Gore volleyed as usual, at the net. Mr Hadow returned the ball and Mr Gore volleyed it again, when Mr Hadow to send the ball over his adversary's head, and made the score deuce. Mr Gore now served two faults, and, after a short rest struck the ball into the net; two games to one Mr Hadow wins. In the fourth game Mr Gore made a mistake at his own game, and volleyed into the net. No incident of importance occurred until 40-30 Mr Hadow wins was reached, then Mr Gore, cleverly dropping a volley close to the net, and the score deuce. Mr Hadow quickly won advantage and game; three games to one. The score in the fifth game soon reached 30-15, when Mr Gore had a slice of bad luck. Returning a difficult ball with a beautiful half-volley, it dropped just an inch out of court, and made Mr Hadow 40-15. A severe return, which Mr Hadow could not get back, made Mr Gore 30; but Mr Hadow won the next stroke after a long rest; four games to one. The next was a love game, Mr Hadow winning four strokes off the service, the last being the only one that was contested, and that very briefly; five games to one. In the seventh game Mr Gore scored first; then a very long and well-played rest was sought to be terminated by Mr Gore, by his usual net volley, but Mr Hadow tossed the ball over his opponent's head. A failure from each player made the score 30 all, then Mr Hadow placed one softly just over the net, and got to 40. A good rest, ended by Mr Gore's volleying out of court, gave the game and set, by six games to one, to Mr Hadow. Two sets love.

The third set, Mr Hadow in the first game won four strokes to one, without much trouble. Thirty all was soon reached in the second game, Mr Gore once again serving two faults. By good play in the next rest Mr Gore scored 40, and Mr Hadow, putting the next out of court, made the set one game all. In the third game Mr Gore volleyed a return at the net; this Mr Hadow got back, but a second volley at the net beat him. Some short rests made the game 30 all. Mr Hadow mis-judging two tosses, put both out of court, and Mr Gore won two games to one. The fourth game, a volley out of court, and a good rest, ended by Mr Hadow's placing a ball in the corner of the court out of reach, made him 30 love. A short rest gave Mr Gore 15. After this a magnificent rest took place: towards the end Mr Hadow tossed a ball when Mr Gore was at the net; the latter ran back about four yards past the base line, and returned it, and Mr Hadow had only to drop the ball gently over the net to win the stroke. He, however, played hard enough to give Mr Gore time to get to the ball, off which he won the stroke; 30 all. Two more fine rests brought the game to deuce, and a strong service made Mr Gore advantage. Two more strokes, and advantage was called again, when Mr Hadow placed another in the far corner, which Mr Gore could not quite return by an excellently tried half volley. Deuce. A fine rest decided the next stroke in Mr Hadow's favour, his last return being scarcely get at-able, though Mr Gore did return it, but out of court. Mr Hadow won the next stroke and game; two games all. The fifth game, an easy service of Mr Hadow's (after a fault) was returned impossible; then a fine rest, well played on both sides, was decided by Mr Hadow. 15 all. A good rest followed, when Mr Gore volleyed at the net, but Mr Hadow returned the ball splendidly over his opponent's head. Another good rest ended by Mr Hadow's returning a very difficult ball out of court. 30 all. Mr Gore killed the next ball with one of his volleys and finally won after deuce had been reached once. Three games to two Mr Gore wins. The next game presented no feature, except a very powerful service of Mr Gore's, until 30 all was called. Then a long rest ended in favour of Mr Hadow, who also won the next stroke. Three games all. The seventh game commenced with a fine rest, including several volleys, which was won by Mr Gore, and Mr Hadow then playing several times into the net, lost the game. Four games to three. Good services by Mr Gore gave him 30 in the next game, and after another stroke, a really good rest ended with a splendid half-volley by Mr Hadow, which Mr Gore could not return. Mr Gore, however, won the game. Mr Hadow putting a nasty one out of court; five games to three Mr Gore wins. A game of little interest followed. Mr Hadow winning it by four strokes to two. The tenth game he also won by the same number of strokes, and might have got more easily, had he not repeated his mistake of playing the ball back too hard, after tossing it so that Mr Gore had to race right past the base of the court to get any return at all. Five games all. Another advantage set had now to be played. In the advantage game a long rest with great returns on both sides was finally won by Mr Hadow. The other strokes were won by midding play, except a rattling half-volley which was placed out of reach by Mr Gore. Finally Mr Hadow won the advantage game, by four strokes to one. The next game Mr Gore won a love game; the first stroke he won after a superb rest, with wonderful returns on both sides; the second was a repetition of the first; next, after a short rest Mr Hadow put a nasty one into the net, and then returned a difficult service out of court. Games all. The next game 15 all was quickly reached, when a volley by Mr Gore, a failure by Mr Hadow at a not very difficult stroke, and a long rest ended by Mr Hadow's putting the ball just out of court, gave Mr Gore the advantage game. Five short rests in the next game made the score 40-30 Mr Hadow wins, when Mr Gore played a not very difficult ball out of court. Games all. Both players now seemed pretty well done up, and there were some rumours of resigning and of adjourning, but after a short interval they got to work again. Mr Gore won the advantage game by four strokes to one, there being nothing very remarkable in the play. The following game Mr Hadow won by four strokes to two, the play being still rather tame, excepting the last stroke but one, which was won by Mr Gore by a well-placed return after a short but good rest. Games all. In the next game, Mr Hadow won the first stroke by a well-judged toss, Mr Gore being at the net. After several uninteresting strokes, a good twist service by Mr Hadow gave him the advantage game. In the last game, after a good rest, Mr Gore volleyed one out of court. Short rests followed until 40-30 Mr Hadow wins was called. Next a great rest occurred, both placing the balls with judgment; finally Mr Hadow put a puzzling one out of court. Deuce. A short rest made Mr Hadow advantage; and then a splendid rest, decided by fine play by Mr Gore, brought the score to deuce again. Another magnificent rest was drawn in favour of Mr Hadow, he placing a return out of reach; but he failed at the next service and deuce was again called. The next two strokes were won pretty easily by Mr Hadow, who thus won this terrific set by nine games to seven. Three sets to love and the match, Mr Hadow wins.

1878 The Field

1879 Rev. John Hartley
beat Vere Thomas St Leger Goold
6–2 6–4 6–2

With Hadow back in Ceylon and not defending his title the Challenge Round was not played in 1879 and the winner of the All Comers final became the men's singles champion. In this final, a crowd of more than a thousand watched **Rev. John Hartley** beat the Irish champion, Vere Thomas St Leger Goold in straight sets.

The 33-year-old clergyman had been fortunate to survive his semi-final match. He had not expected to progress so far in the competition and had failed to arrange for another preacher to stand in for him at his Sunday service. So he had to return to Yorkshire to deliver his sermon and, after a gruelling journey by train, horse and carriage, arrived back at Wimbledon on the Monday with barely enough time to get changed. Hartley duly lost the first set of his semi-final 2–6 but then rain intervened and he recovered sufficiently to win the next three sets with the loss of only two games.

St Leger Goold, an Irish baronet's son, never won a Wimbledon title but he made news of a different kind at the turn of the century. He and his French wife ran into money difficulties while living in Monte Carlo and it was claimed that together they stole some jewels belonging to Emma Levin, a Danish widow. A gruesome sequel occurred in 1907: the Goolds' trunks were searched at Nice railway station and inside was found the dismembered body of Mme Levin.

They were both tried in Monte Carlo and sentenced to life imprisonment. Goold was sent to the notorious Devil's Island prison in the Atlantic Ocean off the coast of Guyana. Just over a year later he died, and his wife died in Montpellier prison in 1914.

LAWN TENNIS.

LAWN TENNIS CHAMPIONSHIP MEETING.
(Concluded from our last.)

THE matches were resumed on Monday, July 14, on the grounds of the All England Croquet and Lawn Tennis Club at Wimbledon. The lawns were again in good order, though slightly wet on the first day after a sharp shower which took place at the conclusion of the first set. About seven hundred spectators viewed the match on Monday between Mr Hartley and Mr Parr, and on Tuesday the large number of eleven hundred were massed round the court, which had been carefully roped off so that the competitors should not be impeded. We never remember to have seen anything approaching this number on the Wimbledon lawns before, and many more people arrived just after the conclusion of the match, and seemed much annoyed at having missed it. Mr P. F. Hadow, the last year's champion, being abroad, was unable to defend his title and cup; so Mr Hartley, besides winning the All Comers' Gold Prize, value 25 guineas, also holds the Champion Cup until next July. The certainty of Mr Hartley's returns are something wonderful as he puts back ball after ball over the net until his adversary gets positively wearied out, and sooner or later returns one into the net or out of court. The play of the winner seemed to improve with each day's competition, and his strokes when playing against Mr St. Leger in the final round were much more severe than on his first appearance on the Wimbledon grounds last Monday week. Curiously enough, the three winners of the Lawn Tennis Championship (Mr S. W. Gore, Mr P. F. Hadow, and Mr J. T. Hartley) are all old Harrow boys, and were also, we believe, all racket players. Mr St. Leger, the Irish Champion, fully sustained the reputation he has in the sister isle, beating all his opponents except the actual winner of the cup. His style of play is very taking, some of his backhand strokes being especially pretty, and also very effective. The round between him and Mr Parr for second and third places was, we think, one of the best matches during the competition, both players showing remarkably good form.

In the Members' Handicap, which has been continued each day this week, Mr Hoare and Mr Myers have each played very well, the severity of the latter gentleman's services being especially noticeable. Mr Ayres' balls have again come in for a great deal of praise, as hardly a stitch in any of them has started all through the matches, and even then there has been no gaping, as the cement still holds the cloth together.

Final Round —The match between Mr Hartley and Mr St. Leger for the All Comers' Gold Prize attracted large crowds, and caused a great deal of excitement; the merits of the two competitors having been eagerly discussed whenever two lawn tennis players came together. Two of the "rests" in this match were of tremendous length—there being thirty-five returns in one of them; and the final rest of the match was wound up in a fitting manner, as forty-nine returns were made, many of the strokes being very severe. In the opening set, Mr St. Leger scored the first game by four strokes to two; Mr Hartley then won the second, after deuce had been called twice, and made the third and fourth love games, also winning the fifth, after advantage had been called to Mr St. Leger once. The latter then scored a love game, but Mr Hartley placed the next two to his credit; the seventh by four strokes to two, and the eighth after being deuce. Six games to two, one set to love; Mr Hartley wins. The second set was very well contested on both sides, three of the games being called deuce. Mr St. Leger won the first game by four strokes to one, and Mr Hartley the second, by four strokes to two. The third was called deuce three times, and was then won by Mr St. Leger, who also took the next game by four strokes to one. Mr Hartley then won the following four games by four strokes to two, four to love, four to two, and the eighth game after gaining advantage three times. Mr St. Leger took the ninth game by four strokes to two, but lost the tenth, though deuce was called twice. Six games to four, and two sets to love; Mr Hartley wins. In the third set, Mr St. Leger won the first game by four strokes to one, and also the fifth after deuce had been called. Mr Hartley won the second and third games by four strokes to one each; the fourth, by four to two; the sixth, by four to one; the seventh, by four to love; and the eighth, by four to two. This making him six games to two, and three sets to love.

In the tie between Mr St. Leger and Mr Parr for second and third places, the latter gentleman won the first set by six games to four; four of them being called deuce; and also the third set by six games to five; three of them being called deuce. Mr St. Leger won the second set by six games to two, and the fourth and fifth by six to four each. Five of the games in the last set were called deuce.

1880   Rev. John Hartley
beat Herbert Lawford
6–0 6–2 2–6 6–3

Rev. John Hartley became the first player to retain the Wimbledon men's singles title when in 1880 he produced another solid performance to beat Herbert Lawford. His safe, patient play wore down the erratic, but sometimes brilliant challenger. Lawford, who was a fine cricketer and all-round sportsman, was to figure prominently in the Championships throughout the 1880s.

The day before the 1880 Championship began, the All England Club committee announced that the admission was going to be increased from 1s. to 2s. 6d. This, however, did not stop the crowds flocking to Worple Road and a record number of 1,300 watched the final. The club's decision to stage a Championship to raise funds was paying handsomely: the profits had risen from £10 in 1877 to £760 three years later.

The 1880 final

THURSDAY.—Travelling down to Wimbledon, the heat was found to be intense, and on arriving at the All England grounds, everyone was saying that it was almost too hot to be playing lawn tennis. Rain had been falling in the early morning, and the lawns were softer than they have been at any time during the present tournament, but still there was little to grumble at about the state of the ground, which had been carefully rolled. The large number of over 1300 people were present to-day to witness the round for the championship, this being by far the greatest amount of spectators that have ever patronised the lawn-tennis grounds. The stands also were filled to excess, and many more reserved seats would have been got rid of, if it had been possible to find room for them. The match commenced shortly after four o'clock, Mr Hartley (last year's champion), appearing to play a trifle nervously at first, but after the third game his play began to be remarkably fine, and he won the extraordinary number of ten games consecutively, by far the best performance that has yet taken place in a champion match; or, indeed, in any other, when we take into consideration the player it was against. During the first set there had been no sun, but on changing ends "his majesty" came out in full force, Mr Lawford thus having rather hard luck, and this happened again in the fourth set to the same player, whilst in the third set, when Mr Hartley faced the sun, there was not much to object to. A splendid rally of 33 strokes took place in the fourth game of the second set, this being the longest that took place during the match. Four of over 25 returns were also reckoned, and taking into account the extreme hardness of the strokes from both competitors, it is wonderful that they succeeded in returning so many. In the third set, Mr Lawford obtained a good start, and his opponent having two sets in hand, and having to face what there was of the sun, judiciously eased up in his play. The fourth set proved what a remarkably strong player last year's champion is, his returns being marvels of pace and placing; indeed they were so hard that Mr Lawford was quite unable to bring his well-known volleying powers into play with any success, and when he did attempt to come up to the net, the placing of the return by Mr Hartley along the side line was a treat to witness. The play all through the match was of the highest order, both winner and loser showing better lawn tennis than has yet been seen in any of the champion matches.

Round for Championship.—Mr J. T. Hartley defeated Mr H. F. Lawford by three sets to one. In the first set the latter player scored the three first games, the third being at deuce; but then Mr Hartley, playing in fine form, took the next six games running, thus winning a love set. The fifth and sixth were love games, though Mr Lawford scored the first and second strokes in the former. Continuing his winning career into the second set, Mr Hartley won the next four games, the third and fourth both being at deuce, and in the latter a splendid rally of twenty-six strokes took place. Mr Hartley finally gaining the ace, amidst tremendous applause. The fifth was a love game to Mr Lawford, his opponent winning the next game to fifteen. Again did Mr Lawford score a love game; but Mr Hartley took the eighth, which gave him the set by six games to two. The score now stood two sets to love Mr Hartley wins. The second set had taken under a quarter of an hour to play. Mr Lawford took the first game in the third set; but the score directly afterwards stood at one game all. The third was a love game to Mr Lawford; and he also placed the fourth and fifth games to his credit, this making the score four games to one in his favour. After the same player had won the first stroke in the sixth game, Mr Hartley made four strokes consecutively, which made him two games to four. The seventh was a love game to Mr Lawford, and he also won the next game, after it had been called deuce, this giving him the set by six games to two. Two sets to one Mr Hartley wins. The fourth and final set, as it proved, fell to Mr Hartley, by six games to three. Mr Lawford won the first game, after it had been called deuce; but then his opponent scored three games running, the last being a love game; and in the third game Mr Lawford twice made two faults. The fifth and sixth games fell to the latter player, his adversary only scoring fifteen in each of them; but Mr Hartley then won the three next games, which gave him the set and the match.

1880   The Field

2 | Willie Renshaw Wins Seven Titles

1881 – 90

Willie Renshaw won six successive singles titles and *The Field* Challenge Cup outright. His seventh victory and that of his twin brother Ernest in 1887 made it eight Championship wins for the Renshaws in nine years. Herbert Lawford was their only challenger; he broke the Renshaws' run of victories in 1887.

The Renshaw twins. In addition to their singles successes the twins Willie (on the left) and Ernest also won seven doubles titles – two at the first venue of Oxford University and five at Wimbledon. They caused a stir by being the first pair to adopt the tactic of one playing at the net with the other serving

1881 Willie Renshaw
beat Rev. John Hartley
6–0 6–1 6–1

The shortest final in the history of men's singles Championship at Wimbledon – just 37 minutes – announced the arrival of **Willie Renshaw**. He totally dominated the ailing Rev. John Hartley who was recovering from ill health. From the start Renshaw volleyed with such power (compared with Gore's tap stroke) that he completely overcame Hartley's lob tactics. Anything short was hammered away overhead and this stroke was immediately christened the 'Renshaw smash'.

It was the second year that Willie and his twin brother Ernest had played in the Championships, although they had entered three times, the first in 1879. On that occasion, the 18-year-olds had been totally overawed by the atmosphere of Wimbledon and were too shy to go on court. In 1880 they both lost to O.E. Woodhouse in the All Comers competition but from that moment they decided to take the sport of lawn tennis very seriously. Their wealthy father had a court built in the grounds of a hotel in the south of France so that they could practise all year round. This investment was instantly rewarded by Willie's outstanding Wimbledon triumph in 1881.

LAWN TENNIS.

LAWN TENNIS CHAMPIONSHIP MEETING.

Mr Renshaw, for the third day in succession, lost the spin for choice of positions, so had to play the first set facing the sun. Play was commenced by Mr Renshaw gaining the opening game by four strokes to one, the winning ace being made by the "Renshaw smash," and the five following games all fell to the same player, who thus won a love set. The second and fourth games were each gained by four strokes to two, and the third, fourth, and sixth were all at deuce, but the two following aces in each game were made by Mr Renshaw; the set taking thirteen minutes' to play. After changing courts, Mr Renshaw gained the first stroke by a tremendous service and won the game by four aces to two, and also the second by the same number; but the winning ace was due to a false bound. The third was a love game to the same player, his final service being a most severe one. Mr Hartley started away with three strokes in the fourth game but then served two faults. The following ace fell to Mr Renshaw, and he also had a lucky stroke which just tumbled over the net, this bringing the score to deuce. Each player then won a stroke, and after Mr Renshaw had gained advantage, one of his well-known "smashes" made him three games to love. After another love game had fallen to Mr Renshaw, Mr Hartley gained the sixth by winning two strokes running when the score stood at deuce. The seventh, however, was won by Mr Renshaw at four strokes to one, thus gaining him the set by six games to one. This set only took twelve minutes' to play. Mr Renshaw opened the third set by winning a love game, and the same player also gained the second by four strokes to two. The third game fell to Mr Hartley, his opponent scoring two aces, but the fourth was another love game to Mr Renshaw. The following game was the best contested during the whole match, two good rallies taking place in it. After the score had been called deuce, Mr Hartley won advantage three times running, only to be brought back to deuce after each hardly gained ace. Then Mr Renshaw scored advantage through Mr Hartley serving two faults, and the game ended with one of the "Renshaw smashes." The sixth game was also called deuce, but then two strokes in succession fell to Mr Renshaw, and he ended up by winning a love game and the set by six games to one. This set also took only twelve minutes to play.

From the foregoing it will be seen that Mr Renshaw only lost two games throughout the match, but, in justice to Mr Hartley, it is only fair to state that he has been far from well during the last day or so. Not that we think it would have made any difference as to the actual result of the match, if Mr Hartley had been playing in his very best form, as the contest was so much a battle of different styles, and it was quite apparent to all who are in any way judges of the game that the one style was vastly superior to the other as a winning game. By many it is thought that volleying has destroyed much of the beauty of the game, as the long rallies from end to end of the court that were seen in most of the contests last season are now very rarely witnessed. But against this it can be said that at times the rallies got very wearisome, there being generally a great sameness about the play, while now much greater variety is introduced into the game, each player striving to keep his opponent as far back in the court as possible, and then, having him at a disadvantage, gradually working his way up to the net in order to kill the ball, as it is called, with a good volley. This mode of play has been brought nearly to perfection by Mr W. Renshaw, and the wonderful way in which he manages to place his volleys, first one side of the court and, if returned, then to the opposite side, was the theme of general admiration. Come the ball where it will, Mr Renshaw always seems there to return it, and this without any great apparent exertion. His play in this match was certainly of the highest order, and he has proved himself *facile princeps* at the game, having won both the English and Irish championships (the latter two years running), the Prince's Challenge Cup, and also, with his brother Mr E. Renshaw, the Double Championship, which takes place at Oxford. Playing from the back of the court, it would be hard to find a better exponent of the game than Mr Hartley, and it is to be hoped that next year he will have picked up the volleying tactics of his opponent, and be able to again show what a really fine player he is.

1882 Willie Renshaw
beat Ernest Renshaw
6–1 2–6 4–6 6–2 6–2

In 1882 the crowds flocked to Wimbledon to see **Willie Renshaw** and his twin brother Ernest contest the Challenge Round final. Wimbledon was beginning to rival Lord's as society's fashionable venue. The twins were popular sportsmen and fine stylists but Willie, the elder by 15 minutes, was a much more aggressive, athletic player compared with Ernest who, at times, seemed to lack ambition. When Ernest won the Irish All Comers earlier in the year he had refused to play the Challenge Round final, and now he did not relish playing Willie. Despite Ernest's initial lead of two sets to one, Willie retained his men's singles title.

The Renshaw twins. The illustration (above right) shows their first Wimbledon final meeting

THE CHAMPIONSHIP MEETING.—July 8, &c.

THE match for the Championship Cup was played off on Monday, July 17, between the brothers Messrs W. and E. Renshaw. Mr W. Renshaw, it may be remembered, gained the championship last year from Mr J. T. Hartley, after having beaten off some very strong players for the All Comers' Gold Prize, and this season his brother carried off the same prize, and was then called on to play the present champion.

MATCH FOR THE CHAMPIONSHIP, best of five advantage sets, the winner to hold the Championship Cup (presented by the proprietors of *The Field*) for the year. If the cup is held by the same player thrice consecutively, it is to become his own property.

Mr W. Renshaw (holder), Cheltenham L.T.C., beat Mr E. Renshaw, Cheltenham L.T.C.

MONDAY, JULY 17.—After so many rainy mornings it was quite refreshing to start the week with some fine weather, but even this could not last out the whole day, as the rain commenced just as a start was made for the final set. The wind was strong all through the match, and at times was very gusty, making it most difficult for the players to place their returns truly. It blew in a diagonal direction from the south-west angle of the court, and this gave the player in the west court a decided advantage all through the match. Something like 2000 spectators gathered round the court and thronged the reserve seats, while every coign of vantage was quickly filled. Mr W. Renshaw gaining the toss, of course chose the west court to play from, and he very easily won the first set by six games to one, only losing the fifth. Deuce was called in the first, fourth, sixth, and seventh games. On changing ends each player gained one game, and then the third fell to Mr W. Renshaw, but this was his last win, as five games in quick succession went to Mr E. Renshaw, who thus gained the set by six games to two. Each player gained one love-game, but only the final game was at deuce. The third was a much better contested set, and was eventually won by Mr E. Renshaw by six games to four, against the wind. At one time the score was called four games to one, Mr W. Renshaw wins; but then, for the second time, did five games running fall to his brother. No less than six of the games in the set were called deuce, including the last three. Having won a set against the wind, it was now generally considered that Mr E. Renshaw would prove the victor, but last year's champion now played up much better, and, in his turn, gained a set from the east court, only losing two games, the second and third, finishing the set with a run of five. Mr E. Renshaw gained one love-game—the third, and Mr W. Renshaw three—the fourth, fifth, and final games. Not one of the games was at deuce. The score now stood at two sets all, and it was agreed upon to change ends at the finish of each game, so as to equalise the chances of the wind. The first three games of the final set were all gained by Mr W. Renshaw, and, after losing the fourth, he added two more to his score. The umpire then called five games to one in his favour. The seventh fell to Mr E. Renshaw, but the eighth brought the match to a close, Mr W. Renshaw thus gaining the set by six games to two. Out of the fifty-one games played, last year's champion won twenty-four, his opponent taking seventeen, while twenty-three games went to the server and eighteen to the striker out. During the match Mr W. Renshaw won 155 strokes and his brother 135. Neither of the Mr Renshaws were playing in their best form, but most of this was no doubt due to the wind, which was decidedly gusty, and made it difficult to keep the balls in court. Every now and then the play was most brilliant, and gained loud applause from those who were witnessing the match. The grass also did not play very true, causing several false bounds.

1883 Willie Renshaw
beat Ernest Renshaw
2–6 6–3 6–3 4–6 6–3

A crowd of 2,500 watched a memorable final that resulted in **Willie Renshaw** winning his third successive Wimbledon men's singles title and *The Field* silver Challenge Cup outright. His twin was once again the opposition and, although the match went to five sets, Ernest did not have the drive to win against Willie. At the foot of *The Field* match report the interesting statistics show that Willie served seventeen aces and hit thirteen winning points with his celebrated overhead smash.

Although the outstanding ability of the twins was causing the number of entrants for the Championship to dwindle, their popularity was doing wonders for the sport of lawn tennis.

The Field Cup. This was won outright by Willie Renshaw in 1883. The All England Gold Cup that is now presented after the singles final on centre court is visible in later illustrations

THE CHAMPIONSHIP MEETING, JULY 7, &c.

THE match for the championship between the two Mr Renshaws at Wimbledon last Monday, July 16, attracted a very large gathering, numbering some 2500, to the All England ground, the reserved seats being well filled, while the space round the courts was completely blocked. The weather was extremely fine, and after the first set the wind, of which there ha l never been much, dropped very considerably, and gave no advantage to either court. The play on both sides was at times very brilliant; but, taken on the whole, it was a trifle disappointing. This we fancy, however, will always appear to be the case when two players so similar in style and play as the brothers come together, as it is only when they are found competing against other methods that the fineness of their play is really seen at the best. It is now quite certain that Mr W. Renshaw is the better all-round player of the two, he being very much more certain in his returns, and, besides, plays with the greater coolness. This makes the third year in succession that he has won the cup presented by *The Field*, so that it now becomes his own property. The cup was given seven years ago, when lawn tennis may be said to have been in its infancy—at any rate as to open matches.

Last year, when the brothers met in the match for the championship, forty-one games were played, W. winning twenty-four games to E.'s seventeen; this time W. again won twenty-four, but E. increased his number to twenty-one. The strokes in 1882 were 155 to W. and 135 to E.; as against this year, 163 to W. and 148 to E. The match took one hour and twenty-eight minutes to play, the shortest set (the fifth) taking fourteen minutes, and the longest (the fourth) nineteen minutes. The server won twenty-three games to the striker-out's twenty-two. Appended will be found full details of the match:

CHAMPIONSHIP ROUND.

Mr W. Renshaw (holder), Cheltenham L.T.C., beat Mr E. Renshaw, Cheltenham L.T.C.

Championship Round.—All the five sets were played in the match between the brothers for the championship, Mr W. Renshaw (the holder), eventually winning the cup for the third year in succession, defeating Mr E. Renshaw by three sets to two. The latter won the toss, and, of course, played with the wind, also serving. The first four games were divided between the players, E. taking the first and third, each by four strokes to two, and his brother the second and fourth each by four strokes to one. Then the next four games in succession fell to E., all of them being at deuce. E. made several fine returns in the sixth game off some especially hard strokes from the back of the court. First set won by E. at six games to two. The wind dropped just before the players changed ends for the second set, W. started away in fine form, scoring the opening four games in fine style, the first and third each by four strokes to one, while the second and fourth were both at deuce. Out of the next four E. won three, the fifth at four strokes to two, and the sixth and eighth after each had been called deuce. The seventh game fell to W. by four to one, and then he placed the set to his credit by six games to three by taking the ninth at four strokes to two, winding up with one of his well-known "smashes." In this set W. made six aces by his service, and eight with "smashes." One set all. There was hardly any wind now, so the sides may be said to have been fairly equal. W. gained three out of the first four games, only one ace in the first and third, and winning a love game for the fourth, while he could only make a single ace in the second, E. scoring three strokes by his services. The next four games were equally divided, the fifth and eighth falling to E. by four strokes to two and six to four, while W. won the sixth at six strokes to four, and the seventh, a love game. The ninth game brought the set to a close, as W. gained it, only losing one ace. The service of both players in this set was extremely good. Score, two sets to one, W. wins. On again changing ends W. seemed rather to slacken in his play, and lost four games out of the opening five, his winning one, the third, being at deuce. E. only lost one stroke in the first game, and two in each of the fourth and fifth, the second being at deuce. The sixth, seventh, and ninth were taken by W., the first and last mentioned both being at deuce, while in the seventh he lost two strokes. E. now brought the score to two sets all, as by winning the eighth game by five strokes to three, and afterwards the tenth at four to two, he gained the set by six games to four. In this set the ninth game was the best contested, E. gaining the advantage stroke twice, and W. three times before the latter won the necessary second ace. W. commenced playing a very strong game in the final set, scoring the opening four games in succession, the first by four strokes to two, the second a love game, and winning both the third and fourth with four strokes running, after his brother had gained the first and second aces in each. W. also won the first ace in the fifth game, but then four strokes in succession fell to his brother, who thus scored the game. The sixth was taken by W. after it had been called deuce, but then E. gained the seventh—a love game—and also the eighth by four strokes to two; but this was the last game he could manage to win, as W. scored the ninth, only losing two strokes, this giving him the set by six games to three, and also the match by three sets to two.

		Games won.	Strokes won.	Won by service.	Won by "smash."	Double faults made.
First Set	W. Renshaw	2	27	3	1	—
	E. Renshaw	6	33	2	1	2
Second Set	W. Renshaw	6	37	6	8	—
	E. Renshaw	3	28	2	—	3
Third Set	W. Renshaw	6	33	4	2	1
	E. Renshaw	3	21	5	—	1
Fourth Set	W. Renshaw	4	39	1	1	2
	E. Renshaw	6	43	2	—	1
Fifth Set	W. Renshaw	6	28	3	1	1
	E. Renshaw	3	23	2	—	1
Total	W. Renshaw	24	163	17	13	3
	E. Renshaw	21	148	11	2	—

1883   The Field

1884 Willie Renshaw
beat Herbert Lawford
6–0 6–4 9–7

1885 Willie Renshaw
beat Herbert Lawford
7–5 6–2 4–6 7–5

1886 Willie Renshaw
beat Herbert Lawford
6–0 5–7 6–3 6–4

With *The Field* cup safely in his possession, **Willie Renshaw** lost none of his enthusiasm for the game of lawn tennis. His all-round play reached new heights as he went on to win his sixth successive Wimbledon men's singles title and the All England Club Challenge Cup outright.

In each of the Challenge Round finals from 1884 to 1886 Herbert Lawford provided the opposition for Willie. The strapping Lawford fought doggedly against the brilliance of Willie in each of the finals but, despite four victories in the All Comers, the Championship victory eluded him.

In 1884 Richard Sears, who won the United States singles title seven years in succession (from 1881 to 1887), played at Wimbledon for the first time. A year earlier the Clark brothers had been the first Americans to play in the Championships.

Also in 1884 the women's singles championship was begun and the All England men's doubles, founded at Oxford University in 1879, was transferred to Wimbledon.

Willie Renshaw. With an unequalled record of wins in Wimbledon men's tennis, he became the first president of the Lawn Tennis Association, which was formed in 1888

Tennis, a game as old as the hills, a pastime once beloved of kings and the great ones of the earth, is now but little heard of. But for the annual match at Lord's for the Gold Racquet, the inter-university matches, and an occasional tussle for the professional championship, the present workaday world knows little of the most ancient of ball games. The Gold Racquet match for the championship was played at Lords on Tuesday last between the Hon. A. Lyttelton and Mr. J. M. Heathcote, and the latter was defeated most signally by three sets to love, Mr. Lyttelton winning the first set by six games to three, the second by six games to five, and the third by six games to five.

The result of the lawn tennis championship match at Wimbledon, between Mr. W. Renshaw and Mr. H. F. Lawford, on Tuesday last, was only in accordance with the anticipation of experts at the game. Year by year Lawford has fought hard for the championship at Wimbledon, but fate, in the combined semblance of the brothers Renshaw, has always been against him. When last week Mr. Grinstead beat Mr. Ernest Renshaw, and then on Monday last suffered defeat at the hands of Mr. Lawford, who thus supplemented his victories in the Irish Championship and L.A.C. tournaments by taking the Wimbledon Gold Prize, it was fondly hoped by the latter's admirers that he might wrest premier honours from W. Renshaw, who has held the title of champion since 1881. He was faulted many times by the base line umpire for serving with one foot off the ground, whilst Renshaw was only once called to account for that defective service. But Lawford played up pluckily and did all he could. Renshaw began well, as he took the first set, a love one, and followed this up by winning set two by six games to four, and finally, in set three, after a prolonged fight, proved victorious by nine games to seven—thus winning the match by three sets to love, and the championship for the fourth year in succession. The first challenge cup became Mr. Renshaw's property in perpetuity last year, and by his victory on Tuesday he is entitled to hold the All England Cup for the present year. His victory was due mainly to his splendid placing and all-over-the-court play, rather than to the celebrated "Renshaw smashes," which he seldom brought into use last Tuesday. I have always kept a special place for Mr. Renshaw in my champions' storehouse, and I am naturally pleased that he has so worthily kept his niche this year.

1884 Evening News

THE LAWN TENNIS CHAMPIONSHIP.

Fully 4,000 spectators, the largest number that has ever witnessed a championship competition, were present yesterday afternoon at the All England Club Grounds, Wimbledon, when the contest for the championship was decided between Mr. W. Renshaw, who had held the title during the four preceding years, and Mr. H. F. Lawford, the winner of the Gold Prize in the All Comers' Competition, which was concluded on Thursday last. Play began in a very even manner, the first set resulting in favour of Renshaw by only seven to five, after 31 minutes' play. In the second set Renshaw was in rare form, winning the first game after deuce once, the second being a love game, and the third to 30. Lawford was successful in the fourth game after deuce twice, and then Renshaw won the fifth and sixth. Lawford again played up well, and the seventh game resulted in his favour to 30, but Renshaw then won the eighth to 30, and the set at 6 to 2, after 18 minutes' play. The third set commenced well for Renshaw, who scored the first three games off the reel, but the champion then had a long run of unsuccessful work, Lawford scoring five games in succession. Renshaw secured the ninth, but the tenth ended in favour of Lawford, who thus won the set, and made the contest stand two sets to one. The next set was splendidly contested, and after 28 minutes' exciting play resulted in a victory for Renshaw by seven games to five, and that gentleman accordingly won the championship by three sets to one. Mr. Renshaw has now won the championship five years in succession. The Ladies' Championship and the gentlemen's "Doubles" will be begun to-day.

EXECUTION AT NEWGATE.—At 8 o'clock yesterday morning Henry Alt, a German, who was convicted at the last sessions of the Central Criminal Court of the wilful murder of Charles Howard, was executed within the walls of Newgate prison, where he had been confined since the passing of the sentence upon him. The motive for the crime, it will be remembered, was jealousy. The prisoner had paid his addresses to a widow, who, however, had refused to marry him, and had engaged herself instead to the deceased man Howard. She told the prisoner one night that she intended to marry Howard, who was present, and Alt thereupon stabbed him several times with a dagger, inflicting wounds to which he succumbed almost immediately afterwards. The prisoner also stabbed the woman and then turned the weapon against himself. He was recommended to mercy by the jury, on the ground that he was acting under a fit of jealousy at the time; and it was said that the German Consul had interested himself in the prisoner's behalf to obtain a commutation of the capital sentence. An intimation to the effect that the capital sentence would be carried out was conveyed to the prisoner on Saturday, and he expressed himself prepared to die. He paid great attention to the ministrations of the gaol chaplain, and in a conversation with that gentleman said he had no recollection of what took place on the night of the occurrence. Mr. Sheriff Phillips arrived at the gaol at half-past 7 yesterday morning, and soon afterwards the ceremony of pinioning the prisoner was performed by Berry, the executioner. The prisoner walked with a firm step to the scaffold, and, while the rope was placed round his neck, he said it was all through a deceitful woman, and that he had evidence ——. He had not time to finish his sentence when 8 o'clock struck, and the signal was given which caused the executioner to draw the bolt. Death was almost instantaneous. A drop of 8ft. was allowed. The black flag was hoisted, and an inquest was afterwards held, at which the usual verdict was returned. The body was buried within the precincts of the gaol.

LAWN TENNIS.

ALL-ENGLAND CHAMPIONSHIP.
SUCCESS OF W. RENSHAW.

The contest between W. Renshaw and H. F. Lawford for the championship of England, which was unavoidably postponed on Monday, was brought off successfully yesterday, at the A.E.L.T.C., Wimbledon, were present. Proof positive of the popularity of Major Wingfield's fascinating pastime was thus adduced. Very little doubts were entertained as to the ultimate destination of the championship, although a close contest was anticipated, but Renshaw undoubtedly had the "call," having won the championship for five successive years. The good opinions formed of his merits were verified yesterday, as he again defeated his old adversary, after a close and exciting contest, thus taking the championship for the sixth time, and the challenge cup, which now becomes his own property. Owing to the recent rain, the courts were in good condition, and this, coupled with the arrangements, left nothing to be desired, and our thanks are due to Mr. Julian "Cavendish" Marshall for the kindly consideration shown our representative. Mr. S. A. Hickson officiated as umpire. Details :—

W. RENSHAW beat H. F. LAWFORD by 3 sets to 1 (6—0, 5—7, 6—3, 6—4).—Lawford having won the toss, the first set was commenced by his obtaining the premier stroke, which his opponent responded to by contributing 3 strokes in succession, Lawford obtaining the next. A clever back-handed return, which the latter failed to reach, won Renshaw the first game by 4 strokes to 2. In the next game Renshaw again scored a victory by 4 to 1 strokes, which he again followed up in the next by adding a similar score. Lawford then won the succeeding stroke in the following game by a clever return, which his adversary responded to by obtaining 4 strokes in succession, which won him the game. Alternate strokes ensued in the fourth game, Renshaw winning by 4 to 2 strokes, and again won the next by 4 to 1. In the sixth game Lawford secured the first stroke from service; two failures from service lost him the next two, Renshaw winning a well-contested game by 4 strokes to 2. This gave him the set at 6 games to love. Strokes played, 35. Time, 10 min. The first game of the second set Lawford again failed to score from service, and Renshaw again further increased his score by 4 strokes to 2. The second game was productive of some good play, Lawford obtaining his first game by 4 strokes to 1, in which he was applauded. Following this up, he secured the third game (4 strokes to 2), and the fourth by a similar score. Some excitement was then infused into the proceedings by deuce being reached four times, in which Lawford became vantage three times, and by judicious "lobbing" won the game. A smart return from service won Lawford the first three strokes of the next game, his opponent from service bringing the score to deuce, when he became vantage, and won the game. Renshaw again secured the next by 4 to 2 strokes, Lawford returning from service by obtaining the next by 4 to 2 strokes, the game being 5—3, Renshaw winning. The ninth game Lawford cleverly sent an irreproachable ball into his opponent's court, which Renshaw failed in returning; the first-named, however, failed in service, and the former won eventually by 4 strokes to 1. The tenth culminated in a love game for Renshaw, which Lawford succeeded by obtaining the next two games by strokes of 4—1 and 4—2, which won him the set amidst great cheering. Strokes played, 77. Time, 30 min. A wonderful return won Renshaw his second love game at the commencement of the next game of the third set. Three times Lawford failed to return from service, but, playing well, obtained the next, only to miss a well-placed ball, which Renshaw served in masterly style, by which he won the game by 4 strokes to 1. In spite of his adversary's clever tactics Lawford obtained the following two games—4 to 1 and 4 to 1 respectively. Deuce was again reached in the next (fifth) game, in which Renshaw won vantage and the game, and the two subsequent games by 4 to 1 and 4 to 1 strokes. The eighth game deuce was reached, Lawford winning the vantage and game. Renshaw easily secured his sixth game and second set by 4 to 2 strokes. Strokes played, 54; time, 21 min. Although Lawford won the opening game of the fourth set by 8 strokes to 6, he showed palpable signs of distress; still, nothing daunted, he played his losing set well, and put forward some capital strokes by which he drew the champion out in his best form. At "Games All!" the excitement was at fever pitch, the fourth game being the crucial one, as it could be seen at this stage that Renshaw was the fresher of the pair, as was proved by his winning the next game, Lawford obtaining the following by 4 strokes to 1. The succeeding game "Deuce!" was called, Renshaw obtaining the vantage and the game by 7 strokes to 5. This he again repeated in his next (sixth) game and set, by which he won the Championship and the A.E.L.T.C. Challenge Cup by 3 sets to 1. Time, 32 min. Duration of match, 1 hour 33 min.

1887 Herbert Lawford
beat Ernest Renshaw
1–6 6–3 3–6 6–4 6–4

1888 Ernest Renshaw
beat Herbert Lawford
6–3 7–5 6–0

1889 Willie Renshaw
beat Ernest Renshaw
6–4 6–1 3–6 6–0

Tennis elbow forced Willie Renshaw to stand down from the Challenge Round final and, for the first time in six years, there was to be a new winner of the Wimbledon men's singles Championship. It was fitting that this final was a match between **Herbert Lawford** (four times a runner-up) and Ernest Renshaw (twice a runner-up), but Lawford's renowned top spin forehand won the day.

The two met again in 1888 and this time the 27-year-old **Ernest Renshaw** made use of his ten-year age advantage to gain a popular victory in straight sets.

Willie Renshaw made a comeback in 1888 and experienced defeat – only his second defeat in a unique history – in the men's singles at Wimbledon. His conqueror was an Irishman, Willoughby Hamilton, whose frail appearance earned him the nickname 'The Ghost'. Ernest Renshaw avenged his brother's defeat by knocking out Hamilton on the way to victory.

In 1889 **Willie Renshaw** won the All Comers final in one of the most sensational matches seen at Wimbledon. Having already saved six match points against Harry Barlow he trailed 0–5 in the final set. Somehow, he levelled the scores and went on to win the last set 8–6 to meet Ernest in the Challenge Round.

As in the previous finals between the twins, Willie won, and set a record of seven Wimbledon men's singles titles.

The Lawn Tennis Association was formed in 1888 and so the All England Club relinquished to them the running of the Championships. The first president of the new Association was the extraordinary Willie Renshaw.

THE LAWN TENNIS CHAMPIONSHIP MEETING.
VICTORY OF H. F. LAWFORD.

OWING to the indisposition of the Champion, W. Renshaw, what would otherwise have been the final game for the 30gs prize and the Single-handed Championship of the All-England Lawn Tennis Club yesterday carried with it the additional honour of the Champion title for the year and the possession of the 100gs Challenge Cup. The rule has been for the winner of the lesser prize to meet the holder of the more valuable trophy and play for the coveted title, but on this occasion it was rendered unnecessary, owing to the resignation of the holder. Therefore the pair left in, E. Renshaw and H. F. Lawford, played for the double honour at the same time. Great interest was evinced in the match, and the centre court at Wimbledon was surrounded by a large gathering of spectators, but contrary to expectation the game proved rather tame compared with some previously witnessed. The weather was brilliantly fine, the heat of the sun being toned down somewhat by a cooling breeze, but the players felt it considerably, and emulating Mr Jingle's famous cricketing companions, had continual recourse to cooling beverages, varied by copious spongings, Renshaw going so far as to give his racquet a bath. Probably it was owing to the heat that neither played up to his best form, and except towards the close Renshaw was anything but brilliant. The games were, however, exciting from the fact of their close character, and right up to the finish either might have won; as it was Lawford, for the first time, became the recipient of the first prize and the Championship, although he has repeatedly been runner-up to "Willie" Renshaw. Play commenced at half-past four, but it was not until after seven that a conclusion was arrived at, owing to the close play. Renshaw began well, and won the first set by six games to one, but in a more determined struggle Lawford took the next by six to three, after "three all" had been called. Again Renshaw was victorious, beating Lawford by six to three, but the fourth set was even closer, as after "four games all" had been reached, Lawford was victorious, winning the next two. The match now stood two sets each, and there was considerable excitement over the rubber. Both played with more life, and "two all" and "three all" were marked, but after hanging in the balance for some time Lawford eventually won the set by six to four.

LAWN TENNIS.

ALL-COMERS' CHAMPIONSHIP.

E. RENSHAW DEFEATS H. F. LAWFORD (HOLDER) AND WINS THE CHAMPIONSHIP.

Undeterred by the unpromising weather, by far the largest attendance yet seen at the All-England L.T.C., Wimbledon assembled yesterday to witness the meeting between H. F. Lawford (holder) and E. Renshaw (winner of the final round of the All-Comers' Singles). As already known, E. Renshaw qualified to meet last year's winner, H. F. Lawford, by winning his ties in the second, third, and fourth rounds, and the final, in which he defeated the Middlesex and Covered Court champion, E. W. Lewis, after a severe and very close struggle. The game yesterday was keenly contested throughout, the long rallies and frequent brilliant passes calling forth great applause, the onlookers being by no means slow to mark, and to show their appreciation of every little bit of good play. Unfortunately, the turf proved to be in a very soft state, due to the continuous heavy rain, and this made the state of the turf anything but agreeable to the players. That Renshaw won on his merits cannot be disputed; still, his opponent being far from a light weight, was severely handicapped on this account, and had to succumb to the superior form shown by his opponent, who won each of the three sets. Details of the play :—

E. RENSHAW beat H. F. LAWFORD by 3 sets to love.

First Set : Renshaw beat H. F. Lawford by 6 games to 3.—The latter won the twist of the racket, and elected to serve, Renshaw opening the initial game by taking two strokes off service, when Lawford by good service won the next stroke, but lost the next after a sharp rally. Renshaw thus taking the game to 30. From 15 to love, Lawford brought play to 40 to 15, and Renshaw by good court play brought play to deuce. Lawford then had to win vantage stroke twice ere he managed to take the second game by 6—4. Renshaw was very sharp on his returns in the third game, and after Lawford had the game at deuce he won by 5 strokes to 3. The fourth, won by Lawford to 40 (deuce once), next saw play at 2 "all." The holder then only scored 1 stroke in the fifth, but made up leeway by taking the sixth to a similar score, 3 all. Several times Lawford lost a stroke through false bounds, whilst Renshaw's arm was ever active in half-volleying dead balls, and never giving his opponent a chance he scored the three following games to 30, 40 (deuce once) and to 15. The last heat won at the fourth stroke, by splendid manoeuvring, thus winning the set in nineteen minutes by 34 strokes to 27.

Second Set : Renshaw beat Lawford by seven games to five.— The turf, instead of improving, got from bad to worse, the hallmark of the players' shoes being very conspicuous by ruts made. This was unavoidable, both consequently having to use no small amount of strategy in circumventing its disastrous effects on the ball and the rebound. Sometimes a ball would drop dead or twist in rising, making it anything but an easy task for the striker to force a ball as he might will it. Renshaw commenced this set by service, and, after making one stroke from a well-sustained rest, lost the next stroke by two points, the game going to his opponent to 15, and the second by a similar score. Again Renshaw lost a stroke by faulty service, and, playing a forcing game, he made his opponent put all his balls into net, and won a hard-fought game to 15. Lawford, from service, next won a game to 30. The fifth game was conspicuous for the many times Lawford sent his balls into net, only scoring one stroke, which he obtained by a well-delivered back-hand cross stroke. The seventh game was started by Renshaw, who, after having the game against him by 15 to 40, brought play to deuce, which was reached no less than five times, when he won the deciding stroke by a well-placed return down the off-side line, taking the game by 9 strokes to 7. So well did Lawford place his return out of reach, that he took the eighth game to 30, which enabled him to bring play to 5—3 in his favour. A 15 game to Renshaw was followed by Lawford bringing the tenth game to deuce, when his opponent gained the vantage stroke by his slipping, the deciding stroke being taken by Renshaw, who took the game to 10, five game all being then arrived at. The vantage game Renshaw was at service, and after taking a couple of strokes, he won two deuces, one from service, taking the game to 15, and the deciding one also to 15, he won the set in 21 min. and 30 sec. by 39 strokes to 28.

Third and Last Set : Renshaw beat Lawford by six games to love. —Lawford was now apparently playing a fatiguing game, and repeatedly sent his balls into the net, just missing the top cord by a few inches, whilst Renshaw, evidently seeing his opportunity, just skipped his balls, and by placing them beyond his opponent's reach, he won the set by twenty-five strokes to eight. Time, 10 min. 30 sec., scoring nineteen games against eight made by Lawford. Duration of match, 58 min. 21 sec.

LAWN TENNIS.

THE MATCH FOR THE SINGLES CHAMPIONSHIP.
DEFEAT OF LAST YEAR'S WINNER.

AFTER the interesting and exciting battle on Saturday afternoon between H. S. Barlow and W. Renshaw in the final round of the Open Singles at the All-England Club inclosure at Wimbledon, it was generally anticipated that the meeting between the two brothers Renshaw for the Championship of 1889 would result in another close struggle. The meeting was fixed for yesterday afternoon in the specially-fitted centre court, and undeterred by the threatening aspect of the weather there must have been upwards of two thousand spectators in attendance. Fortunately the rains that descended in the metropolis did not extend with equal force to the south-western suburbs, and the turf, which has all along been in splendid condition, was in no way harmed. Mr Herbert Chipp again mounted the umpire's chair to officiate, and both players were accorded a hearty greeting as they made their way into the court. Willie Renshaw won the spin of the racquet and elected to start service. The Champion scored well in the returns and won the opening game to 30. During the second event both men played in splendid form, the rallies being especially smart. Eventually after deuce had been reached eight times Willie made the winning stroke and the umpire called the score—one game all. The play continued to be very even, Ernest securing the third and Willie the fourth games, but the Champion getting the fifth and sixth, crossing over with four games to two in his favour. This advantage was soon disposed of by Willie, who brought the score to "four all," and winning the ninth and tenth, credited himself with the first set with a total of six games to four; time, 19min 55sec. The first game of the second set was won by Ernest, but Willie, who commenced to display by far the superior form, won six games in succession, and the set by 6 to 1 ; time, 14min 55sec. In the third set the service of Ernest Renshaw was far from good, but after bringing play from forty to thirty in his favour, he lost the next stroke, and deuce being called, his brother took the game to forty. Ernest made amends in the second game, which he took by four strokes to two. In the third, in which deuce was reached once, W. Renshaw displayed some very fine passing, which his brother found impossible to reach. As the match progressed, however, Ernest showed in much better form, as he succeeded in taking the fourth, fifth, sixth, eighth, and ninth games, and the set by 6 to 3. Time, 18min 41sec. The fourth and what proved to be the last set was the outcome of some very brilliant play on the part of both. However, Willie proved himself by far the superior, his playing being too difficult for his brother to circumvent, and although Ernest made many plucky efforts to get on terms. Willie won by six games to love, and thus regained the Championship honours, and became holder of the 100gs Challenge Cup, amidst applause, by scoring three sets to one (6—4, 6—1, 3—6, and 6—0). Time, 10min 10sec. Duration of the match, 1 hour 5min 30sec.

Appended are the previous winners of the Championship :

The following is the result of the draw for the Four-handed Championship, which commences to-day at the All-England Lawn Tennis Ground, Wimbledon, at four o'clock :—W. Watkins and R. K. Micklethwaite, H. S. Scrivener and H. W. Carlton, G. R. Mewburn and G. Gore (byes), Cramer-Roberts and H. C. Smith v. F. L. Rawson and H. S. Stone, E. W. Lewis and G. W. Hillyard, P. B. Brown, and G. E. Brown, C. J. Stanley and A. Walker, W. Baddeley and H. Baddeley (byes).

1890 Willoughby Hamilton
beat Willie Renshaw
6–8 6–2 3–6 6–1 6–1

Willie Renshaw's decade of dominance came to an abrupt end in the 1890 Challenge Round final. He led **Willoughby Hamilton** by two sets to one but, disappointingly, was only able to win another two games.

So the Renshaws' era ended (although Ernest did reach the All Comers semi-final in 1891) and Willie's record in ten singles Championships was: seven titles and only three defeats (by O.E. Woodhouse in 1880 and twice by Hamilton, in 1888 and 1890).

Irishman Hamilton was unable to defend his title in 1891 because of blood poisoning. He never recovered enough from this illness to be able to play at Wimbledon again.

Willoughby Hamilton. He had the distinction of being the only player to beat Willie Renshaw in a Wimbledon men's singles final

W. J. HAMILTON v. W. RENSHAW, FOR THE CHAMPIONSHIP.

W. J. HAMILTON WINS THE CHALLENGE CUP.

Yesterday afternoon fine weather favoured the closing day of the All-England Lawn Tennis Championship Meeting at Wimbledon, a large concourse of spectators surrounding the centre court, where, at half-past four, W. J. Hamilton, of the Fitzwilliam L.T.C., Dublin, challenged the holder of the 100-guinea challenge cup for the trophy and title of Champion of All-England, which have been held for a year by W. Renshaw, who defeated Ernest Renshaw in 1889. Hamilton had been in splendid form on Saturday, when he met H. S. Barlow in the final tie of the All-Comers' Singles, and a good match with the champion was confidently anticipated. The arrangements were excellent, thanks to the exertions of the courteous hon. secretary, Mr. H. W. W. Wilberforce, and the hon. referee, Mr. B. C. Evelegh. The past winners are:—1877, S. W. Gore; 1878, P. F. Hadow; 1879, J. T. Harkey; 1880, J. T. Harkey; 1881, W. Renshaw; 1882, W. Renshaw; 1883, W. Renshaw; 1884, W. Renshaw; 1885, W. Renshaw; 1886, W. Renshaw; 1887, H. F. Lawford; 1888, E. Renshaw; 1889, W. Renshaw; 1890, W. J. Hamilton, Fitzwilliam L.T.C., Dublin, beat W. Renshaw, All-England L.T.C., by three sets to two (6–8, 6–2, 3–6, 6–1, 6–1). Details of play:—

Renshaw commenced service, Hamilton taking the first game to 30, the next, a deuce game, falling to his opponent. Alternate games were then scored, when Renshaw, with a love game, brought games to four all. Hamilton, reversing this state of affairs with a 15, brought games to five all. Hamilton won the vantage game, but play was again brought level by a deuce game to Renshaw, who scored a second advantage game and set by eight to six. In the second set each player scored a couple of games, in which deuce was reached four times. Hamilton, then playing well up to the net, and passing his opponent very smartly from right to left, succeeded in taking four games (3–6, 4–1, 6–4, and 4–1), and the set at six to two. The third set was very closely contested for the first four games, the fore-hand volleys and cross drives, and passing being a conspicuous feature in the play. Renshaw, securing no less than four games, lost the eighth to 30, but won the ninth to a similar score, bringing play to two sets to one in his favour. A very protracted struggle ensued in the opening games of the fourth set, Renshaw being at vantage four times ere he won the game by twelve strokes to ten. Hamilton then rallied, and out-pacing his opponent by his half-volleys and placing, took six games right off the reel, bringing play to two sets all. In the decider, Hamilton played so well, that his opponent never had a chance of getting to the net, his play repeatedly calling forth well-merited applause, no less than six games, with the exception of the fourth, being taken against his hitherto unbeaten opponent. He scored the match by six to one, and the match, championship, and challenge cup by three sets to two, and 27 games to 18. Duration of play, 1 hour 43 min. Mr. G. W. Hillyard was umpire.

The 1890 All Comers semi-final. The match between Harry Barlow and Ernest Lewis
is featured in the centre of this Illustrated Sporting and Dramatic News extract.
Wimbledon was beginning to make its mark on the social scene, which explains the
particular attention drawn to the spectators and their dress

3 | The Youngest Champion for Nearly a Century

1891–96

Wilfred Baddeley became the youngest men's singles champion in 1891. He held this record until Boris Becker shocked the tennis world by winning the title at the age of seventeen in 1985. Baddeley and the Irish doctor Joshua Pim contested four successive finals between 1891 and 1894.

Wilfred Baddeley. Along with his younger twin brother Herbert he won four Wimbledon men's doubles titles to add to his three successes in the singles

1891 Wilfred Baddeley
beat Dr Joshua Pim
6–4 1–6 7–5 6–0

At the age of 19 years 5 months and 23 days **Wilfred Baddeley** became the youngest winner of the Wimbledon men's singles Championship – a record that stood until 17-year-old Boris Becker's victory ninety-four years later.

Baddeley, the son of a London solicitor, took the title in the All Comers final by defeating the Irish doctor Joshua Pim. The two players were to contest the next three Challenge Round finals (from 1892 to 1894).

Baddeley had an identical twin brother, Herbert, who also played tennis and the pair were at first considered as the Renshaw twins' possible successors. The Baddeleys won the men's doubles four times but Herbert's tennis was not up to his brother's standard and he never reached the later stages of the men's singles.

LAWN TENNIS.

ALL-ENGLAND LAWN TENNIS CLUB.
THE SINGLES CHAMPIONSHIP.

BRILLIANT weather favoured the executive of the All-England Lawn Tennis Club on Saturday, when the closing scene in the first act of the Championship meeting was enacted at Wimbledon. Despite the fact that from various causes the leading players—with the exception of Ernest Renshaw, who suffered defeat at the hands of W. Baddeley on Thursday—were absent from the competition for the Singles Championship this year, a deal of interest was manifested by the public in the affair, and that this was sustained right up till the close was amply proved by the large company that gathered round the centre court whilst the play was in course of progress. In former years it has been customary for the winner of the All comers' competition to meet the holder of the Cup to decide who should have the right to dub himself Champion during the twelve months ensuing, but inasmuch as Mr Hamilton, last year's victor, is not sufficiently well to defend his title, the winner of Saturday's match becomes entitled to hold the A.E.L.T.C. Challenge Cup until June next year without having to run the gauntlet of further opposition. The twain left in to contest the all-important final match were W. Baddeley and J. Pim. Expert opinion was to the effect that a close struggle might be anticipated, and for once in a way the components were correct in their surmises, as although Baddeley won by three sets to one, thirty-nine games were played in the course of the match. Of these it may be interesting to note that Baddeley won twenty games to his rival's fifteen, and altogether scored 122 strokes to 102. Details are appended :

SINGLE-HANDED CHAMPIONSHIP.
FINAL MATCH.

W. BADDELEY beat J. PIM by three sets to one (6—4, 1—6, 7—5, and 6—0). Pim opened well, taking the first two games of the opening set at 4—1 and 4—2, but Baddeley then commenced playing in very effective style, and carried off the ensuing three games by four strokes to one. Pim then equalised after deuce had been once called, following which Baddeley won two games at 4—2 and 4—1 respectively. Pim played remarkably well in the ensuing game, which he secured by five strokes to three. The tenth game, however, was a love one in favour of Baddeley, who won the set by six games to four. Second set: Pim only allowed his rival to score one stroke in the preliminary game, but was beaten at the next time of asking after deuce had been twice called. Pim took the third game at 4—2, the fourth at 5—3, the fifth at 4—2, the sixth at 4—1, and finished off the set in grand style with a love game. Third set: At the outset Pim maintained his form of the previous set, opening with a love game. He only reached 30 in the second game, but won the third by four strokes to 2, the fourth by 6—4, and the fifth by 4—2, thus bringing his record to four games to one. He then fell off considerably in his play, and allowed Baddeley to take the next two games, the first to fifteen and the ensuing one to love. Pim won the eighth game after deuce had been once called, but Baddeley then scored four successive victories (4—2, 4—0, 8—6, and 8—6), and took the set at seven games to five. Fourth set: This was all in Baddeley's favour, Pim being tired and totally unable to cope with the other's effective service. It is worthy of note that with the exception of the third Baddeley won every one of his games at 4—2; the third being a love one in his favour.

1891   The Sportsman

Dr Joshua Pim. A popular Irishman, Pim decided to concentrate on his career as a doctor in Dublin rather than attempt to win the Wimbledon singles for a third successive year

1892 Wilfred Baddeley
beat Dr Joshua Pim
4–6 6–3 6–3 6–2

1893 Dr Joshua Pim
beat Wilfred Baddeley
3–6 6–1 6–3 6–2

1894 Dr Joshua Pim
beat Wilfred Baddeley
10–8 6–2 8–6

Wilfred Baddeley and **Dr Joshua Pim** contested four successive finals for the Wimbledon men's singles title and, in the end, honours were even. Baddeley won the first two meetings (1891 and 1892) and Pim the next two (1893 and 1894). The decider was avoided by Pim's retirement from tennis; he wanted to concentrate on his profession as a doctor.

The two players had completely contrasting styles. Baddeley was a good mover around the court and settled for a steady, solid game. Pim, on the other hand, was a flamboyant strokemaker and attempted as many different and difficult shots as possible. He perfected the drop volley and it was said that his shots were so accurate that he could hit the ball so precisely against the top of the net cord as to make it drop lifelessly on his opponent's side, impossible to recover.

LAWN TENNIS.
THE CHAMPIONSHIP MEETING.
GENTLEMEN'S SINGLES.

The lawn tennis enthusiasts who thronged the Central Court at Wimbledon yesterday were fated to witness only a very one-sided contest. After the sensational match on Saturday it seemed not unreasonable to expect that the victor on that occasion would make a determined fight with W. Baddeley for championship honours. During the first set, indeed, which Pim won after 20 minutes' play, there appeared some promise of a struggle worthy of the occasion; but in the second set Baddeley speedily settled down to play a beautiful game, winning stroke after stroke with automatic regularity. The winner secured the last set—with a fine stroke down the side line—in 14 minutes, the whole match occupying one hour and a quarter. Thus W. Baddeley by three sets to one upheld his right to the championship.

GENTLEMEN'S DOUBLES.

First Round.—E. W. Lewis and H. S. Barlow beat W. Milne and "Spyers" by three sets to love (6—3, 6—1, 6—1).

Second Round.—E. W. Lewis and H. S. Barlow beat O. S. Campbell and G. W. Hillyard by three sets to love (6—2, 6—4, 6—2.)

In the gentlemen's doubles some alterations in the arrangements, as announced on Saturday, have been deemed necessary in order to bring the meeting to a close to-morrow. The matches for to-day will be:—J. Pim and H. S. Mahony v. A. W. Gore and A. Palmer; E. W. Lewis and H. S. Barlow v. winners.

The pair left in will be called upon to play W. and H. Baddeley to-morrow for the championship.

LADIES' SINGLES CHAMPIONSHIP.

Miss Shackle beat Miss Steedman by two sets to love (6—4, 6—3).

Mrs. Hillyard beat Miss Martin by two sets to one (1—6, 6—3, 9—7).

The final round between Miss Shackle and Mrs. Hillyard will be played off to-day at 4 30, the winner to meet Miss L. Dod to-morrow.

THE ALL-ENGLAND CHAMPIONSHIPS.
SEVENTH DAY.
THE IRISH CHAMPION SECURES THE SINGLES.

There was hardly a vacant seat in the large stands at the All-England Lawn Tennis Club's prettily situated grounds at Wimbledon yesterday (Monday), when the seventh day's play was commenced. Although the card was not an extensive one, only a couple of matches being down for decision, the spectators were amply rewarded by one match, that wherein J. Pim, the Irish champion, met and defeated the holder of the title, W. Baddeley. The latter, however, appeared somewhat "off colour," and certainly did not play with that dash and finish so characteristic of him. Pim, however, was certainly a bit above himself as judged by his previous performances, but he thoroughly deserved his victory. In the Doubles Pim and Stoker proved victorious over A. W. Gore and A. Palmer in the penultimate tie of the Doubles, and will now have to meet the brothers Baddeley in the final. Mr. B. C. Evelegh again ably discharged the duties of referee. Details:—

GENTLEMEN'S SINGLES CHAMPIONSHIP.
CHAMPIONSHIP TIE.

J. PIM (challenger) beat W. BADDELEY (holder).

First Set.—In this the holder raised the hopes of his friends by winning at 6—3, but still upon going into figures there was not much in it, as he only scored 33 strokes to Pim's 26, the scoring being 4—1, 4—2, 6—4, 5—3, 4—2, 2—4, 2—4, 2—4, and 4—2. Duration of set, 17 minutes.

Second Set.—A change came o'er the scene in this set, the holder only winning one game, Pim taking the set at 6—1 (27 strokes to 13), the scores being 4—1, 2—4, 4—1, 5—3, 4—2, 4—1, and 4—1 Time of play, 10 minutes.

Third Set.—The Irish champion having won the preceding set, matters were thus even—one set all. Pim again played well, and won at 6—3, 43 strokes to 34, the games being as follows :—8—10, 4—2, 4—2, 4—1, 4—2, 2—4, 7—9, 4—0, and 6—4. Time of set, 21 min.

Fourth Set.—In this set Pim once more demonstrated his superiority, as playing with all his usual dash, he won at 6—2, taking 31 strokes to 21, the figures reading 4—1, 3—5, 4—2, 4—2, 5—3, 4—1, 2—4, 5—3. Duration of play, 15 min.

Pim thus, for the first time, won the championship by three sets to one, 21 games to 12, and 127 strokes to 101.

Appended will be found a list of previous winners :—

YR.		YR.	
1877	S. W. Gore	1886	W. Renshaw
1878	P. F. Hadow	1887	H. F. Lawford
1879	J. T. Hartley	1888	Ernest Renshaw
1880	J. T. Hartley	1889	W. Renshaw
1881	W. Renshaw	1890	W. J. Hamilton
1882	W. Renshaw	1891	W. Baddeley
1883	W. Renshaw	1892	W. Baddeley
1884	W. Renshaw	1893	J. Pim
1885	W. Renshaw		

GENTLEMEN'S DOUBLES CHAMPIONSHIP.
PENULTIMATE TIE.

J. PIM and F. O. STOKER beat A. W. GORE and A. PALMER. The first-named couple went away well, gaining the first set at 6—2, and, though their opponents took the second at 7—5, they won the third at 6—1, and the fourth at 6—4, thus qualifying to meet the Brothers Baddeley in the final by three sets to one. . . .

1892 The Times

1893 The Sporting Life

ALL ENGLAND LAWN TENNIS CLUB.
THE CHAMPIONSHIPS.
J. PIM RETAINS THE SINGLES.

Not for many years have so many spectators attended the series of championship matches at the Wimbledon ground as was the case yesterday. It was fortunate that no play was arranged for Monday, when the weather turned out very showery, and with the exception of a rather stiff breeze it was very pleasant yesterday afternoon, the large company present being favoured with bright sunshine. The chief item on the programme was the deciding tie in the Singles Championship, in which J. Pim, the holder, met W. Baddeley. In addition to this event there was the final for the Ladies' Championship, and two matches in the Doubles Championship. The ladies' game was first played, the centre court being surrounded by a throng of followers of the game, principally ladies, who applauded the players enthusiastically. Mrs Hillyard, who ran up to Miss L. Dod last year, was opposed by Miss Austin, and although the latter played well she was no match for her opponent, who won easily, Mrs Hillyard now becoming entitled to the championship, as the holder, Miss Dod, has retired. The Gentlemen's Championship followed,

and in this there was some brilliant play. Mr Pim, the holder, was the smarter, however, and he had no great difficulty in retaining his title. The semifinal round of the Doubles was very protracted, occupying nearly two hours. In the end Messrs Barlow and Martin, who had previously beaten Chaytor and Ball Green, proved successful over Hausberg and Hatton, and to-day meet the brothers Baddeley in the final, the holders, J. Pim and F. O. Stoker, having retired. The umpires were A. Walker, H. Chipp, and H. B. Lawford.

GENTLEMEN'S SINGLES CHAMPIONSHIP.
J. PIM (holder) beat W. BADDELEY by 3 sets to 0.

The holder played with admirable judgment, and won the first set by 10 games to 8, Baddeley commencing well by winning the first two games. The second set fell easily to Pim, who won by 6 games to 2; but the third was closely fought out, and Pim winning by 8 games to 6 secured the championship for the second year in succession. The scores in the first set were: 0—4, 2—4, 5—3, 4—1, 2—4, 4—2, 1—4, 4—2, 3—5, 5—3, 2—4, 5—3, 0—4, 4—1, 4—6, 4—2, 4—0, 5—3. In the second: 4—1, 5—3, 3—5, 1—4, 4—2, 4—2, 4—0, 6—4. In the third: 4—2, 4—2, 3—5 5—3, 4—1, 1—4, 2—4, 4—2, 1—4, 2—4, 2—4, 0—4, 4—2, 4—1.

1894   The Sportsman

1894 programme. This is an example of an old-style Championship programme. On the reverse side there are full details of the men's singles draw

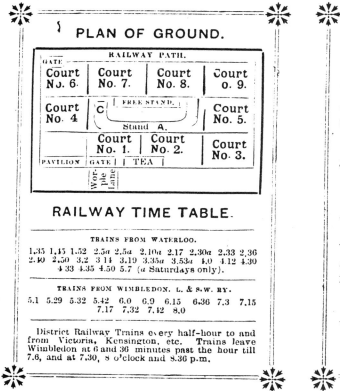

1895 Wilfred Baddeley
beat Dr W.V. Eaves
4–6 2–6 8–6 6–2 6–3

1896 Harold Mahony
beat Wilfred Baddeley
6–2 6–8 5–7 8–6 6–3

Despite being within a point of a straight-sets defeat **Wilfred Baddeley** went on to win his third Wimbledon's men's singles title in 1895. In the All Comers final – playing for the Championship as Dr Pim had retired – Baddeley stood at match-point down against W.V. Eaves. An Australian by birth but a pioneer of international play – he was to be runner-up in the United States men's singles championship in 1897 – Eaves failed to take this advantage and eventually succumbed to Baddeley's determination.

In two consecutive years Baddeley was involved in a thrilling five-set final match. As 1895 champion he qualified for the Challenge Round in 1896 but this time he came off second best to **Harold Mahony.**

The friendly Irishman Mahony was as popular with the Wimbledon crowds as his fellow countrymen St Leger and Dr Pim had been. His long legs and arms suited his powerful volley game, but he was so weak on the forehand that often he ran round to take a ball on his stronger backhand side.

In 1896 the All England Plate was introduced for the first time and was open to first- and second-round losers in the men's singles. This attracted an entry of thirty-one – the highest since 1881. Spectator attendances had fallen following the retirement of the Renshaw twins and for the first and only time a loss of £33 was recorded by the All England Club following the 1895 Championship.

LAWN TENNIS.

THE CHAMPIONSHIPS.—JULY 8, &c.

SATURDAY, JULY 13.—Those who were present at Wimbledon to-day will long remember the splendid struggle between Mr W. Baddeley and Mr Eaves in the final round of the All Comers' Singles, and in what really was also the championship round, as it was well known that Mr Pim did not intend to defend his title. The weather was again bright and fine, but there was rather too much wind. Mr Eaves was in astonishing form when he commenced his match against Mr Baddeley, and, wonderful to relate, forced the game to such a degree, that he seemed to take all the usual accuracy out of his opponent's play. The opening set was won by Mr Eaves after ten games had been contested, and the same player gained an easy victory in the second in this set, only losing two games. The play in the third set was much more, even as one, three, four, and five games all were called. Mr Eaves gained the advantage game, and in the following game was 30—love and 40—30, and then put a lob just over the base line, and this seemed to be the turning point of the match, as afterwards Mr Baddeley seemed to get back all his old accuracy, and won the last three sets in succession—a most wonderful performance. It certainly was hard luck on Mr Eaves to be within one ace of being champion for the year, and then to lose after such splendid play as he had shown in the first three sets. Certainly Mr Baddeley is greatly to be congratulated upon the great pluck he showed in struggling on when to all appearances the match was practically over. Many players would have given it up as a hopeless task, but he persevered, and Mr Eaves having almost played himself out, Mr Baddeley gradually got on terms, and being a good stayer, eventually gained the victory, thus once again winning the championship. The score of the match was three sets to two; twenty-six games to twenty-three, and 167 aces to 149.

All Comers' Singles.—Final Round : The opening ace of the match between Mr Baddeley and Mr Eaves was taken by the former ; but the next four in succession were all gained by Mr Eaves, thus crediting him with the first game ; and then followed two love-games to Mr Baddeley, but the fourth fell to Mr Eaves by four strokes to two, while Mr Baddeley secured the fifth by the same number. The sixth—once at deuce—was taken by Mr Eaves, but that player could only gain one ace in the next game, the score now standing at four games to three in favour of Mr Baddeley. Some very brilliant play was now seen from Mr Eaves, his returns, both volleying and from the back of the court, being exceedingly well placed and very close to the lines. The eighth game Mr Eaves took after it had been at deuce once, the ninth, at deuce twice, while in the tenth he only lost one ace. Mr Eaves won thirty-one aces to his opponent's thirty. Three of the games were at deuce, and Mr Baddeley won two love-games. Playing even still better in the second set, Mr Eaves only lost two games (the second and seventh), Mr Baddeley taking these by five strokes to three and four to two respectively. Mr Eaves only lost one ace in each of the first and sixth games, whilst the second and fourth games he won by four strokes to two. In the fifth game deuce was called three times, and in the eighth once. Mr Eaves won thirty-three points to Mr Baddeley's twenty-three. The third was the best contested set of the five, as fourteen games were played before it was won by Mr Baddeley, one, three, four, and five games all being called. Mr Eaves secured the opening game by four strokes to two, and then Mr Baddeley took the second after it had been at deuce twice, the third at deuce once, and only lost one ace in the fourth. Mr Eaves now had a turn, and gained three in succession, by four strokes to one, five to three, and a love-game respectively. Two consecutive games were then made by Mr Baddeley, he only losing one ace in each, making the score five games to four in his favour; but Mr Eaves, by taking the tenth at four strokes to two, caused an advantage set to be played. At this point of the set each player had scored thirty-one aces. The advantage game was taken by Mr Eaves by four strokes to two, and the score was also called 30—40 in his favour in the next game, making him within one ace of the match. In lobbing the following stroke over Mr Baddeley's head, his return just went over the base-line, or in all probability he would have won the match, as, even supposing Mr Baddeley had been able to return it, his opponent was up at the net, and would most likely have killed the ball. Mr Baddeley by making the next two aces brought the score back to games all, and then in turn won the advantage game after it had been at deuce once, and only losing one ace in the next game, thus won the set by eight games to six. Mr Baddeley won forty-seven aces to Mr Eaves's forty-two. Five of the games were at deuce. A change now came over the game, Mr Baddeley playing decidedly the better, and after Mr Eaves had gained the opening game by four strokes to two—one ace being made after he had fallen over a ball in the court and recovered himself—his opponent took five games in succession, only losing one ace in the second, fourth, and fifth, while the third he won by five strokes to three, and the sixth was a love-game, Mr Eaves only lost one ace in the seventh game, but was unable to follow this up, Mr Baddeley then finishing off the set and match with a love-game. In this set Mr Baddeley won twenty-eight aces to his opponent's fourteen.

Harold Mahony. Like his fellow Irishman Pim, he was very popular with the Wimbledon spectators

The 1896 final. This was a thrilling match between Wilfred Baddeley and Harold Mahony, illustrated for the Daily Graphic

LAWN TENNIS.

THE CHAMPIONSHIPS.
SEVENTH DAY.
MAHONY SECURES THE SINGLES.

Yesterday (Monday) the biggest crowd that has yet assembled at the grounds of the All England Lawn Tennis Club during the progress of the present meeting put in an appearance. The chief attention was the championship round of the gentlemen's singles, wherein the holder, W. Baddeley, met H. S. Mahony. The former unfortunately was far from well or he would undoubtedly have retained his title, as in the fourth set he was within one game of taking the set and match, but after this he played in a very weak fashion, whilst Mahony appeared to improve, and ultimately won the championship, but not until the whole of the five sets had been played. The Brothers Allen for once in a way appeared all abroad in the doubles, and were easily beaten by Doherty and Nisbet, who now have to meet W. and H. Baddeley for the championship. Mr. B.C. Evelegh is officiating as referee, and Mr. A. J. Chitty is hon. sec. Brief details:–

GENTLEMEN'S SINGLES CHAMPIONSHIP
CHAMPIONSHIP ROUND

H. S. Mahony (challenger), All-England L.T.C., beat W. Baddeley (holder), All-England L.T.C. – First Set. – The holder took the first game, but Mahony secured the next three, and after Baddeley had taken the fifth game, Mahony secured the sixth, seventh, and eighth, winning the set at 6-2. Second Set. – Baddeley won the opening game, and Mahony the next two. The holder, however, won the fourth and fifth, the next three fell to the Irishman. Baddeley, won the ninth and tenth, and Mahony the eleventh, but Baddeley winning the twelfth, thirteenth and fourteenth, took the set at 8-6. Third Set. – Playing in fine form Mahony won the first four games, Baddeley took the fifth and Mahony the sixth, after which the holder, playing grandly, carried off the six following games and won the set at 7-5. Fourth Set. – Baddeley won the first game and Mahony the second, but after the holder of the title had secured the third, Mahony placed the next three to his credit. The seventh and eighth games went to Baddeley, Mahony winning the ninth, but after Baddeley had taken the tenth and eleventh, Mahony secured the next three and thus won the set by 8-6, making it two sets all. Fifth Set. – After Baddeley had won the opening game, Mahony, playing with much confidence, took the next five. Baddeley won the seventh and eighth, but Mahony securing the ninth took the set at 6-3, and the match and championship by three sets to two.

1896 The Sportsman

4 | The Doherty Brothers Dominate

1897–1906

Reggie and Laurie Doherty won nine singles titles between them – four and five respectively – in ten years. Wimbledon's main gates are named in their honour.

The Doherty Brothers. Like the Renshaw twins, Reggie (on the left) and Laurie had an outstanding record in men's doubles winning eight Wimbledon titles between 1897 and 1905. Their elder brother – William Vernon – captained Oxford University at lawn tennis but then decided to pursue the career of an Anglican priest

1897 Reggie Doherty
beat Harold Mahony
6–4 6–4 6–3

1898 Reggie Doherty
beat Laurie Doherty
6–3 6–3 2–6 5–7 6–1

1899 Reggie Doherty
beat Arthur Wentworth Gore
1–6 4–6 6–2 6–3 6–3

1900 Reggie Doherty
beat Sidney Smith
6–8 6–3 6–1 6–2

The Doherty brothers' ten-year dominance of the men's singles Championship began in 1897. **Reggie Doherty** won through the All Comers and beat Harold Mahony in the Challenge Round final without dropping a set, thus equalling Frank Hadow's achievement in 1878.

In 1898, Reggie met his younger brother by two years, Laurie, in the Challenge Round final. Laurie had scraped through the All Comers final by beating Mahony 14-12 in the last set. Reggie, at 6 ft 1 in. was taller than his brother and, unlike the Renshaw twins, they enjoyed playing against one another. Their match was billed ' "Big Do" v. "Little Do".' In the end, the final was considered a good game rather than an exciting one, with Reggie winning in the final set.

A year later Laurie missed the Championship and Reggie was challenged by Arthur Wentworth Gore, who himself was to become something of a Wimbledon legend. Reggie was not in the best of health following a car accident and Gore won the first two sets. However, Reggie fought back and kept the ball on Gore's weaker backhand to retain the title for a third successive year.

Reggie met yet another different challenger in 1900 as Sidney Smith beat Gore in the All Comers final. Hailing from Gloucestershire, he was known as 'Smith of Stroud' and had the distinction of being the first men's badminton champion in England. Smith won the first set but once Reggie settled down and tamed his powerful forehand, the holder only lost six games in the next three sets.

After a drop in profits in the

WEDNESDAY, JUNE 30.—Owing to Mr R. F. Doherty having made his way into the championship rounds of both the Singles and Doubles, it was deci ed that the two matches should not take place on the same afternoon, so to-day's play was confined to the Championship Singles of the tournament proper, but in addition to that competition, it was agreed that the final round of the All England Plate should also be played. In this Mr H. Buddeley defeated Mr Crawley by three sets to one, the latter player taking the third set after twelve games had been contested. Turning to the Championship Round, Mr Doherty defeated Mr Mahony three sets in succession, ten games being played in each of the first and second sets, and nine in the third. Mr Doherty won eighteen games and 106 aces to Mr Mahony's eleven games and 88 aces. During the match Mr Doherty gained four love-games, but only seven were at deuce. During the earlier part of the play the light was very bad, and then just as the second set was concluded a little rain fell, but only for a short time, and when the game was resumed the light luckily became much better. The game was not of a very brilliant description, but each player took full advantage of his adversary's shortcomings, both playing with their heads, if one can put it so, as well as with their rackets. At times Mr Mahony did well by rushing up to the net to volley, but in the long run Mr Doherty beat him well with his returns, time after time scoring by placing the ball just where the service line cuts the side line. Mr Doherty also scored well with his volleying when he did go up to the net, his short volleys being most effective, and especially well placed.
Gentlemen's Singles.—Championship Round: Mr R. F. Doherty defeated Mr H. S. Mahony three sets in succession. In the opening set Mr Mahony secured the first game, after it had been once at deuce ; but the second was a well-contested game, and was eventually won by Mr Doherty, after the advantage ace had been scored three times by each player. The next three games were also gained by Mr Doherty, the third after it had been at deuce once, the fourth by four strokes to two, and the fifth by four to one, this making the score four games to one in his favour. In the sixth game Mr Mahony only lost one ace, and in the next two, this making him only one game behind. The eighth game was won by Mr Doherty by four strokes to one, and then, after he had lost the ninth to two strokes, he finished off the set by gaining the tenth by the same number, thus winning the set by six games to four and 39 aces to 34. The first three games were all at deuce, twenty-seven minutes. In the opening game of the second set Mr Doherty could only obtain one stroke ; but he gained the next eight in succession, and so won two love games. The fourth was taken by Mr Mahony by four strokes to two, but the next was gained by Mr Doherty after being at deuce twice, and then the score became once more level, when the holder secured the sixth game after losing one ace. After deuce had been called twice in the seventh game, Mr Doherty gained it, and then had the game called five games to three in his favour by taking the next game by four aces to one. Mr Mahony secured the ninth game by four strokes to two, but lost the next game after it had been once at deuce, Mr Doherty thus winning the set by six games to four and 34 aces to 31. Time of set, twenty-three minutes. In the third set, as in both the previous sets, Mr Mahony gained the opening game, but lost the next three in succession, the second and third both being love games, while in the fourth he only lost one ace. Each player gained a game by four strokes to one, and then Mr Doherty took the seventh after it had been at deuce twice, and when his opponent had secured the eighth by four strokes to two, finished off the set and match in the ninth game, the aces being seven to five in his favour. Mr Doherty in this set won 33 aces altogether to Mr Mahony's 23, while the duration of the set was seventeen minutes.

1897 The Field

LAWN TENNIS.

THE CHAMPIONSHIPS AT WIMBLEDON.

R. F. Doherty yesterday succeeded in retaining possession of the Lawn Tennis Championship, which he won for the first time a year ago. The honour could not be in safer keeping. There may be those who doubt whether he is the best of the players now to the front ; none can question the statement that he is the most stylish. But as a matter of fact, he combines with a beautiful style a skill that very few of his compeers can even approach. His ability is not at once apparent when he is seen in the court. He has a rather nonchalant manner that is apt to deceive the onlooker, but a careful scrutiny of his performance reveals eventually the superb quality of his play. It is very seldom that he lets himself "go," and plays all he knows ; there is nearly always a reserve of force to be drawn upon if occasion demands. Though he may not have taken Pim for his model, certain it is that he most forcibly reminds one of that famous Irish player. Both play with the same ease, the same grace, and with an almost equal strength. More than that one cannot say in commendation of Doherty, for lawn tennis has not yet produced a finer exponent than Dr. J. Pim when he was at his best, say, five years ago.
Doherty yesterday had to play his brother H. L. in the championship round. We were solemnly assured beforehand that the match was to be a fight "to the death." It may have been, but there were a good many onlookers who had their doubts. And there were many little things that drove one to the conclusion that it was little more than an exhibition game. For example, play was started without linesmen ! Then, again, neither of the players seemed very particular whether the ball boys were on or off the court when they started serving. True, it turned out to be a five-set match—that made it look well ; but surely R. F. Doherty could have won without losing a set ? At any rate, granting that he could not under any circumstances have beaten his brother in the third he had the fourth practically at his mercy when he was leading at 5—4 for in the next game he was four times within a stroke of winning the match. The full score read 6—3, 6—3, 2—6, 5—7, 6—1 in the champion's favour. Both players relied mainly on ground strokes, only very occasionally resorting to volleying. Some of the passages were very pretty and entertaining, but the spectators—of whom there was a very large company—took but a languid interest in the affair, it seemed so patent that R. F. Doherty could assert his supremacy at any moment he chose. The match was twice interrupted by rain, and several games were played in a heavy downpour. Altogether it was not an inspiriting occasion.
Owing to the decision of Mrs. Hillyard not to defend the championship she wrested last year from Miss C. Cooper, the contest in the final round of the ladies' event was invested with all the greater importance. The competitors were Miss Cooper, of Surbiton, and Miss Martin, of Dublin. It so happened that they met at Liverpool nine days previously, and on that occasion Miss Martin won at 10—8, 6—4. Yesterday, however, the Irish lady quite failed to do herself justice, and Miss Cooper scored a comparatively easy victory at 6—4, 6—4, and thus regains the title or lady champion which she held in 1895 and 1896. She is to be congratulated on her success.
The final in the gentlemen's doubles was a tame business. Nisbet and Hobart took the first prize by defeating Hillyard and Smith at 2—6, 6—2 6—2, 6—3. The combination of the victors was very much superior to that of their opponents. This afternoon at half-past four, or thereabouts, Nisbet and Hobart will play the Dohertys for the doubles championship.

1898 Pall Mall Gazette

1890s, the All England Club once again benefited from the outstanding performances of two brothers at the Wimbledon Championships. They built a new pavilion for £1,200 and renamed themselves the All England Lawn Tennis and Croquet Club.

Come rain or shine. This Wimbledon centre court crowd scene was taken during a men's singles final at the turn of the century

CHAMPION ONCE MORE.

GREAT DAY AT THE LAWN TENNIS TOURNAMENT.

("Daily Mail" Special.)

Mr. R. F. Doherty is for the third year in succession the lawn tennis champion of All England.

He fought for the honour at Wimbledon yesterday, and he won. His opponent, Mr. A. W. Gore, gave him a hard struggle and a long one. At one time, if anything so vulgar as betting were known at a lawn tennis tournament, the odds would have been in Mr. Gore's favour. After years and years of tennis, he was at last within a hair's-breadth of the supreme distinction of the game.

But youth will be served. Mr. Gore's natural claim on the championship is past. Mr. Doherty added brilliance to precision, and litheness to vigour; and he left the court as he entered it—the Champion of All England—a distinction which among lawn tennis players, is a shade higher than that of the see of Canterbury.

The tennis ground at Wimbledon is laid out for use rather than for beauty. Its adornments consist of a railway embankment and a few gaunt stands. But for the handsome finery of the ladies, the scene would have been about as picturesque as the Oval. Everybody flocked to the championship court, for everybody wanted to see the contest for the high priesthood of the game.

Lawn tennis runs in pairs—twins for preference. As the competitors came on the ground there were some who looked with curiosity to see which of the Dohertys the champion might be. The Dohertys only resemble each other in their lawn tennis. This was the

TALL AND HANDSOME ONE,

with the curly locks—the slim Greek god of the pair. The other brothers of the game are more difficult to distinguish. One of the Aliens sat in the seat of judgment to declare the "faults" and proclaim the score. Which of them he might be—E. R., the stout and ruddy, or C. G., the ruddy and stout—nobody would venture to say.

It was an excellent match, hard, keenly fought, and determined. Mr. Gore, the elder player, played a vigorous game, grim and precise. His strokes are terrific. They skimmed the net, and generally alighted just on the hither side of safety. His game was steady rather than brilliant. He played the obvious stroke whenever it was possible, and raced yards to escape a "back-hand" return. He seldom volleyed, and he seldom allowed his opponent to volley. He tried few experiments, preferring to rely on agility and strength of wrist.

If he made a mistake, it was in returning too frequently to Doherty's left. Doherty's back-hand strokes were

MODELS OF PRECISION.

He did not skip about to catch the ball in direct flight. He stretched out his long arm, jerked his flexible wrist, and sent the ball flying back to the uttermost end of the court, generally on the side which caused Gore to race round for his favourite return.

In the finesse of the game, the dainty placing of the ball out of reach, Gore was beaten in the end by his brilliant opponent.

Gore served from the outermost edge of the court—very fast, very low, but generally to about the same spot. Doherty seldom served two balls alike. He threw the ball high in the air, he gathered up his long body for the smite, he smote hard, and whether the ball alighted in the centre of the court or at the outer edge, or set the net shaking, was a thing to be discovered, but not to be foretold.

At first Gore had the match all his own way. He won the first set by six games to one, and the second by six to four. As the match was the best of five, he only required another set to win. From this point Doherty steadily crept back to his lost form. Style began to tell and energy to wane. Doherty ventured to volley, and his volleys generally scored. He won the next three sets (6—2, 6—3, 6—3), and a final cheer announced the fact that Mr. Doherty was champion once more.

LAWN TENNIS.

TWO EXCITING FINALS AT WIMBLEDON.

It looked as if the championship finals at Wimbledon would have to be postponed again yesterday, but the weather cleared up just after lunch, and play began about three o'clock.

The centre court had been covered with tarpaulin all the morning, so, compared with the spongy condition of the other courts, it was dry. The stands round the court filled up quickly, but people were a little shy of standing on the grass.

The final for the ladies' championship was played first, Mrs. Hillyard (holder) beating Miss C. Cooper. The play was exciting, and for some time it seemed as if Miss Cooper would win. Her play was more brilliant than Mrs. Hillyard's, but she had not the same staying power. She fell off badly in the last two games, while Mrs. Hillyard's only worry was the proper adjustment of her gloves.

There was great applause for every point made by each lady, and opinion was fairly divided as to which was the better player.

In the gentlemen's championship Mr. S. H. Smith entered the final for the first time. His opponent was Mr. R. F. Doherty, who has been in several.

The game was followed with the keenest interest, and it was funny, in watching the stands, to see all heads moving together like a row of cavalry.

Both players started very carefully, and it was some little time before they worked any spirit into the game. Smith won the first set, getting in some very pretty play, and "placing" beautifully.

But he was no match for Doherty. He failed altogether in his backhand strokes, keeping his racquet too close to the ground. Doherty's victory was a foregone conclusion after the first set, in spite of the fact that some of the games were very long. This is R. F. Doherty's fourth consecutive win.

1901 Arthur Wentworth Gore
beat Reggie Doherty
4–6 7–5 6–4 6–4

Reggie Doherty was an outstanding athlete who had also excelled at football and cricket while at Westminster School. However, throughout his life he was plagued by ill health and prior to the 1901 Challenge Round final he had been advised by his doctor not to play.

He had intended to scratch if his brother Laurie Doherty had won the All Comers final, but it was the redoubtable **Arthur Wentworth Gore** who had won through to become his opponent. So Reggie decided to play but, after winning the first set, he grew weaker and weaker and Gore was able to take the next three and the title. At the end of the match Doherty was so overcome with with exhaustion he could hardly stand.

So Gore avenged his defeat of 1899 and Reggie decided that in future he would only play in the men's doubles event with his brother Laurie.

Gore, nicknamed 'Baby' after winning a tournament at the age of twelve, graced the Wimbledon scene from 1888 until 1927, the year before he died. A baseline player, he was very strong on the forehand.

Gore, militant.

The contest for the English championship between the holder, R. F. Doherty, and the challenger, A. W. Gore, was, in a way, disappointing. Although Gore won, and on the day's play thoroughly deserved his victory, there are few who will contend that he is really Doherty's superior. The latter was quite off his game yesterday, after the first set. I had been told that he was not "up to the mark," and was, therefore, prepared for what happened. Now and again Doherty played with that brilliancy and wonderful grace that have usually distinguished his performances at Wimbledon, but, generally speaking, he utterly failed to do himself justice. Gore, on the other hand, was simply wonderful. The longer he played the more vigorous he became. There was a dash and a business-like air about his operations that foreshadowed the result. The most noticeable feature of his game—apart from the steadiness which always distinguishes it—was the manner in which he passed Doherty when the latter ventured up to the net. His placing was marvellously accurate. Never before have I seen Doherty run about so much. Gore put the ball first on one side of the court, and then on the other, and no doubt Doherty's exhaustion at the finish was largely the result of these tactics. As a rule, he makes his opponents do the running. The upshot of it all was that Gore won the match at 4—6, 7—5, 6—4, 6—4, and was declared English champion. There was much enthusiasm displayed at the close, and both players were loudly cheered as they left the court, particularly Doherty. He has had a good innings, having held the championship for four years. It is in the best interests of the game that the honour should change hands occasionally.

Then came the fight in the Doubles final, which was easily won by the American champions, Ward and Davis. I had heard so much about this pair that I was very curious to see them in the court. It was a most interesting experience. For a long time I have wondered what the next development of the game would be. They have supplied it. Their play affected me much in the same way as a tonic. This is the last day of the tournament. Ward and Davis this afternoon play the Dohertys for the Doubles Championship. If there is any lawn-tennis player reading this column who has not yet been to Wimbledon and seen the American pair play, let me urge him to take the first train out from Waterloo, for he will obtain a liberal education by watching their movements. Their methods are not those we have become so accustomed to; the effectiveness of their methods is shown by the fact that they have won the first prizes. That mighty swipe across the court, with which Davis now and again electrifies the onlookers, is something to be remembered, and so are his smashes and his services. Ward is not so brilliant, but he is very sure, and his lobbing is excellent. The lob plays a large part in the Americans' game. I happened to see them practising in one of the outer courts just before they played their match yesterday. I soon realized how Davis had developed that swipe of his. It seems to me that we shall have to go to America to learn the knack of training lawn-tennis players as well as horses.   SENTINEL.

1901   Pall Mall Gazette

Arthur Wentworth Gore. In this shot (above right) he displays the fullness of his powerful forehand stroke

1902   Laurie Doherty
beat Arthur Wentworth Gore
6–4 6–3 3–6 6–0

1903   Laurie Doherty
beat Frank Riseley
7–5 6–3 6–0

1904   Laurie Doherty
beat Frank Riseley
6–1 7–5 8–6

1905   Laurie Doherty
beat Norman Brookes
8–6 6–2 6–4

1906   Laurie Doherty
beat Frank Riseley
6–4 4–6 6–2 6–3

Arthur Wentworth Gore had broken Reggie's run but he was confronted once again by a Doherty in the Challenge Round final in 1902. **Laurie Doherty** won through the All Comers although he had a dramatic clash in the semi-finals with Harold Mahony, the 1896 champion. After winning the first two sets, Mahony looked set for victory but Laurie came back to win the third 8–6. Despite an advantage of two sets to one Mahony only lasted another two games before having to retire through exhaustion.

By beating Gore in the Challenge Round final, Laurie began a run of five Wimbledon singles victories, going one better than his older brother. Despite this achievement, it was often rumoured that Reggie still had the better of him in friendly matches.

In 1903 and 1904 Laurie won straight-sets victories over Frank Riseley, a strong server and volleyer from Clifton. Riseley also made the final in 1906 and at least won one set from Laurie, as did Norman Brookes in 1905.

In 1903 Laurie became the first overseas player to win the US Championships – a milestone in the history of tennis. Reggie was a beaten finalist the previous year but Laurie made up for this by beating W.A. Larned who won the title seven times. However, Willie Renshaw's record of six successive singles victories remained   *(cont.)*

LAWN TENNIS AT WIMBLEDON.

H. L. DOHERTY DEFEATS LAST YEAR'S CHAMPION.

After an interval of a year the name of Doherty is once more supreme in the lawn tennis world, as yesterday at Wimbledon Doherty the younger wrested the title of champion from Mr. A. W. Gore, who defeated his elder brother last year after he had held the title for four years in unbroken succession. Yesterday's contest attracted a large attendance to the Wimbledon Tennis Club, and when the match began the inner or championship court was occupied to the full.

The sun, which poured down with furnace-like intensity, alone prevented the conditions from being perfect at the beginning of the match. The sun, however, was obscured by a bank of clouds during the latter half of the contest—a relief which was welcomed as gladly by the spectators as by the players.

Doherty, who started a strong favourite, opened rather wildly, and lost the first game without scoring a point. Quickly settling down to his game, however, he took the next two games, and finally won the set by six games to four. He followed this up by winning the second set by six games to three, mainly by his superb volleying at the net.

In the third set Gore turned the tables on his opponent, and won by six games to three. In the fourth set, however, Doherty again reasserted himself, and won a love set. By thus winning the best of five sets H. L. Doherty won the championship for the first time.

From the start there was no doubt as to which was the better man, but Gore is a player who furnishes such unexpected surprises that he is never beaten until the final point has been decided. His tireless energy and tremendous pluck have often before enabled him to beat an adversary his superior in skill.

The styles of the two players in yesterday's contest were in marked contrast. Doherty plays with that ease and grace and apparent lack of effort which characterise the master. Gore, on the other hand, is a stiff and comparatively awkward player. The one is a born player, the other is manufactured.

The most interested spectator of yesterday's contest was the elder Doherty, who watched, with an appreciative smile on his face, his younger brother retrieving the family fame.

In the final round of the Doubles Championship S. H. Smith (Stroud) and F. L. Riseley (Clifton) beat G. W. Hillyard and C. H. L. Cazalet (All England) by four sets to one. Smith and Riseley play the holders, R. F. and H. L. Doherty, for the championship to-day.

Miss M. Robb defeated Miss A. M. Morton in the final round of the Ladies' Competition, and will now have to play the holder, Mrs. Sterry, for the championship. Mrs. Sterry and Miss A. M. Morton beat Mrs. Hillyard and Miss Steedman in the semifinal round of the Ladies' Doubles.

In the third round of the Mixed Doubles Competition C. H. L. Cazalet and Miss Robb beat M. J. G. Ritchie and Miss Thomson, while H. L. Doherty and Mrs. Sterry defeated H. S. Mahony and Mrs. Hillyard. In the semi-final round Cazalet and Miss Robb defeated C. H. Martin and Miss D. K. Douglass.

1902   Daily Mail

DOHERTY HOLDS HIS OWN IN LAWN TENNIS SINGLES.

The attendance at the All-England Club, Wimbledon, yesterday was again far above the average, over 2,500 people witnessing the contest between H. L. Doherty and F. L. Riseley in the challenge round of the singles championship—the great lawn tennis event of the year.

Though Doherty was somewhat erratic at the outset he soon found his game, and as the match went on the vast difference between the players became more and more apparent.

The champion finally got into form, and, playing in irresistible fashion, he won the second set at 6—3 and the third at 6—0, and so secured the match by three sets to love, finishing with a run of ten games off the reel.

The victory of Miss Douglass over Miss Thomson in the final of the ladies' competition decided the championship, as Miss Robb is not defending her title.

The challenge round of the doubles will be played to-day. Results:—

Singles Championship.—Challenge round: H. L. Doherty (holder) beat F. L. Riseley (winner of the all-comers' competition) by three sets to love (7—5, 6—3, 6—0).

Ladies' Championship.—Final and championship round: Miss D. K. Douglass beat Miss E. W. Thomson by two sets to one (4—6, 6—4, 6—2).

All-England Plate.—Final round: A. W. Gore beat C. Hobart by two sets to love (7—5, 6—3).

Ladies' and Gentlemen's Open Doubles.—Third round (concluded): C. Hobart and Miss Bromfield beat M. J. G. Ritchie and Miss W. A. Longhurst by two sets to love (6—4, 6—4). Semi-final round (concluded): C. Hobart and Miss Bromfield, w.o., F. L. Riseley and Miss D. K. Douglass scratched. Final round: S. H. Smith and Miss Thomson beat C. Hobart and Miss Bromfield by two sets to love (6—2, 6—3).

1903   Daily Express

LAWN TENNIS.

THE CHAMPIONSHIPS.

The challenge round of the Singles Championship attracted a large attendance to Wimbledon yesterday, while perfect conditions for lawn tennis prevailed, the weather being bright with an absence of wind. At the outset of the match Mr. Riseley was quite off his game, and Mr. Doherty playing with great steadiness took the first set at 6-1. In the second set Mr. Riseley improved, but his opponent always appeared to be master of the situation. The former won the first game, but Mr. Doherty placing across the court with accuracy went to four games to one. Mr. Riseley at this stage began to find his game, his severe first service repeatedly coming off, but, after five games all had been called, Mr. Doherty secured the set. The third set was also advantage one, but Mr. Doherty, with his greater steadiness, never looked like losing. Mr. Riseley showed all his customary brilliancy at times, many of his drives from the back of the court and smashes being extremely severe. The challenger won the first three games, but Mr. Doherty equalized, and after "six all" was called, he won the set and the rubber. The results were:—

Singles Championship – Challenge Round – Mr. H. L. Doherty, holder, beat Mr. F. L. Riseley, challenger (6-1, 7-5, 8-6).

Doubles Championship – Semi-final Round (concluded) – Mr. S. H. Smith and Mr. F. L. Riseley beat Mr. G. Greville and Mr. M. J. G. Ritchie (6-1, 7-5, 6-1).

Ladies Championship – Final Round – Mrs. Sterry beat Miss A. M. Morton (6-3, 6-3). Mrs. Sterry will play the holder, Miss D. K. Douglass, for the championship to-day.

1904   The Times

unchallenged because Laurie decided to retire after the final of the men's doubles in 1906. The brothers, with eight doubles victories to their name, were beaten in a traumatic five-set match by Sidney Smith and Frank Riseley. After sixty-three competitively fought games, Smith and Riseley won the last set 11-9.

Reggie's poor health had again been the weak link and the Doherty brothers' mother – who watched all her sons' matches – made them promise after this marathon final not to play at Wimbledon again. Reggie died four years later.

The entry for the men's singles Championship reached seventy-one in 1904 and this included three Australians, four Americans and players from Belgium, Denmark, Sweden and South Africa. Wimbledon was becoming truly international and, in 1907, the men's singles title went abroad for the first time.

Laurie Doherty. His five victories are legend

H. L. DOHERTY TO THE RESCUE.

After a short interval, during which the spectators sat wondering whether the Men's Championship was also going over the seas, N. E. Brookes and H. L. Doherty passed through the barrier amid a roar of greetings.

The Australian challenger, with a grim look on his lean face, wore his sun hat, as usual, but the holder bared his sleek head to the fray.

Brookes opened the engagement by completely deceiving his rival with his jumping left-handed service, and when "three all" was called, there seemed every prospect of a near thing. Doherty's deft volleying was often hooked back successfully by the Colonial, who showed more tricks than his adversary. When the challenger led 6—5, and reached "deuce" in the next game, the Commonwealth supporters were rapturous. But the champion's reputation was at stake, and he made a supreme recovery which eventually gave him the set at 8—6. Had Brookes won this bout a very different tale might have been told at the finish. It was the first set he had lost in England in a single, and the knowledge of the fact seemed to weaken his attack.

Doherty showed magnificent generalship in the next round. Recognising that the Australian was quite his match at close quarters, he lobbed on the slightest provocation, and then neatly placed the return which his opponent sent over. Doherty was "four—love," and soon had placed the second set to his credit at 6—2.

In the third round the Colonial braced himself, and somewhat modified his running-in tactics. Nevertheless, he failed to catch the Englishman, and though taking both the seventh and eighth games, Brookes missed several "sitters" in the ninth—mistakes which ultimately lost him the championship by 3 sets to love and 20 games to 14.

38

At the championship meeting at Wimbledon Mr. H. L. Doherty defeated Mr. F. L. Riseley by 3 sets to 1, and so retains his title of champion for the fifth year in succession. The late Mr. W. Renshaw held the championship for six years. On the left, Mr. Doherty, in the foreground, returning the ball. On the right, the players leaving after the match, Mr. Riseley in the foreground. (Daily Mirror photographs.)

'Little Do' in action

DOHERTY STILL CHAMPION.

BY F. B. WILSON.

" What I have I hold " should be H. L. Doherty's motto. He had the lawn tennis championship of the world yesterday, and held it against F. L. Riseley. Riseley played magnificently; but H. L. proved himself, like the Maltese cat, past-pluperfect prestissimo judge of the game.

Riseley's service was magnificent, his agility wonderful, and his resource infinite: yet, " Little Do " won, and won easily. His network was wonderful, and his head-work was unsurpassable.

Nobody knows how good Doherty is, except, perhaps, Riseley. " When we go down the vale " we may meet a better player: but it will not avail much to talk much rot, and lose many matches. The score in Doherty's favour was 6—4, 4—6, 6—2, 6—3.

Miss Douglass and F. H. Wilding beat Miss Eastlake-Smith and R. F. Doherty, after a grand game. The winners should win the mixed doubles against Miss Thomson and A. W. Gore.

The charity cricket match, between Catford tradesmen yesterday, resulted in a victory for Perry Hill, who beat Stanstead-road by 10 runs—96 to 86. F. Bisney scored 41 for the winners, and Sweet made 33 not out for the losers.

1906 Daily Mirror

39

5 | Last Championships at Worple Road

1907–21

In the period either side of the First World War the illustrious names of Tony Wilding, Arthur Wentworth Gore and Bill Tilden appear on the champions' roll. The title went abroad for the first time when the Australian Norman Brookes won in 1907. Following the 1921 final the Championships were switched to the new venue at Church Road, Wimbledon – just over a mile away.

Worple Road. This aerial photograph shows the layout of the courts at Worple Road – the venue of the Wimbledon Championships until 1921. By this time the event had become so popular that the site was ridiculously overcrowded, with a capacity for only 8,000

1907 Norman Brookes
beat Arthur Wentworth Gore
6–4 6–4 6–2

Norman Brookes, an Australian, became the first overseas winner of the Wimbledon men's singles Championship when he defeated Arthur Wentworth Gore in the All Comers final. He did not have to play the Challenge Round because of Laurie Doherty's retirement, and he became the first left-hander to hold the singles title.

Nicknamed 'The Wizard' because of his all-action game, Brookes had played in the 1905 final which many observers described as the most skilful match in the first thirty years of the Championship's history. This year, after beating Gore in straight sets, he had a break from Wimbledon and did not enter the men's singles again until 1914.

The Prince of Wales, later George V, paid his first visit to Worple Road in 1907. He and his wife watched Brookes' victory and the following year, as president, he donated the President's Cup for the All Comers Wimbledon singles champion.

The Prince and Princess of Wales. They attended the 1907 men's singles final

LAWN TENNIS CHAMPION.

MR. N. E. BROOKES BEATS MR. A. W. GORE.

LADIES' TURN TO-DAY.

Up till four o'clock yesterday afternoon the lawn tennis "blue riband" had never been won by any player who was not either an Englishman or an Irishman. But at that hour, on the centre court at Wimbledon, England's fate was sealed, and Mr. Norman Brookes, of Melbourne, became the champion of 1907. His defeat of Mr. A. W. Gore, England's last survivor, in the final was severe and conclusive, and without question revealed the famous left-hander as the greatest exponent of the year. He does not possess the same polished style as Mr. Doherty, nor has he that combination of accuracy and effortless action which that inimitable champion commanded. Mr. Brookes is almost clumsy in court compared with "H. L.," but he has great strength, infinite cunning, and quite the Doherty-like power of anticipation.

Mr. N. E. BROOKES.

He has the supreme satisfaction of knowing that no "homelander" who ever won the blue riband scored so freely and with less anxiety against every opponent of English birth whom he met. It can be said with truth that of the eight competitors Mr. Brookes defeated at Wimbledon only two made him really go, and one of these came from New Zealand and the other from America—the two youngest players engaged.

Mr. Gore did not play so well as he generally does. Probably he was put off his drive in some measure by the wind, but a more feasible reason for his comparative collapse was simply that he had forgotten what he had learnt about his opponent's methods, especially about his service; and no opportunity to resume relations with this embarrassing attack had occurred. He could not tackle the Victorian's swerves with anything like the facility he did two years ago. Once or twice he got the measure of an opening and banged the ball past the Colonial's fore-hand as he came craftily up, but more often he made an impotent return.

As for Mr. Brookes, he improved as his position became more secure. Opening in a gingerly fashion, he mysteriously failed to pick up some of Gore's simple-looking services, and the Englishman led 3—2. The sixth, seventh, and eighth games were all captured by the Australian, and he won the tenth game to love and the first set by 6—4.

A MATTER OF BRAINS.

After that there was only one player in it. Starting by capturing his opponent's service, Mr. Brookes actually took the next three games without the loss of an ace. There was brain behind every shot; his court-craft was eminently sound. Only once did he relax his stern expression, and that was to apologise to his opponent for a brilliant hook-volley grazing the top of the net. Otherwise his face never relaxed;

Mr. A. W. GORE.

there was grim determination in every line and a self-confidence worth alone three games in every set. Altogether this wonderful player won six love games—one right at the end of the match. His opponent won one at the beginning and one in the middle.

The first "foreign" holder of the lawn-tennis title was born thirty years ago in Melbourne, Victoria, where his father is a prosperous merchant, devoted to Norman, the only son now at home. He has played lawn tennis and other games since he was a boy at the Church of England Grammar School, and twice reached the final of the Victorian championship before he won and held it for several years.

To Dr. Eaves, who is Australian born and a former champion of New South Wales, the new champion ascribes much of his phenomenal advance. It was Dr. Eaves who encouraged him to come to England two years ago to try for the championship, and who backed him to win the "All-Comers." Though Mr. S. H. Smith led him 4—2 in the final set of the final round in 1905, the grim Australian was the first winner of the Renshaw Cup, and only Mr. H. L. Doherty stopped him from carrying off the championship he has now gained.

Mr. Norman Brookes is an outdoor man in every sense of the word. He is a fearless rider and a really capable golfer, while his versatility extends to billiards and singing. His family, by the way, are allied to the Deakins, one of the new champion's brothers having married a daughter of the Commonwealth Premier.

WILL THE LADIES' TITLE FOLLOW?

This afternoon, when the great tennis carnival at Wimbledon comes to an end, Miss Sutton will play Mrs. Lambert Chambers, the holder of the title, for the ladies' championship. Yesterday, in the final of the ladies' singles, Miss Sutton was in great form, defeating Miss Wilson in such a confident manner as to suggest the possibility of the ladies' blue riband also leaving the country. Miss Wilson made some beautifully crisp shots and her capture of the eighth and ninth games in the first set did her infinite credit; but she failed over several comparatively easy volleys at the net and was inclined to toss where a chop would probably have served better.

1908 Arthur Wentworth Gore
beat H. Roper Barrett
6–3 6–2 4–6 3–6 6–4

1909 Arthur Wentworth Gore
beat M.J.G. Ritchie
6–8 1–6 6–2 6–2 6–2

Arthur Wentworth Gore made the most of Norman Brookes' absence

in 1908 and won a five-set All Comers final against H. Roper Barrett. A finalist again in 1911, Roper Barrett had more success in the men's doubles and won three titles. He remains the most successful Davis Cup captain Great Britain has ever known.

The following year, Gore retained the singles crown in another long five-set final. This time he trailed by two sets to M.J.G.

Ritchie but showed extraordinary stamina to win each of the last three sets 6–2. By doing so at the age of forty-one, the remarkable Gore became the oldest Wimbledon men's singles title holder (and remains so today).

The 1909 Championship witnessed the worst weather conditions so far in the event and, for the first time, the Wimbledon fortnight ran into a third week.

LAWN TENNIS.

CHAMPIONSHIP FINALS.

"AS IN 1901."

By Our Special Correspondent.

The champions of 1901 are the champions of 1908. Yesterday, at Wimbledon, before 4,000 people, who watched the rallies with the keenest appreciation, Mrs. Sterry and Mr. A. W. Gore became the respective holders of the lawn tennis titles after an interval of seven years. In the hiatus Mrs. Chambers and Miss Sutton, H. L. Doherty and Norman Brookes, younger players than their forerunners and their successors, have held the highest honours. The natural deduction is that, with the exception of these four, the last generation has failed to produce a champion.

It is many years since the struggle for the men's championship yielded such a close and strenuous final as yesterday's engagement between Gore and Roper Barrett. Brookes and S. H. Smith contested a five-set all-comers' final in 1905, but the championship, as the Australian had good reason to remember, did not hang on that result; H. L. Doherty was waiting in the challenge round. In all the five years that "H. L." reigned supreme, the limit of sets was never reached, and (except for an "exhibition" challenge round, which I think the Dohertys "contested" in 1898) we must go back to 1895, when Dr. Eaves came within one ace of beating Wilfred

Baddeley in three straight sets, only to lose by the odd bout, to find a parallel for yesterday's momentous final.

Until the match had run half its course there was no outward sign of a thrilling finish; only a secret conviction, born of recollection, that Barrett had something in reserve. In the first two sets, which were very similar in character, Gore's hurricane drives, sound judgment, and superior accuracy held his opponent at bay. He could make no adequate response, either by stopping back, where his length was comparatively poor, or by coming up, when he was adroitly passed. That at this early stage he did not advance more often was doubtless due to the fact that he relied on his ability to drain Gore's resources, and then in the next three sets, when his adversary's drives had weakened, administer the death draught by small doses of volleying at the net. How near this campaign came to a successful issue the subsequent sets demonstrated. After Gore had taken the first two games in the third set, deluding many of his supporters into the belief that he was a safe man, Barrett began to unfold his scheme, and for the next hour we saw the process of adjusting the balance slowly, but surely, proceeding. Barrett's main objective was his opponent's left-hand corner, to which he gained access by low and oblique backhand drives—for Gore was also shooting across the court. Following the deepest of these efforts to the net, and carefully guarding possible loopholes, he executed some sparkling volleys, now a swift forehand cross-volley, next a back-hand stop volley. Naturally, with the high premium placed on accuracy, Barrett had risks to face—he was frequently passed, especially after he led 5—2 in the third set.

But he took the bold line, and fortune favoured him. Instead of relaxing his efforts in the fourth bout, Barrett spent his energies freely, his obvious desire being to gain a substantial lead as quickly as possible. For when a man is waging a stiff uphill battle and waging it with success, the slightest quarter invests his enemy with fresh confidence. He loses the all-potent moral effect. Again Barrett reached 5—2, mixing his game judiciously and profiting in some measure by the loose returns of his opponent. Though Gore was now shaping like a man who had come precious near the end of his tether—he would thrust his left hand anxiously through his hair at the close of each rally—his friends never despaired of his capacity to save the situation, conscious that the veteran had a reserve of stamina for the last set. The crisis was soon to come. By plucky and accurate driving, Gore reached 3—1, a commanding lead which would have upset the morale of most players. But excitement quickly simmered again when Barrett, by dint of audacious volleying, won the next three games in succession, the last from 15.40. For the first time in the history of the final the North Londoner held the lead. Had Gore faltered at this moment the end must have soon come. His heroic fortitude deserved the championship. He won Barrett's service game from 15.40; then annexed the ninth game without the loss of an ace. The tension was now very high, but was to reach an even higher pitch when Barrett converted 15.40 against him into deuce. Gore reached the 'vantage point three times before he ran out. Yesterday I ventured to say in the *Telegraph* that the issue would be fought out to the last ace. I think that forecast was justified.

1908 The Daily Telegraph

LAWN TENNIS

THE CHAMPIONSHIP.

The challenge round of the singles championship at Wimbledon yesterday was disappointing. The lawn tennis never rose to a standard worthy of the occasion, and at times it was quite mediocre. In the first set, especially, both players were off their game. Ritchie lacking his usual steadiness, while Gore's chief asset, his severe sweeping fore-hand drive, was seldom in evidence, his well-meant endeavours to finish the rest almost invariably finding the net on the outside of the court. Ritchie was better in the second set, while Gore was still lamentably weak, and when the challenger was two sets up and a couple of games to the good in the third, the match looked all but over. From this point, however, Ritchie dropped his game in a remarkable manner, and with a corresponding improvement on the part of the holder, so considerable

a change came over the aspect of the match that Gore took the set without further loss. Ritchie made no attempt to retrieve it towards the end and created the impression that he was reserving his powers. As it happened, he never once got going again, and with Gore in the last two sets driving with much of his old pace and precision, the challenger had to suffer defeat. Throughout, Ritchie kept to the base line, but Gore showed at times enterprise in going up to the net to finish the stroke. Results:

The Singles Championship Challenge Round.—A. W. Gore (holder) beat M. J. G. Ritchie (winner of All-Comers' Competition), 6—8, 1—6, 6—2, 6—2, 6—2.

Open Mixed Doubles, Semi-final Round (concluded). —H. Roper Barrett and Miss Morton beat C. P. Dixon and Miss A. N. G. Greene (11—9, 6—3).

The All-England Plate, Third Round (concluded).— R. B. Powell, w.o.; D. M. Hawes, scratched. Fourth round: R. B. Powell beat G. Gordon Smith (6—2, 6—1). Semi-finals: R. B. Powell, w.o.; L. Billake, scratched; H. A. Parker beat A. E. Crawley (6—2, 6—2). Mr. H. S. Scrivener is referee.

1909 The Sunday Times

1910 Tony Wilding
beat Arthur Wentworth Gore
6–4 7–5 4–6 6–2

1911 Tony Wilding
beat H. Roper Barrett
6–4 4–6 2–6 6–2 ret'd

1912 Tony Wilding
beat Arthur Wentworth Gore
6–4 6–4 4–6 6–4

1913 Tony Wilding
beat Maurice McLoughlin
8–6 6–3 10–8

Tony Wilding, a New Zealander of English parents, was the next to dominate the Wimbledon Championships in the same way as Willie Renshaw, and Reggie and Laurie Doherty had. He won four successive titles between 1910 and 1913 with a strong dedication to lawn tennis that developed while he was at Cambridge University.

At the age of seventeen Wilding had won the New Zealand championship but, during his debut appearance at Wimbledon three years later in 1904, he realized he would have to improve his backhand and volley. He practised hard and before every important match he would study his opponent and have a training session in preparation for the contest.

Wilding's distinguished reign began in 1910 with the defeat of the title holder, Arthur Wentworth Gore. The following year he retained the title under strange circumstances when Roper Barrett, suffering from sunstroke and loss of movement in his legs, retired with the score at two sets all.

Gore won through the All Comers in 1912 to reach his eighth final. Although he lost to Wilding in four sets, Gore's victory in the All Comers against Frenchman André Gobert, the Stockholm Olympic lawn tennis gold medallist, was a great achievement. The crowd gave the 44-year-old a standing ovation as he beat a player half his age.

In 1913 it was rumoured that Challenge Round final tickets were being sold on the black market for £10. This was mainly due to (*cont.*)

NEW LAWN TENNIS
CHAMPION.

As was expected after his victory over Mr. Beals C. Wright (America) in the final of the all-comers competition, Mr. A. F. Wilding (New Zealand) won the lawn tennis championship at Wimbledon yesterday, defeating Mr. A. W. Gore (England), who has held the title for the last two years, by 3 sets to 1.

Mr. Gore won his first prize in a lawn tennis tournament three years before Mr. Wilding was born, and he accomplished a wonderfully fine performance yesterday by putting up so magnificent a fight against so fine a player as the young New Zealander, who, in addition, was perfectly trained. The general anticipation was that Mr. Wilding would win easily, but there were some who, knowing Mr. Gore's wonderful pluck and tenacity, and relying upon the fact that he always rises to a great occasion, particularly on his favourite centre court at Wimbledon, prophesied his victory. These hopes were flattered by the veteran's splendid start. Mr. Gore, being in his best driving mood, got the first four games, and had 40—15 on his own service.

A long rally followed. Mr. Gore followed to the net a deep drive, Mr. Wilding replied, and the ball just hitting the top of the net made Mr. Gore miss an easy volley, bringing the score to 40—30. Another long rally and Mr. Gore got a short ball and he went for it, but just missed the line by a few inches. Mr. Wilding took courage from this and won the next two points and his first game. Mr. Gore led by 4 games to 1, however, and his supporters were still jubilant.

Mr. Wilding now got more power behind his shots, and coming to the net much oftener took game after game and won the set 6—4. Mr. Gore was unlucky in not winning the game that would have made him 5—0. He also, when at 4 all, got to 40—15. This seemed to be the critical period of the game for the holder, and he evidently realised it. His stroke afterwards became more timid—it certainly had less pace and length on it—and this enabled Mr. Wilding to get in his drive and get up to the net, where he was most effective.

In the second set Mr. Gore had another slice of hard luck. He led 3 games to 2 and 40—15, when again he seemed to falter. The knowledge of the importance of that game to him doubtless made him too anxious, for 4—2 is such a different position from 3 all. Mr. Wilding hit the top of the net and made what would have been an easy volley difficult. Mr. Gore missed it and a double fault made it "deuce." Mr. Wilding got that game and the next, making the score 4 all, and it was afterwards called 5—4 in his favour. Mr. Gore, however, got back his pace and amid great cheering got to 5 all, but the effort seemed too much for him, and the second set went to the New Zealander.

MR. GORE'S FINAL EFFORT.

Mr. Wilding started the third set with great confidence, and volleying with nice judgment went to 4—2, and it seemed all over bar "shouting." However, Mr. Gore, true to his traditions, now played his very best form. Going for everything, especially the return of Mr. Wilding's service (which didn't seem to bother him at all), and missing nothing (especially volleys, which before he was losing), he crept up to Wilding and the excitement grew intense as he got to 5—4. In the tenth game Mr. Gore got to 30—15, then 40—15, and won the set by a side-line shot that left Mr. Wilding standing still. It was a great performance winning four games off the reel at a critical moment.

The spectators were beginning to wonder whether this recovery of Mr. Gore's would have a moral effect on Mr. Wilding. To his credit, however, Mr. Wilding rose to the occasion and, playing better than ever, won the fourth set 6—3, and the match and the championship.

DEFEATED BY ILLNESS.

SICK MAN'S FIGHT FOR LAWN TENNIS HONOURS.

The spectators who gathered round the centre court at Wimbledon on Saturday to watch the struggle for the lawn tennis championship of the world between Anthony F. Wilding, the holder, and H. Roper Barrett, the challenger, witnessed an exhibition of pluck on the part of the latter which will be remembered as long as the game is played.

Barrett retired with the score at two sets all—each man winning exactly the same number of games—but not until the limits of human endurance had been reached.

Barrett came on the court with a temperature of 102, and throughout the match it was clear that there was something very wrong with him.

His face was drawn and grey—the face of a man battling with sickness, but who is determined to go through with it while he can stand.

People who did not know looked upon his languid movements and long pauses between services as part of a cunning scheme of bluff to lure his opponent into the belief that he was already a beaten man.

TWO OPPONENTS.

But Roper Barrett was not only fighting one of the most perfectly trained athletes living—he was grappling with the human weakness which makes a man just long to give up and sink down and allow the waters of deadly tiredness to close over his head.

To those who grasped how things were it was a spectacle of fascinating tragedy. How long could this suffering little man keep it up? Was it possible that he might yet win through, in spite of the numbing illness that seemed to shackle his limbs with heavy irons?

And the amazing thing was the way in which, in spite of revolting nature, the little man's genius for the game asserted itself. Only half-conscious as he was, he yet moved automatically to the position he ought to occupy to meet a return, and some subconscious power that lurked within him made him make the proper reply. Time after time he would lurch across the court, and his wonderful back-hand stroke would leave his opponent standing, baffled and beaten.

And all the while Barrett made Wilding play the game he wanted him to. Some people described the play as "pat-ball," and so it was to a certain extent, but it was pat-ball simply because Barrett preferred to have it so, and Wilding had unwillingly to acquiesce. The holder was afraid to let himself go, for as soon as ever he attempted to become dashing, just as certainly would he suffer for it.

Wilding won the first set at 6—4, and Barrett the next at the same score. In spite of his ever-increasing weakness, Barrett was brilliant in the third set, which he won at 6—2.

Then it became painful to have to watch him. His effort had overdrawn his balance and his cheque was returned. He could not respond, and Wilding won the fourth set at 6—2.

SYMPATHETIC SILENCE.

Then the great-hearted little man had to give in. He sorrowfully shook his head, and with anguished eyes tottered blindly off the court. And the tense, sympathetic silence that followed showed that at last everybody understood.

For years Roper Barrett has been striving to win the championship. In the has played better this year than ever before, and victory seemed fairly within his grasp. The pity of it!

the fact that 'The Californian Comet' Maurice McLoughlin had qualified to meet Wilding. McLoughlin, the US champion, was the originator of the cannonball service and he played well in his only Wimbledon final. However, Wilding had been watching him play in earlier matches and had worked out the best way to win.

The New Zealander decided to take the cannonball serve early by standing inside the baseline and attack McLoughlin's backhand at every opportunity. These tactics proved very successful and Wilding recorded the best of his Wimbledon victories in three hard-fought sets.

Although lawn tennis had featured in the Olympic Games from 1896 it was not until 1912 when the International Lawn Tennis Federation was formed that the sport gained worldwide status. Until then the British LTA had been the world governing body as far as was possible and their chairman, Mr R.J. McNair, became the ILTF's first president.

Several overseas players were now competing at Wimbledon and, in 1913, the entries reached a pre-war high of 116.

LAWN TENNIS.

CHAMPIONSHIP ROUNDS

FRENCHMEN LOSE DOUBLES.

By Our Special Correspondent.

New Zealand retains the Championship Singles, England regains the Championship Doubles. Such was the net result of the two challenge rounds at Wimbledon yesterday, the closing matches of a fortnight's memorable meeting. The crowd that cheered the victors and which paid tribute to Mr. Gore's heroic defence of his title was the largest ever seen at the headquarters of lawn tennis—a keenly animated crowd, too, that picked out the best strokes and the best coups and followed them with deafening applause.

Mr. Gore's challenge round against Mr. Wilding had the same result as that in 1910, the Englishman (who was then the holder) winning the third set in 4 and making a bold but unsuccessful bid for the other three. But the play yesterday was faster, more stimulating, and it exhibited the resources of both men to better advantage. Strange as it may appear in one who should show declining prowess, Mr. Gore hit harder and braced more persistently than he has ever done on the centre court. When he was thoroughly set—that is to say, making full use of his forehand ordnance—he attacked and Wilding defended; and it was only by concentrating every fibre in his body to the task in hand that the champion eventually wore down the determined assault. As a fact, Gore played finer tennis in the first two sets, which he lost, than in the third, which he won. This was because Wilding allowed himself to be temporarily upset—his will-power relaxed—by a slight incident associated with a service decision.

At the time he was 40—15 on his own service in the ninth game, each man having won four games. The third set looked to be going the way of the first two. This mental harking back to the past when the present claimed undivided attention left Gore in possession of the court and caused the fight to be extended. But one does not want to suggest that Gore's play, admirable in tactics, consistent in vigour, and deep in resource, did not deserve the recognition of a set. Indeed, but for the fact that the holder, by splendid mobility and cool judgment, kept many a rally alive that many less endowed physically would have abandoned, Gore would undoubtedly have reaped a richer reward.

DETERMINED PLAYERS.

Both men seemed determined to set a fast pace at the start; they were both all out to draw first blood, and as Gore's eye was right in and his passing shots in perfect trim he delighted his supporters by taking a 4—2 lead. He scored some beautiful winners across Wilding's forehand when he came to the net, shots so accurate and forceful that the champion was beaten outright; again, he added to his points by deep hurricane drives off the service down the line into that famous left-hand corner which has ever been Gore's "pepper-box." He has been making the same shot with the same deadly effect for a score of years, and yesterday it was better than ever. But Wilding's vitality was unshaken. The feature of this set, as of the other four, was his capacity to respond to the spurts of his opponent, to breast him in the race and eventually to pass him. The effort placed a great strain on his backhand resources, and he was often forced to lob in order to recover a winning position. It was the excellent length of these tosses and his alert intelligence in anticipating the direction of Gore's smashes that saved both the first and second sets. Once he caught Gore in the first Wilding played his best, and he won the ninth and tenth games to love.

In the second set Gore got away with a 3—0 lead. Wilding appeared to have two bad decisions in the third game, but Gore's tenacity was irresistible, and his drives of splendid length. Wilding did not make Gobert's mistake in the fourth game. He continued to come up, and, finding Gore's shots less accurate, won it from him. But the champion's defensive backhand strokes, some of which fell short, allowed Gore to find that corner again, and he reached 4—2. More, he got to 'vantage in the seventh game—a long and brilliant duel. Once level at four-all Wilding, as in the first set, ran out with concentrated brilliance. But the tenth game was the longest in the match, and Gore was 'vantage four times.

In the third set the pace visibly slackened, but more on Wilding's side than on Gore's. The latter, coming to the net on his best drives, scored with forehand volleys, and led 3—1, and then 4—2. Another brace by the champion brought him level, but then, as I have indicated, he had a bad lapse, and Gore was out, 'mid a tornado of cheers, at 6—4. The first game in the fourth set fell to the challenger, the next four to the holder, but the fight was not yet finished. Gore made a spirited and final rally, pounding the service with his old-time vigour. This heroic effort won him three games, but the champion was not to be denied his triumph, and he took the last two games and the match with the loss of only three points.

1912   The Daily Telegraph

Tony Wilding and Arthur Wentworth Gore. The 1912 men's singles final was Gore's eighth and last appearance in a Challenge Round final

Tony Wilding. The four-times Wimbledon champion displays his strokes in this Illustrated Sporting and Dramatic News *extract*

A GREAT LAWN TENNIS MATCH.

DEFEAT OF THE AMERICAN.

BRILLIANT PLAY BY MR. WILDING.

CROWD OF 10,000.

By three sets to love (8—6, 6—3, and 10—8) Mr. A. F. Wilding, the New Zealander, successfully defended the lawn tennis championship yesterday against Mr. McLoughlin, the Californian, and so retains the championship which he has held for the past three years.

The bare fact sounds as if the victory were hollow, as if Mr. McLoughlin were at every point outplayed. This was not so at all. Every game was hardly fought. Both men played with magnificent energy and judgment. The largest crowd of spectators ever collected in the famous ground at Wimbledon saw one of the finest matches ever played. Fully 2,000 people were present on the ground who never caught a glimpse of the play.

From half-past nine enthusiasts, mostly athletic young women in knitted coats of all colours, waited for the gates to open. At midday a very large number were admitted, and a steady stream flowed in until after two o'clock. Before two the policemen at the entrance were warning people that all seats were gone and that there was no standing room. But the hope which "springs eternal" made them put down their half-crowns, believing they would find some corner still.

"A MAN AND A BOY."

At 2.15 two-shilling seats in the stands were being sold for a sovereign each, and when the players appeared there was not a foot of space vacant anywhere. "Ten thousand admissions" was the figure bandied about. There were many left outside, though. Only between six and seven thousand can have seen anything of the match. That, however, is a record easily. The previous "best" was in 1905, when Mr. Brookes played Mr. H. L. Doherty. Since then the interest in match lawn tennis has been on the increase all the time. It has spread to other nationalities. There were many French spectators yesterday. Here and there one heard German. Americans, of course, were numerous, and they went away rather sad.

Yet there was really no reason for them or for their champion to be downhearted. When Mr. McLoughlin settles down—he is only twenty-three yet—he ought to be the finest lawn tennis player the world has seen. Yesterday's match was a match between coolness and inexperience, between a Man and a Boy.

MR. WILDING'S GRACE.

The difference between the players expressed itself in their appearances even. Mr. Wilding is at twenty-nine a sunburnt, clean-cut type of the healthy open-air Briton. His air of quiet distinction never drops from him. He is always graceful in his strokes. He appears to play with perfect ease. The only moments when he can be seen to make any effort come when he pulls himself together to deal with a loose ball. Then his frame quivers tensely and the ball is whacked into its place, his opponent standing miserably apprehensive like a rabbit waiting for boa-constrictor to strike!

Mr. McLoughlin has a powerful frame, topped by a strong lion-like red head. He plays hard all the time. He personifies vigour rather than grace. His service, when it comes off, is terrific, very swift and very low. His judgment is mostly brilliant, but it breaks down occasionally and betrays him badly. His placing is uncanny in its precision, but he can be worn down by steady returns. Time after time Mr. Wilding manoeuvred him into a bad position and ended a rally with a quiet little pat.

All through the sets Mr. Wilding steadily improved. At first he was worried by Mr. McLoughlin's service. But quite soon he got on easy terms with it, and his quiet mastery increased with every game. The Californian, the "Boy," was never so good as at the start. Although he pulled off wonderful "shots" he got wilder and wilder, and revealed his growing discouragement by little gestures of annoyance over his "misses," which grew more and more frequent towards the end.

1913 Daily Mail

1914 Norman Brookes
beat Tony Wilding
6–4 6–4 7–5

Norman Brookes and Tony Wilding, great colleagues in Australasian Davis Cup victories, met in the last final of the men's singles Championship before the First World War. Brookes was making his first appearance at Wimbledon since his victory in 1907 and he had to win a tremendous battle in the All Comers final before he could challenge Wilding. At one point he was leading two sets to love and 5–3 but his German opponent Otto Froitzheim fought back with great determination. Finally, after a long fight, Brookes took the last set 8–6.

In the Challenge Round final he had a much easier match against Wilding and won in three sets. It prevented the holder claiming a fifth successive title; it was said this may have been because Wilding had not trained for the match in the same way as he had for previous Wimbledons.

Wilding never played at Wimbledon again. At the beginning of the war he was killed by shell-fire in Belgium at the age of thirty-one.

BROOKES BEATS WILDING.

Surprise for the Lawn Tennis Champion.

SOME WONDERFUL PLAY AT WIMBLEDON.

(By HERBERT L. BOURKE.)

When Wilding beat McLoughlin last year he told me he had played the game of his life. Brookes beat Wilding in Saturday's challenge round, and said the same thing. In each case it was very true; the prophets came down all of a heap, and I must confess that on Saturday it took me some time to extricate myself from the débris. Norman Brookes, the man hustled by veteran Gore, and nearly beaten by the delicately persuasive methods of Froitzheim, had shown no form like this in his earlier matches, but the genius that baffles us was all there in Saturday's challenge round, even as it was when Wilding played that inspired game against America's champion in 1913.

"The Mighty Brookes."

It was said that Brookes, in those uneven and rather unconvincing matches of his, had been exploiting the strokes which he best considered suitable to the discomfiture of Wilding. Furthermore, he had discovered to his intense satisfaction that his experience of the Froitzheim match had left him physically well equipped for a five-set ordeal. With him it is not so much a question of stamina as an occasional recurrence of dyspepsia, a complaint likely to assert itself at critical times. On Saturday, when he had astonished everybody by finishing off Wilding in three sets, he looked fresh enough to begin all over again. And he had played wonderful lawn tennis; the game of supreme stroke control that marked the master mind and the master hand. He was simply too good for Wilding; Wilding admitted it, and there we have it in a nutshell. It was "The Mighty Brookes," as we called him in 1907.

The Splendid Game.

We have seen Brookes this season faulting repeatedly with his first service and have seen his second service collared; we have seen his overhead play indecisive, and we saw his game all in a tangle when Gore was passing him with those slashing drives and Froitzheim was getting him grappling overhead or chasing those insidious lobs. But on Saturday that second service was seldom called for. His first service had power and precision, deadly in effect, and he played it so well that he was able to follow it to the net and take up his position where he anticipated the return and where he almost invariably got it. Occasionally Wilding would make a return to the service with a powerful drive that would have gone clean through most men, but there was Brookes's, just in the right place, and it mattered not whether the volley was on the forehand or backhand, the ball was caught clean in the middle of the racket, and Wilding was out-positioned by the direction of the return. Brookes's footwork was supreme. He was never on the wrong foot, and Wilding often was.

Defective Lobbing.

There was little need for powder overhead when Brookes was placing so well, but he applied the extra pace when the occasion required. As for driving through him when he was commandeering the net, that seemed impossible, so Wilding endeavoured to lob him as Froitzheim had done, but between Froitzheim's lobs and Wilding's lobs there was a difference as wide as the poles. Wilding simply could not do himself justice with his lobs; he was usually over or short, and it was noticeable that Brookes did not speculate with the few good ones by groping for them in the air, but he let the ball come down and took it on the bound, the response generally being a telling deep drive. The spin on the majority of Brookes's strokes had Wilding mistiming his lobs, and whilst I thought the holder, having regard to Brookes's supreme skill at the net, might have lobbed more, he certainly should have played this stroke better.

The Mascot Cap.

With all these fine qualities of Brookes asserting themselves, how came it that Wilding took thirteen games in the three sets against his conqueror's nineteen? The fact was that Wilding lost the first four games before he had felt his feet. His practice form had not pleased him, and he was not wholly confident. He was obviously troubled by the glare of the sun, and it puzzled me that he should have removed the big white hat with which he came into the court. Brookes wore his grey-peaked cap throughout, and it must have been worth something to him. After this faltering start, Wilding made a bold fight, but it was an uphill one all the way. He reached 3–4 and was at 4–5 after being led by 3–5, but Brookes took the set at 6–4.

By the same figures Brookes won the second set, but Wilding was at 1–0 and 3–2, and then a lob that fell inches out lost him the sixth game. Despite a double fault he won the seventh game from 15–40, and led by 4–3, but Brookes broke through his service in the ninth game, and next won the set at 6–4.

Wilding's Spurt.

Wilding appeared to be finding himself when he went to 2–0 in the third set. He was going up, and volleying well, but by losing the third game when serving he lost his best chance of the match. And yet he led by 4–3 and 5–4, the tennis at this stage being of fine quality all round, a topping reverse service winning Wilding the last stroke of the ninth game. Superb judgment in leaving a ball that went just out took Brookes to 6–5, but even then it was thought that Wilding might capture the set, and he helped by his fine condition to win the match. How Wilding fought for the last game of all was something to remember. Twice he redeemed the match point—Brookes was at 40–30 and next at vantage—but finally hitting a ball wide of the side line the champion for four years had to relinquish his title.

Naturally ignoring himself, Wilding recently ranked M. E. McLoughlin as the world's best player, and it would be interesting to know how he would now rank Brookes after this great display. It is true that Wilding was not himself, as apart from his defective lobbing he could not get his back-hand passing shot into working order or hit on the forehand with quite his customary power, but it is equally true that Brookes had him indecisive by superb lawn tennis. Brookes, who is 37 years of age, has thrice played through the all-comers singles at Wimbledon, and twice won the championship, his previous success having been achieved in 1907. Since he was last in England he has been beaten by Wilding, Parke, and Doust, and that he should have risen again is to his lasting credit. Saturday's scores were 6–4, 6–4, 7–5.

Norman Brookes and Tony Wilding. Both players were acknowledged in the world outside the tennis court. Brookes (on the left) was knighted in 1939 and Wilding was awarded the Military Cross

1914   Daily News and Leader

1919 Gerald Patterson
beat Norman Brookes
6–3 7–5 6–2

The Wimbledon gates were closed for five years but the popularity of tennis was booming when the Championship resumed in 1919. Applications for tickets were so great that the now-famous ballot had to be introduced.

Some of the men's tennis was undistinguished – so many players being involved in the war – and the Challenge Round final was, for the first time, an all-Australian clash. **Gerald Patterson**, a 23-year-old with a cannonball service, proved too strong and young for 'The Wizard' Brookes who was eighteen years his senior.

King George V and Queen Mary visited the Championship twice in the summer of 1919. Wimbledon proved to be a great reunion event for players and supporters from all over the world.

THE CHAMPIONSHIP.

It was a disappointing match. Mr. Patterson beat Mr. Brookes in three sets, with the loss of only 10 games—and that without increasing his reputation. He made more mistakes than in his previous matches—and several blunders not to be accounted for by the cumulative strain of long rallies. He stands very much where he did. He had proved himself the best player in the All Comers beyond cavil; but in a lean year; the match with the much-travelled champion of 1914 was to show his comparative rank. He beat Mr. Brookes, but not the Mr. Brookes of 1914. There have been matches this year when other players have shown themselves for a time Mr. Patterson's equals in the rallies; and the Mr. Brookes we knew of old—admittedly the superior of Mr. Barrett and Mr. Ritchie—was expected to do better than they had done with his famous service to help him.

Mr. Patterson served in the first game and won it; what was much more significant he won the next. But Mr. Brookes retaliated in the third with his old masterful placing, and "two all" promised a tussle. But it was not forthcoming. Mr. Brookes's strokes were intercepted, and they did not look so difficult to intercept. "Own kin are the worst friends," said the fox when he saw the dogs after him, and Mr. Brookes must have thought the same at finding another Victorian with his own power of attracting the balls to his racket. But the balls came higher or slower than formerly. Mr. Brookes was on the defensive; he could not get past Mr. Patterson and keep in. Mr. Patterson reached 5–3, 40–15 on his service. Then he missed an easy kill, made two faults, scored with a fluke, and won the game. It was an inglorious end to the first set of a challenge round.

At the beginning of the second set Mr. Brookes drew level at 2 all, after one or two of the rallies one had been hoping for. Three all. The seventh game—Mr. Brookes serving—was a crucial but rather lucky gain to Mr. Patterson. Mr. Patterson reached 5—4, 40—15 on his service, and then made two faults. These were nothing against him as a match player, rather the contrary, but to miss two easy volleys as he proceeded to do suggested nerves. He redeemed himself by promptly winning Mr. Brookes's service, and then his own. He was confidence itself in the third set. In one game he made Mr. Brookes a canvas for a master-piece. He passed the first of that redoubtable man's services across him forehanded; did the same by the next backhanded; took the third point when at the base line by a drive straight at him and too fast to be volleyed, and the fourth with a low sudden push that entangled him in his own foot. He won the set 6—2, and with it the championship.

He has earned it; and it may well be that in criticizing it as one has done one has been unjust to two players each compelled by the other's punishing power to take great risks. Whether or no he be now the equal of the greatest players of the years before the war, Mr. Patterson must surely become so; the finality of his smashing, the reach and range on the volley, his resolution off the ground, and his fast swirling, beautifully delivered service stamp him as a worthy champion. If he did not realize all our hopes that is his own fault for raising such high hopes. To be criticized after beating Mr. Brookes in a challenge round 6—3, 7—5, 6—2 is, after all, a compliment. But it was a sad match. There was little of the joy of battle about it—such as one associates with Mr. Gore —and one felt as in some boxing matches, as if one was looking on at the discomfiture of a famous veteran rather than acclaiming the rise of a new star.

1919   The Times

1920 Bill Tilden
beat Gerald Patterson
2–6 6–3 6–2 6–4

1921 Bill Tilden
beat Brian Norton
4–6 2–6 6–1 6–0 7–5

William Tatem Tilden was, and is, regarded by many experts as the finest-ever male tennis player. He arrived at Wimbledon from the USA for the first time in 1920 at the age of twenty-seven and soon displayed his genius by crushing his first three opponents. The 6 ft 3 in. Tilden, 'Big Bill' as people called him, then had a close five-set match with Algy Kingscote before beating the Japanese number one Zenzo Shimizu in the All Comers final.

In the Challenge Round final, Tilden lost the first set to Gerald Patterson. However, he settled down and attacked the champion's backhand to become the first American to win the Wimbledon men's singles title. He was also the first player since Laurie Doherty in 1903 to win both the Wimbledon and United States titles in the same year – a feat that, remarkably, he repeated twelve months later.

It did not seem possible at one stage that 'Big Bill' could retain his Wimbledon title in 1921 for, as the Championship entered its second week, he was ill in hospital. He was discharged four days before the Challenge Round final and was restricted in his practice.

Tilden promptly lost the first two sets to the 21-year-old from South Africa, Brian 'Babe' Norton. He then showed tremendous courage to level the score at two sets all. The South African – a great admirer of Tilden – had a match point in the last set at 5–4 but failed to take advantage and 'Big Bill' won the next three games.

This was the last men's singles final played at Worple Road and the 1922 Championships were moved to their existing site at Church Road, Wimbledon. The new complex, which cost £140,000 and took two years to build, had a centre court with a capacity for 14,000 spectators. Number one court could hold 5,000 and there were another thirteen outside courts.

An important change that coincided with the move was the abolition of the Challenge Round. Thus the scene and the organization of the Championship were by 1922 much the same as we know them today.

A DAY OF SUCCESSES FOR THE AMERICANS.

By Hamilton Price.

In spite of a sensational report that W. T. Tilden would be unable to challenge Gerald Patterson, the holder of the world's championship, owing to his injured knee, would-be spectators began to line up outside the gates at an early hour on Saturday morning. Tilden was not only able to play, but he also accomplished a feat which no other American has succeeded in doing since the inception of the championships in 1877. That he deserved the great ovation accorded him as he left the centre court at the conclusion of a comparatively poor match is beyond dispute.

Tilden owed his win to his greater versatility of stroke and the rough treatment which he meted out to Patterson's tornadic service. The holder has made the service the backbone of his game. One can just imagine his feelings when he found Tilden hitting it down the side lines and across the court with equal facility on both wings. It would be enough to demoralise even greater players than Patterson. Then, again, that back-hand weakness which the sturdy and dour Australian betrayed last summer was exploited to the full by Tilden, who drove, chopped, and volleyed 75 per cent. of his returns into this vulnerable corner. The American also wisely eschewed the lob when the sun was not behind his back. When Patterson faced the rays of the sun he found perfect lobs floating over his head. He either had to make a tentative kill or allow the ball to drop. This move of Tilden's showed what an astute lawn tennis brain the American has cultivated.

MANY MIS-HITS.

I have seldom seen so many mis-hits made by two players of such high standard. Tilden was not at his best, but Patterson was only a shadow of himself. The loser, to my mind, was over-trained, and he appeared to lack sufficient energy persistently to chase the clever wide cross-court volleys of his opponent. It is perfectly true that the holder won the first set at 6—2 after a lead of 4 games to love, but the second and third sets were always dominated by the keen-witted American. Patterson made a laudable attempt to stem the tide of adversity in the fourth set, in which he lost the third game after being 40—love with a lead of two clear games. Tilden led at 5—4 and won the tenth game, the match, and the championship.

Although volleying with but little accuracy Patterson went in on every possible occasion. This extraordinary tactical blunder was like good wine to the American. He drank his beverage with avidity, and passed his man with yards to spare. Tilden is a very worthy champion, and I learned with pleasure that we shall see him at Worple road next summer unless something very unexpected turns up to prevent him crossing the Atlantic. For the sake of the statistical experts the run of the games is appended:—

First Set.—Patterson: 4–0, 4–0, 5–1, 5–2, 6–2).

Second Set.—Tilden: 2–0, 2–0, 4–1, 5–2, 5–3, 6–3).

Third Set.—Tilden: 0–1, 1–1, 1–2, 2–2, 4–2, 6–2.

Fourth Set.—Tilden: 0–2, 1–2, 2–2, 2–3, 4–3, 4–4, 5–4, 6–4.

Number of Aces.—Winner, 112.
Number of Aces.—Loser, 99.

1920 The Sporting Life

NORTON'S BID FOR THE TITLE.

MY NARROW VICTORY AT WIMBLEDON.

LUCK THE ARBITER.

By W. T. TILDEN
(World's Lawn Tennis Champion).

Wimbledon is over.

Next year may find the world's lawn tennis championships held at the new grounds, and the famous centre court, on which the Renshaws, the Dohertys, Brookes, Gore, Wilding, and those other great stars made tennis history, will be but a memory.

It is sad to contemplate its passing, but the old order changeth, and even the centre court must go before the public demand for more seating capacity.

The championships in 1921 hold many pleasant memories, and, for me, a few regrets. It is pleasurable to recount the splendid tennis of Mlle. Lenglen, who, as always, held the gallery by the perfection of her strokes.

It was a splendid exhibition that Miss Ryan gave on her victorious way to the

B. I. C. NORTON (the challenger) on left and W. T. TILDEN (the champion) are close friends, and appeared equally pleased with the result of the match on Saturday, in which Tilden retained the title.

challenge round. It was a shame she fell off so badly there.

Mrs. Mallory justified her great reputation, and while no one denies Miss Ryan full credit in her victory, one feels that Mrs. Mallory should have beaten her. Surely Mrs. Mallory's first set against Miss Ryan was the best tennis played by any woman during the meeting.

The hero of 1921 is undoubtedly B. I. C. Norton, the "babe" of the meeting. He played tennis of a type that fully justified his position as challenger, and if the luck which smiled on me had been equally gracious to him his name would worthily join those of the famous players of the past as champion. I admire above all else his sportsmanship and generosity in victory or defeat.

Norton, after winning the first two sets and losing the third, went all out for the early games of the fourth set. Fortunately for me I struck my best tennis of

the match, and gained a 3—0 lead by virtue of two very lucky recoveries. Norton made what proved an error of judgment owing to his underestimating my stamina, and was content to lose the set for the sake of running me a long distance.

It very nearly proved excellent tactics. Norton was clearly fresher, and by pushing the pace, led at 4—2. I called on my last bit of reserve, and managed to pull even at four all after facing 'vantage twice. Norton took the lead at 5—4, and my service to follow.

EXCITING MOMENTS.

"Point-set-match" came up at advantage. We had a long rally. Finally I hit a backhand shot down the line. It seemed as if it were going out, and my heart stood still. The ball fell on the edge of the line. Norton's return was out, and I had another chance. Again Norton gained "Point-set-match," but a good service saved the rally as Norton hit out. Finally I pulled out the game. I broke Norton's delivery at 15 for 6—5, and led 40—0 on my own for the match. Norton gamely saved it twice by remarkable recoveries, but a fast service down the line ended the struggle, and I was again champion.

Manuel Alonso, who came so close to the challenge round, is, like Norton, a player of infinite promise, and a charming personality, whose genial court manner deservedly made him a favourite.

Zenzo Shimidzu, as always, was the sterling sportsman and wonderful little fighter. He is a greatly improved player over last year, and should cause a real sensation in the Davis Cup matches this year.

The men's doubles hardly reached the high level of former years, but in Lycett and Woosnam a strong combination succeed Garland and Williams.

Lycett and Miss Ryan regain the mixed doubles title, lost last year to Patterson and Mlle. Lenglen, while the champions, Mlle. Lenglen and Miss Ryan, easily took the women's doubles.

Personally, I regretted my own inability to take part in the men's doubles, for I enjoy any opportunity to play before the sporting spirit of the British public, and this year my chances were all too few.

LUCK OF THE GAME.

I feel that "Babe" Norton deserved to win the championship, for he out-played me, but fate smiled on me and frowned on him in the crisis, and allowed me a chance to return again to defend my title.

The tournament was run with the perfect efficiency that always characterises it, and Mr. Burrows, the referee, Commander Hillyard, and his able committee deserve the highest praise. The weather and the great galleries joined in making Wimbledon a tremendous success, and I know that for one I bid "Farewell, a long farewell" to the old grounds, and hope with all my heart that the new Wimbledon will enjoy the great success it deserves.

I trust that I may have the pleasure of assisting in the first championship on the new courts.

1921   **Daily Express**

Bill Tilden. He achieved a great Davis Cup record for the United States, winning thirteen consecutive challenge round singles in the early 1920s

6 | The French Connection

1922–29

Two years after King George V opened the new Wimbledon venue the French began to dominate the Championship. From 1924 until 1929 there was only one year in which a non-Frenchman qualified for the final. Jean Borotra, Henri Cochet and René Lacoste each won two singles titles and, together with the doubles specialist, Toto Brugnon, they were labelled 'The Musketeers'.

Church Road. This picture, taken from the balcony of the main Wimbledon building, shows play in progress on an outside court at the Championships' new venue

1922 Gerald Patterson
beat Randolph Lycett
6–3 6–4 6–2

1923 Bill Johnston
beat Frank Hunter
6–0 6–3 6–1

On 26 June 1922, King George V officiated at the opening of Church Road, Wimbledon and the new venue was greeted with bad weather which lasted throughout the fortnight.

The men's singles final was eventually played on the third Monday and **Gerald Patterson** beat Randolph Lycett to win his second title in three years. Bill Tilden was taking a five-year break from playing in Europe and, in 1923, **'Little Bill' Johnston** made the most of his absence to win a one-sided final for the loss of only four games against Frank Hunter. 'Big Bill' had beaten 'Little Bill' in five US finals.

In 1923 the acceptances for the men's singles exceeded 128 for the first and only time. The first round contained 133 players and there were 123 byes to the second round. Johnston was included in the byes and, in the seven rounds he played to win the title, he only lost one set.

PATTERSON WINS

Mediocre Game in Lawn Tennis Final

By "REFEREE"

That human catapult, G. L. Patterson, became the champion of the world for the second time at Wimbledon yesterday, when he defeated R. Lycett by 6–3, 6–4, 6–2, before the smallest crowd of the whole tournament. The game itself never rose above mediocrity, for it was extremely dull and tedious.

Even when Lycett, standing far beyond the base-line, took Patterson's hurtling services with great cleverness, and got to within a point on two occasions of 5–2 in the second set, it was obvious that Patterson had a lot in reserve. The champion played well within himself, but the sun seemed to bother him a good deal.

The chop drives of Patterson worked their effect on Lycett's ground play. The loser was never really at home in dealing with them. Double faults—five in a single game—were seen from Patterson's racket at intermittent periods.

NO UNDUE EXERTION

This defect did not affect the result in the least, for Patterson could afford to take any risks. In fact, his play was almost leisured, and he never unduly exerted himself. Lycett, on the other hand, had to run miles in a fruitless chase. Fast as he is on the court, he was unable to reach many of Patterson's stop-volleys.

They were what Tilden would term "peaches." Patterson is a great match-winner, to use a hackneyed phrase. He is a fighter of the first degree, and his great physique is made full use of by this Australian giant.

Patterson's honour was richly deserved, for he had all the great players in his portion of the draw. For sheer determination and grit the champion is unequalled. He concentrates his whole mind on the business at hand, and, above all, he is an excellent sportsman.

A great battle with a 15–13 set thrown in was waged between T. M. Mavrogordato and P. M. Davson and J. O. Anderson and R. Lycett, which the latter pair luckily won. For clever tactics Mavrogor-

dato was always conspicuous, but Davson drove cleanly and freely throughout. Anderson was almost a travesty of his real self. He netted ever so many smashes and missed many volleys, and Lycett worked with heroic enthusiasm and fairly carried his partner home. If Davson and his partner had shown a little more enterprise, victory would have been theirs. They were solid and sagacious, but they lacked the stroke-power of the opposition.

A LUCKY ESCAPE

Speed, and only speed of stroke, saved the winners from what would have been an unexpected defeat. The losers tossed admirably, and retrieved some wonderful balls. It was a very lucky escape for two men who do not combine as they ought.

Another defeat for Mrs. Mallory at the hands of Mlle. Lenglen was recorded. This time it was in a mixed double. O'Hara Wood was much better than Dean Mathey, whose back-hand play was very poor.

Wood showed a nice wrist in his volleying, which was oblique and incisive. Suzanne was supreme in all that she did.

KENT'S EASY VICTORY

Northants Outed for 80 by Woolley and Freeman

Kent declared with their Saturday's total of 345 for two against Northants at Tunbridge Wells. The visiting team found the wicket badly against them, and were dismissed for 150. C. N. Woolley and Walden made a stand and later Lake scored a few runs, but the rest of the batsmen fell easily to Woolley, who took six for 87.

Northampton followed on and suffered a crushing defeat, being dismissed for the small total of 80, Kent thus winning by an innings and 115 runs. It must be said in excuse for the collapse that the wicket was very tricky and entirely suited to Woolley and Freeman, who took 5 for 56 and 5 for 26 respectively.

1922   Daily Herald

THE WINNERS AT WIMBLEDON.

A WORLD'S TITLE FOR W. M. JOHNSTON.

By FRANK POXON.

The King and Queen were at Wimbledon on the final day, and their presence gave the requisite finishing touch to a meeting which has been a sustained success. Fine weather and huge crowds have been the accompaniments to the lawn tennis day by day, and the only thing lacking has been a larger proportion of matches in which the issue was open. I think a "seeded" draw would be advisable next year, for it is a perfectly legitimate proceeding, tending to give enhanced interest to the closing stages.

The champions of 1923 are:

Men's Singles.—W. M. Johnston (America).

Women's Singles. — Mlle. Lenglen (France).

Men's Doubles.—R. Lycett and L. A. Godfree (Great Britain).

Women's Doubles. — Mlle. Lenglen (France) and Mis. Ryan (California).

Mixed Doubles.—R Lycett (Great Britain) and Miss Ryan (California).

The expected happened in the final of the men's singles, for W M. Johnston became the world's lawn tennis champion on grass by defeating his fellow countryman, F. T. Hunter, in three straight sets at 6—0, 6—3, 6—1. Quite early in the game it became apparent that Johnston was too strong for his hard-hitting opponent and the chief interest for the spectators consisted in watching Johnston display his brilliant and varied ability.

Would Johnston Beat Tilden?

I found myself comparing him with Tilden, and the comparison was in Johnston's favour, for I think Johnston played better at this Wimbledon than Tilden ever did during his last trip to England.

The ease with which Johnston returned Hunter's hardest drives was impressive; he not only returned the ball, but went for winners down the side lines, and more often than not got them. His placing and his crisp volleying were deadly, but there was less volleying than usual.

I do not think the match calls for any extended comment, for it was too one-sided to be really gripping. Johnston left the court as a man who had very decisively proved his right to the championship; at this Wimbledon he was just as much in a class by himself as Mlle Lenglen was. Each was incomparable.

When I congratulated Johnston on his success he said, with that quiet modesty which has so favourably impressed everybody. 'Thank you all for your kindness to me. I have enjoyed Wimbledon so much, and I hope I have given pleasure to the folk who have made me feel at home."

A Win for England

England had a look in when Lycett and Godfree won the men's doubles, defeating the Spanish pair, the Count de Gomar and E. Flaquer 6—3, 6.—4, 3—6, 6—3. I have seen de Gomar play better than he did in this match, for he was lacking in consistency. Lycett was a fine "skipper," and Godfree backed him up well with some deadly "killing" at the net. Lycett and Godfree thus avenged their Davis Cup defeat at Manchester, where de Gomar and Flaquer beat them; England has every right to be proud of her doubles pair.

The big crowd got most delight from the women's doubles final, in which Mlle. Lenglen and Miss Ryan beat Miss Colyer and Miss Austin 6—3, 6—1. The two English girls played delightfully free and "taking" lawn tennis with Miss Colyer much the more consistent. The all-round strength of the formidable pair opposed to them prevailed, but some of the honours of a bright match certainly went to the losers.

Another very powerful doubles combination, R. Lycett and Miss Ryan, won the mixed, beating L. S. Deane and Mrs. Shepherd Barron 6 4, 7 5.

1923   Daily News

Bill Johnston. His was a one-sided victory in 1923

1924 Jean Borotra
beat René Lacoste
6–1 3–6 6–1 3–6 6–4

1925 René Lacoste
beat Jean Borotra
6–3 6–3 4–6 8–6

1926 Jean Borotra
beat Howard Kinsey
8–6 6–1 6–3

The next six years of the Wimbledon men's singles Championship were dominated by three Frenchmen: Jean Borotra, René Lacoste and Henri Cochet. They were dubbed 'The Musketeers', and each of them won the Wimbledon men's singles title twice. Collectively, they carried their country's flag with the same pride as Suzanne Lenglen had done in winning the women's singles title at Wimbledon between 1919 and 1923.

Jean Borotra, 'The Bounding Basque', won in 1924 and, in a repeat final, **René Lacoste** gained immediate revenge the following year.

In 1926 Howard Kinsey had the distinction of being the only non-Frenchman to play in a men's singles final between 1924 and 1929. An American, Kinsey kept pace with **Borotra** in the first set but was unable to mount another serious challenge.

Fittingly, Borotra became the Jubilee Wimbledon men's singles champion. He was a great showman who always wore a beret while playing and he captivated the English crowds in much the same way as Ilie Nastase was to do some fifty years later.

Lacoste withdrew from the 1926 Championship and was therefore unable to set up a third successive final clash with Borotra. He was troubled by ill health throughout his short but brilliant career and finally had to retire at the age of twenty-seven.

Lawn Tennis.

THE CHAMPIONSHIPS

BOROTRA SUCCESSFUL.

ENGLAND WIN MIXED DOUBLES

ALL TITLES CHANGE HANDS.

By W. L. I.

Wimbledon, Saturday.

It was an historic day at Wimbledon to-day, as not only did we have an all-French final of the Men's Singles, but, as a natural and obvious corollary, we had, for the first time in the history of the game, a Frenchman winning the championship at Wimbledon. Another interesting feature of the day was that all five championships changed hands, but it should be remembered that this was partly on account of Mlle Lenglen having to scratch in the three events in which she was engaged, in two of which she was the holder. There would have been a different tale to tell if the famous French girl had been able to "carry on." The crowds at this year's tournament have beaten all previous records, and from an early hour this morning would-be spectators were lining up in queues, with the result that there was hardly a vacant space round the centre court. The Royal Box was occupied by many well-known people, including Lord Balfour and Mrs Asquith. Summing up the results, France won the Men's Singles through J Borotra; Miss K McKane took the Ladies' Singles for England; America captured the Men's Doubles by V Richards and F T Hunter; another American success was gained in the Ladies' Doubles by Miss Helen Wills and Mrs Wightman, while Miss McKane and J B Gilbert won another victory for England. J Condon won the All-England Plate for South Africa.

BOROTRA'S RAPID SET.

In spite of the fact that it was an all-French final, that in no way affected the interest of the spectators, and the stands were packed from top to bottom when the players came into court. Mr C B Sharp was the umpire. There was little of that preliminary "knocking-up" which is becoming such a nuisance in first-class lawn tennis, and it was obvious that both men, especially Borotra, were eager to "get on with it." There is a dash and vivacity about this Frenchman that is in great contrast to the easy-going, lackadaisical manner of certain other players. Lacoste, too, is quick, but he does not win the hearts of the spectators as does Borotra, with his happy smile. About 3.5 p.m. Lacoste began to serve, and a long game ended in victory for the server. It was some time, however, before this 20-year-old youngster won another, for in double quick time Borotra proceeded to rattle off the set in less than ten minutes, and won seven games right off the reel. Hitting hard and smashing with terrific force, running about all over the place, driving and lobbing in turn. Borotra was absolutely brilliant. Lacoste, it may be, was watching points, but, as somebody sagely observed, he did not win many!

A CHANGE IN THE GAME.

In the second set, however, the boot was on the other foot, and we saw a complete change in the situation. Borotra's play deteriorated, and as he fell away so Lacoste improved. The younger man, by some clever placing and hard passing shots, reached 3—1 and 5—2. Everything seemed to go right for Lacoste, and, by the same token, everything seemed to go wrong for Borotra, who managed to win another game before Lacoste took the set at 6—3. Borotra in this set hardly looked a champion, as he was decidedly erratic, frequently over-hitting the ball or sending it outside the side lines. But surprise followed surprise in this match. For Borotra changed the quality of his play as a chameleon changes his coat. Once more in the third set he rattled through, with the loss of only one game in just over ten minutes. Here again Lacoste played just about as well as his opponent allowed him to. But on play like that, Borotra would beat Lacoste (and a good many other people) every time. There was one fine trait about the younger man—he never gave up trying to the bitter end, and when he got a chance he was quick to take advantage of it. But in that third set Borotra gave him very few opportunities.

ANOTHER SURPRISE.

Followed another surprise in the fourth set. Eastman was clearly "all out" to win it, Borotra so as to finish off the match, Lacoste to make the score two sets all. The older man served with great pace in the first game, which he won. Lacoste followed by taking his service game, and becoming "one up" off his opponent's service. Borotra retaliated by taking Lacoste's service game and going ahead to 3—2 on his own. Lacoste equalised and ran out with a sequence of four games, taking the set at 6—3, and, making the score two sets all. The final set saw some exciting play. Each man won his service game in turn. One had almost written "with monotonous regularity," but that would scarcely be the phrase, for the keen duel between the two men kept the crowd on the tenterhooks or excitement as to see which would "break through" first. Every ace was fought out at a great pace, and there were some long rallies, though whenever Borotra got a chance he made no mistake about "putting it away." At last, after the score was 4—all, Borotra succeeded in winning the ninth game off his opponent's service and then by taking the next, won the set, the match, and the championship.

A THRILLING MATCH.

It was not a great match, but it was a thrilling one. It lasted just an hour and twenty minutes. It was probably Borotra's greater experience, as well as his pace, that gave him the victory. It should be remembered, too, that Borotra had already defeated Lacoste twice this season, and that knowledge has a moral effect on a player. There were times when it seemed as if Lacoste would win the day by his quiet, but persistent, and really clever play. But even his remarkable lobbing and skilful driving could not beat the wonderful volleying and pace of his opponent. It is of interest to recall the fact that the best previous by a Frenchman was in 1912, when A H Gobert was beaten in the All-comers' Final by A W Gore. Noone can begrudge the French victory. The French people have been striving for some years to win the highest honours, and they are to be congratulated on their success this year. There could be no more worthy holder of the title than J Borotra, one of the most cheery of sportsmen, and France could have no better representative.

LACOSTE WINS BRILLIANT FINAL.

UMPIRE'S REBUKE TO SPECTATORS.

By OUR LAWN TENNIS REPRESENTATIVE.

In the presence of His Majesty the King France both "won and lost" the Men's Singles Championship at Wimbledon yesterday, for in the final J. Borotra, the holder, went down before his young compatriot, R. Lacoste. Lacoste, a phenomenal player for his years, won a match that had many remarkable features—sensational in the persistent footfaulting of Borotra by a most courageous linesman—by 6—3, 6—3, 4—6, 8—6.

There have been younger champions in the national events of other countries, and also younger ones in the ladies' singles at Wimbledon, which Miss May Sutton, of America, won when she was seventeen; but Lacoste has established a new record as the most youthful player to secure the men's singles title.

And a right worthy champion Lacoste is. One of the classic players of the game. He has the rhythmical ease of the late H. L. Doherty, plus accentuated stroke power, and the ideal temperament for the game. In short, a boy with a man's brain.

Lacoste's achievement of yesterday was all the more noteworthy because he had in Borotra one of the most difficult men to beat. Since he won the championship last year, largely on his brilliant volleying, Borotra has stiffened his ground strokes. As ever, he is still, with his cat-like activity, one of the quickest men on the court, both on foot and alacrity of mind. Above all players, he has an exceptional capacity for getting an opponent guessing. It redounds to the credit of Lacoste, however, that, although he sometimes found himself unexpectedly trapped, and was frequently enticed into error while losing the third set, he stood his ground unruffled, and gradually mastered a combination of great stroke play and exceptional athletic attributes.

There was something majestic in the manner in which Lacoste could "pull out" in critical issues.

Masterly Strokes.

His game was replete with masterly ground strokes; lobbing of the highest order, while he had in reserve a potent service of a break variety which he skilfully combined with a plain and well-placed fast service. Somehow or other, I never thought at any stage during the match that Lacoste would lose, but to what extent the result was influenced by Borotra's troubles with foot-faulting is a matter for speculation.

The match had many dramatic incidents, and it opened in unique fashion, for one of such importance, Borotra twice double-faulted, and Lacoste was at 20—love without having played a stroke. Borotra also double-faulted twice in the third game, but he compensated by winning the fourth game against the service, making the scores "2 all." In the fifth game Borotra was foot-faulted, and then each man won to love on service. Borotra was again foot-faulted in the last game, Lacoste taking the set at 6—3.

There were more foot-faults by Borotra in the second set.

Foot-Fault Perplexities.

It occurred to me that sometimes he had both feet off the ground, and at others dragged a foot over the line, but he appeared to be perplexed and once interrogated the linesman. There were some great rallies while Borotra was going to 2—1, some of the backhand sweeps in front of an advancing volleyer being exquisite strokes. Then he became defective in the length of his ground strokes, and several "cuts" helped Lacoste to a 4—2 lead, Borotra double-faulting and foot-faulting in the sixth game. When Lacoste was at 5—2 it was dis-

covered that there was a hole in the net, but the players agreed to continue. When, however, Lacoste had won the set at 6—3, a new net was requisitioned.

Obviously concerned over his numerous penalties, Borotra was indecisive in service for the greater part of the third set. Again he foot-faulted, and again double faulted. His game, generally, however, increased in intensity, and by a courageous attack he reached 3—0. In this set, which Borotra won by 6—4, Lacoste made several errors in the way of mistiming, but he fought the last game tenaciously, pulling his man down from 40—30 and set point.

It took fourteen games in the fourth set to settle the issue before Lacoste ran out at 8—6. After Lacoste had won the first game against the service, there was a halt through Borotra having some trouble with his shoes—it was his day of trouble! Despite two more foot-faults and two great stop volleys by Lacoste, Borotra won the third game to lead by 2—1. He then proceeded to 4—1, and there were possibilities of a fifth set. He was smashing well and cleverly steering low drives of varied length. Then, however, Lacoste braced up, producing some beautiful back-hand strokes.

The seventh, which took Lacoste to 3—4, was a vital game, but Borotra once more obliged with a double fault. Lacoste was ahead at 5—4—yet another double fault by Borotra! —but then, with his great chance to finish the match, Lacoste dropped his service game, leaving a ball that fell just in instead of out. Borotra was at 6—5, but the best Lacoste captured the next three games, to claim the championship at 8—6. In these games he brought up his volleying forces with fine effect.

1925   The Sunday Times

René Lacoste. The Frenchman was a popular champion in 1925 and 1928

BOROTRA WINS TENNIS TROPHY AGAIN.

AMUSING CONTEMPT FOR "CUT" SHOTS.

By FRANK POXON.

FRANCE again won the men's singles championship at Wimbledon yesterday, Jean Borotra beating H. O. Kinsey, of America, in straight sets with the score 8—6, 6—1, 6—8. Borotra thus repeated his success of 1924, and for the third year France has taken the lawn tennis blue riband.

Borotra devoted the first set to a study of Kinsey's cut strokes. I have seldom seen the Basque so quiet and subdued as in this set. It was interesting to watch his thoughtful study of his opponent.

Then Borotra seemed to come to the conclusion that there was nothing terrible in Kinsey's "cut," and from that point he "went for" Kinsey in a way that swept that good player off his feet. In a contest between brilliance and studious consistency, brilliance won hands down. Kinsey never saw the way Borotra went in the last two sets.

SPELLBOUND CROWD.

There was half an hour or so of "wonder lawn tennis," and the crowd was so spellbound by the dazzling overhead play of Borotra that they even forgot to applaud. Borotra smashed and volleyed his way to victory, and his pantherish speed about the court was thrilling.

Kinsey tried to check Borotra's rushes to the net by lobbing, but Borotra electrified all by taking those lobs in mid-court. His "kills" were so deadly that, more often than not, it would have been sheer futility for Kinsey to have attempted to get to the ball.

Both men played scrappily the first few games. Borotra was going up on practically every shot. Borotra stopped storming the net, and it was 3—3, 4—4, 5—5, and 6—6. Borotra took the next two games for the set at 8—6.

A COMIC TOUCH.

In the second set with Borotra, the real Borotra, and, gaining an early lead, all Kinsey's craft and all his heavily cut ground strokes were of no avail. Borotra stormed ahead to win 6—1. The third set was always going in favour of Borotra, and Kinsey accepted the inevitable during the last two games.

There was one moment of comic relief when Borotra dashed at full speed to the umpire, asked him to remove a fly from his eye, then shook the umpire by the hand, and raced back to do more unkind things to Howard Kinsey.

Mrs. Godfree and Miss Evelyn Colyer, in the women's doubles final against Miss Ryan and Miss M. K. Browne, the Americans, were overwhelmingly defeated 6—1, 6—1. Their display was pitifully weak.

To-day's final in the women's singles will be between Senorita E. d'Alvarez and Mrs. Godfree. There is the possibility of a most exciting match.

1926   Daily News

1927   Henri Cochet
beat Jean Borotra
4–6 4–6 6–3 6–4 7–5

The return of Bill Tilden to the Championship coincided with the introduction of full seeding. With six successive United States titles to his credit between 1920 and 1925 Tilden, playing at New Wimbledon for the first time, was ranked number two.

René Lacoste had the honour of being the number one and with Jean Borotra (3) and **Henri Cochet** (4) there were three Frenchmen in the top four seeds. The All England Club committee got it right the first time as all four came through to the semi-finals.

At this time Wimbledon witnessed one of the most sensational matches in the Championship's history. Cochet had already won his quarter-final against Frank Hunter after being two sets down when he came up against the great Tilden for a place in his first final. This looked impossible as 'Big Bill' raced into a 6–2 6–4 5–1 lead against his much smaller opponent. Cochet then had a run of seventeen consecutive points that pulled him back to 5–5. He took the third set 7–5 and, with Tilden totally dispirited, won the next two and the match.

'The Little Lion of Lyon' had pulled off a remarkable victory and he kept his advantage over Tilden, losing only twice in nine tournament meetings.

Borotra had beaten Lacoste in the other semi-final and predictably he won the first two sets against Cochet. Back came Cochet again to win the next two sets and level the match but, in the final set, Borotra built up a commanding 5–2 lead. It did not seem possible that Cochet could come back from such a position in a third successive match but this he did, saving six match points in the process. From 5–5 he won the next two games and the Wimbledon men's singles title for the first time.

NEW   WIMBLEDON   CHAMPIONS.

COCHET'S PLUCK AND LUCK.

DOUBTFUL STROKE WINS HIM THE TITLE.

Henri Cochet (France) won the lawn tennis " blue riband " in the championships at Wimbledon on Saturday, when he defeated his countryman and previous holder, J. Borotra, by 3 sets to 2.

Cochet made a doubtful stroke in the fifth set and received the benefit of the umpire's decision. If this had gone against Cochet, Borotra might still have been champion.

The day was dull, but the quality of the lawn tennis and the tenseness of the matches made up for the state of the weather. Once again Cochet proved himself a wonderful fighter.

For the third successive match he found himself in a losing position and yet won. In his matches against Tilden and Hunter, however, although he lost the first two sets he was never within a point of losing them.

On Saturday against Borotra, Cochet had that dreaded (and to Borotra the elusive) point six times to save. Borotra had won the first two sets at 6—4, 6—4. He had been the master of the match until then.

His tactics were to manœuvre until he received the ball in the centre of his court, then to direct it to Cochet's backhand and rush to the net to cut off Cochet's return—generally across the court—with a dazzling volley.

BOROTRA EASES UP.

In the third set Borotra, who had taken a lot out of himself, purposely eased up so as to be able to go all out for the fourth set.

The real fight began when Borotra led by 4—2 in this fourth set. Cochet's fighting qualities never let him acknowledge defeat. He was uncanny in the manner he saved strokes and clever in his passing shots, which had to be extra good because Borotra was in his best volleying mood.

Cochet pulled this set up, and won it without losing another game.

With two sets all and with the reputation that Cochet has for winning in the fifth set, it was thought that he had the match won. How near he came to losing it will make this match an historic one. Borotra went to 5 games to 2 in this fifth set. Cochet served in the eighth game, and was 40—0. Borotra, making a gallant effort, obtained the advantage point and needed but one point for match. Instead of gaining this he feebly returned the ball into the bottom of the net.

But there was worse to come. Borotra still had his service and his following volleys to depend on. Borotra led at 40—30. He served, and came in. A long rally followed, and Cochet placed the ball to the feet of Borotra, who netted it.

The crowd wanted Borotra to win yet admired Cochet's grit. Borotra twice more gained the match point, and in a volleying duel for the fourth time Cochet made a doubtful stroke (hitting the ball twice), but

Jean Borotra (on the left) and Henri Cochet. This picture was taken before their dramatic men's single final in 1927 (London News Agency)

the umpire, after Borotra looked at him, gave it as a fair shot.

Still Borotra persevered and twice again got to within an ace of victory. But he could not break through that wonderful tenacity and courage of his smaller opponent.

At length Cochet not only saved that crucial game but won it through Borotra double faulting.

Borotra hardly made a fight for the remainder of the set, and so Cochet, now playing perfectly, won the next three games for the match and the championship.

Borotra took his defeat magnificently, and in the dressing-room said that Cochet was too good for him, and passed over lightly that doubtful double hit.

1928 René Lacoste
beat Henri Cochet
6–1 4–6 6–4 6–2

1929 Henri Cochet
beat Jean Borotra
6–4 6–3 6–4

In 1928 the semi-finals again consisted of three Frenchmen and the American Bill Tilden. This time **René Lacoste** accounted for 'Big Bill', then went on to win his second Wimbledon singles title by beating Henri Cochet in the final. Lacoste's victory was particularly sweet as he had lost to Cochet in the French championship earlier that year.

The next Wimbledon, in 1929, had a British player seeded for the first time. Colin Gregory (8) unfortunately did not figure in the later stages but the unseeded H.W. ('Bunny') Austin reached the semi-finals. Austin put up a great fight against Jean Borotra before losing in four sets and Cochet again defeated Tilden in the other semi-final. **Cochet** then enjoyed a much easier victory in the final over Borotra than he had in 1927.

At the end of their six years of dominance, 'The Musketeers' had each won two singles titles. For six years they had provided the adoring Wimbledon crowds with a great spectacle, along with skill and charm. None of them, however, ever again reached a Wimbledon men's singles final, although Borotra (in 1930 and 1931) and Cochet (in 1933) were beaten semi-finalists. In their own championships they shared eight wins from its inauguration in 1925 – Cochet (four), Lacoste (three) and Borotra (one).

A fourth 'Musketeer' was the outstanding doubles player Toto Brugnon. He won four men's doubles titles – two with Cochet (in 1926 and 1928) and two with Borotra (in 1932 and 1933).

So 1929 was the end of the French manipulation of the men's singles. It was in the same year that a certain Fred Perry entered the Wimbledon Championship for the first time and reached the third round.

LACOSTE WINS
TAME FINAL

Cochet Far Below His Best Form

AMERICANS BEATEN

Crawford's Brilliant Play in Mixed Doubles

By MRS. GODFREE (Kitty McKane)

In defeating Cochet, the holder of the title, in the final of the men's singles at Wimbledon yesterday, Lacoste played magnificent lawn tennis, and carried out to perfection a very determined attack on Cochet's backhand.

Lacoste's ability to retrieve difficult balls is almost uncanny, and many of Cochet's strokes, that against any other player, would have been winners, were returned with interest by his relentless opponent.

It is only fair to add that Cochet was far below his best form, for not only did his back hand let him down badly, but his net play, usually so brilliant, was most uncertain.

In the mixed doubles America suffered another blow when Helen Wills and F. T. Hunter went down to Miss Ryan and P. D. B. Spence. It was Miss Ryan's splendid play at the net that gave her side the victory, for Spence was always a little uncertain.

Miss Wills drove and served with her usual skill, but she and her partner did not find their way to net position quickly enough, and they were always on the defence.

Favourites Defeated

The most fancied pair for the mixed doubles championship, Cochet and Miss Eileen Bennett, were defeated by the Australian pair, Crawford and Miss Akhurst, who have now to meet Spence and Miss Ryan in the final.

Crawford served excellently and aced Cochet's fiercest cannon-ball services continually by brilliant passing shots to his backhand.

Thanks to the victory of Mrs. Watson and Miss Saunders over Miss Ryan and Mrs. Licett, the final of the women's doubles will be contested by two English pairs, the other finalists being Miss Harvey and Miss Eileen Bennett.

The final of the women's singles between Miss Wills and Senorita de Alvarez is the big event to-day. But the Senorita must be under a heavy handicap owing to her illness, from which she has not yet completely recovered

CHAMPION'S DEFEAT

Cochet Informed of Mother's Serious Illness

Behind the surprisingly poor and listless display by Cochet, both in his final of the singles and the semi-final of the mixed doubles on the Centre Court yesterday, lies a poignant story (writes a special correspondent).

Since Thursday his intimate friends have noted a change in his demeanour, and the secret leaked out yesterday that Cochet had received a telephone message from his home town, Lyons, late on Wednesday night that his mother was dangerously ill.

His secret anxiety was undoubtedly reflected in his play on Thursday when, for the first time since he has been playing with Miss Bennett, he failed to be the dominant partner.

Cochet himself denied strenuously that the bad news he has had had anything to do with his defeat by Lacoste. Indeed he was insistent that Lacoste won on his merits.

Cochet intends to leave Wimbledon for Lyons immediately on the conclusion of the doubles final to-day.

COCHET AGAIN

When Cochet and Borotra came on for the final of the singles they were cheered and "shot." The knocking up consisted of a rapid exchange of volleys, and then rain came on, the players left, and in their stead men relaid the tarpaulin. It was soon fine again, and the match began. Cochet was out for blood, for revenge; he had much to wipe out. Beaten in Brussels by Borotra, beaten in the Paris championships by Borotra, beaten in the doubles in Paris by Borotra and Lacoste, beaten at Wimbledon in the doubles (by Allison and Van Ryn), beaten in the Wimbledon mixed by Collins and Miss Fry . . . high time that Henri Cochet came back. The match as a match was not very exciting; Borotra was far from being his brilliant best, and he was footfaulted and that put him off, though, as far as one could judge, he was very properly footfaulted. The worst of the footfault rule is that it so often lies in abeyance until the final round. Cochet was very much the grand Cochet, stalking majestically with measured gait to his baseline between the rallies, not speaking to the ball boys, and if a rally ended in his sending a ball that he considered hopeless to chase, after Borotra had dealt with it, he did no more than watch Borotra deal with it. True economy of effort, and economy of effort is the keynote of Cochet's game. As the match progressed Cochet dominated it more and more, and time after time in the final set he wrung from Borotra the "Ah! Oui!" that spoke the admiration of an untakable shot. In the last set Cochet's ground shots were on a par with his lovely volleying.

In the first set the games went to three all and four all. Cochet took the next on his own service, and Borotra lost a love game on his having been footfaulted. When the second set was at three-all Cochet became the aggressive Cochet, his ground shots justified his rush for the net, and the end came with Borotra netting the return of a second service. In the third set Cochet was ahead at 3—love, and the spectators cheered Borotra, not wishing to see his favourite thus roughly handled without doing something to hearten him. So Borotra obliged with a game, but Cochet went to 4—1, Borotra again singing his "Ah! oui" song. Cochet served, and Borotra got another cheer and obliged with another game 4—2, Borotra served and was love-40, but won, amidst very loud cheers, 4—3. Cochet then made his effort and won his service, Borotra falling, but in some mysterious way saving his trousers from being marked. Borotra served and Cochet missed two consecutive services. It was to be a fight after all! Cochet, however, won his own service from love—30, and all was over. Borotra, of course, bounded over the net, and the next moment hands were wrung and Cochet was apparently protesting to Borotra that he (Borotra) was quite off his game and that it really did not count and was a shame and so forth. And so protesting the two left the court. Cochet is champion for the second time, having won before in 1927.

1928 Daily Sketch   **1929 Manchester Guardian**

7 | Perry's Hat-trick

1930–39

Following the abolition of the Challenge Round in 1921, Fred Perry became the first to win the men's singles title three years running. The next player to repeat this feat was Bjorn Borg over forty years later. In 1937 the American Don Budge became the first man to win the Wimbledon triple crown – singles, men's and mixed doubles victories all in the same year.

Fred Perry. In addition to his singles victories, he also won the mixed doubles with Dorothy Round in 1935 and 1936

1930   Bill Tilden
beat Wilmer Allison
6–3 9–7 6–4

1931   Sidney Wood
walked over Frank Shields
(scratched)

'**Big Bill' Tilden** capped his amateur career by winning his third Wimbledon singles title – his first at the new venue – at the age of thirty-seven. He had a lot to thank his final opponent for, as Wilmer Allison had surprisingly beaten Henri Cochet – Tilden's bogeyman – in the quarter-finals. Allison thus became the first unseeded player to reach a men's singles final but he was no match for 'Big Bill'.

Following his victory Tilden turned professional. In six Wimbledons he had won three singles titles (1920, 1921 and 1930).

The next year the final did not take place following a semi-final injury to American Frank Shields. He fell badly when playing Jean Borotra and, although he carried on to win the match, his Davis Cup captain insisted that he withdraw from the final.

So the 1931 Championship went to **Sidney Woods** whose semi-final win over Fred Perry was more important than he had first realised. Shields was the number three seed while Woods was the number seven.

Frank Shields. Nursing an injury, he had to withdraw from the 1931 singles final

TILDEN WINS WIMBLEDON SINGLES

Allison Defeated in Finals Before King and Queen.

WIMBLEDON, England, July 5 (A.P.).—Tall Bill Tilden, at age of 37, today came back for the Wimbledon tennis title he last won, nine years ago, and by defeating Wilmer Allison, the slender Texan, in straight sets, 6—3, 9—7, 6—4, again climbed to the singles champion's throne.

King George, Queen Mary and Prince George, the latter president of the All-English Club, in a generous sporting gesture came to Wimbledon to see the Americans scrap over the historic spoils. Having no Englishmen at all to cheer for, the crowds vented their enthusiasm on their monarchs. The queen, in a pink gown topped by a tall toque of pink beige with pastel tints around the crown, and the king in a summery suit and light gray derby, were cheered lustily as they were seated just as Tilden and Allison started warming up.

"They Never Come Back" Wrong, Tilden Shows.

"They never come back," according to a well-worn epigram of sports but Tilden did—and with all the convincing mastery of old. Allison played brilliant tennis, without doubt as brilliant as he played in toppling Henri Cochet, the Wimbledon title holder, on Wednesday, but Tilden's genius at a game calling for youthful stamina, delicate skill and lightning judgement, enabled him to dominate today's play throughout most of the match. The plaudits of a gallery of nearly 15,000 were for the great defense of the agile Texan rather than the hope held out that he could win.

Again Tilden's tremendous speed from service served him well. In long games Allison was fighting to save his service, while Tilden's smashing service aces always were in reserve to be unloosed in the moment of crisis. Allison's speed at times was more marvelous than Tilden's. From his almost frail physique he drew shots that left his tall opponent standing.

Tilden, displaying a beautiful assortment of strokes, won the first two games. Allison, serving, had the advantage in the third game and his first serve, which the linesman called out, having been good, according to Tilden's view, Big Bill deliberately hit Allison's second service outside and gave the Texan the game.

The American champion took the next from deuce, whereupon Allison served a love game. Tilden answered with a love game of his own to lead at 4—2.

Allison won the seventh from 30 with a service ace for the final point. Tilden served another love game to lead 5—3. The ninth game was deuced five times, but Allison lost it and with it the set, although he played some great tennis in a gallant effort to save it.

Allison Puts Up Best Fight In Second Set.

In the second set the Texan made his greatest fight and clear to deuce ten games went on service. Four of them from Tilden's racquet were love games, an indication of the value of Big Bill's cannonball delivery.

Games went with service in the second set and they were deadlocked at 5-all.

Tilden served his third love game of the second set to take a lead of 6—5. Allison led Tilden at 40—30 in the twelfth game, tried a streaming second service for the next point and double faulted, but won the game to go 6-all.

Tilden again led at 7—6, then at 8—7 with a fourth love game. Allison fought magnificently to draw level again and the game was deuced three times, but the Texan foot-faulted at a critical moment, and Tilden carried the set.

Tilden broke through Allison's service in the sixth game of the third set to lead at 4—2. The blond youth from Austin, Tex., came right back to break Tilden's delivery and cut his lead to 4—3, but Tilden again won Allison's service and the games stood at 5—3. Tilden went after the ninth game with a will, but Allison, rushing to the net on every point, took the game with a series of spectacular placements.

Allison, serving in the final game, soon found himself at love-40. He grabbed the next point, then over-hit the baseline to lose the game, set and title.

1930   Washington Post

1932 Ellsworth Vines
beat Bunny Austin
6–4 6–2 6–0

1933 Jack Crawford
beat Ellsworth Vines
4–6 11–9 6–2 2–6 6–4

During the Wimbledon men's singles tournament in 1932 **Ellsworth Vines** produced some of the most scintillating tennis ever

seen. It was his first appearance in the Championships and the power with which the 20-year-old Californian hit the ball startled the crowds. He improved almost daily during the fortnight and in his semi-final and final matches lost only twelve games in six sets.

At match point in the final against Britain's Bunny Austin he served an ace that Austin claimed afterwards he didn't see and couldn't even say which side of him it had gone.

In 1933 the 6 ft 3 in. Vines showed he had lost none of his serve and volley strength as he reached a second final. This time Australian **Jack Crawford** – the number two seed – was his opponent and those fortunate enough to see the match said it was one of the finest played at Wimbledon.

The first set went to the top-seeded Vines but the brilliant Crawford concentrated on the rallies and won the second 11–9. Crawford

(cont.)

VINES CRUSHES AUSTIN.

WIMBLEDON FINAL WON BY YOUNG AMERICAN.

(By SIR F. GORDON LOWE, Bart., the Famous International.)

A great international programme, with leading representatives from the chief tennis nations engaged, brought enormous crowds to Wimbledon yesterday for the final day, and provided a fitting finish to a splendid fortnight's tennis.

The outstanding attraction was, of course, the match for the Blue Riband between Bunny Austin, the first home player to break through to the final since 1923, and Ellsworth Vines, the young American, who, with his super-tennis, has taken Wimbledon by storm at his first appearance, the only man, except Tilden, to do so.

The King and Queen arrived just in time for the match, which, to everyone's disappointment, provided after all an easy straight-set victory for the American.

Vines, on his way to the final, struck form superior and more sustained than anything he had previously shown in his own country, and yesterday against Austin was no exception. Vines proved himself a worthy champion.

Austin quite failed to produce the perfect tennis he had shown against Shields.

"DAVID AND GOLIATH."

The match certainly did not come up to expectations. Vines played wonderfully well, but, at the same time, after the first set Austin seemed incapable of putting up a real fight. In his top form, Vines should never be able to beat Austin as easily as he did yesterday, deadly as the American is.

Both Vines and Austin seemed to feel the importance of the occasion at the start, but the former soon warmed to his work and was driving and serving at a tremendous speed toward the end of the first set.

It was the fact that he could not take Vines lethal cannon-balls, which, I am sure, depressed Austin and eventually got on his nerves and upset his concentration. Austin's service, so good against Shields, was in-

Bunny Austin. He made history in 1933 – the first man to wear shorts in a centre court match at Wimbledon

effective against Vines, and his length throughout the match was poor, he was only half-way down the court with his drives, and he served too many double-faults.

Vines, on the other hand, was keeping a perfect length and continually hitting deep into the corners of the court. This prevented Austin from getting up to the net and gave Vines many opportunities to do so. It is impossible to have rallies with Vines, he either wins the point outright in two strokes or he misses it.

Austin played down the centre of the court at the start right at Vines, and it is a pity he did not persevere with these tactics. Vines plays a very unusual game, and after a few more matches against him Austin will be more at home in such hurricane tennis. At this Wimbledon this 6ft. 4in. young American certainly played a robot game with a vengeance.

At the beginning of the first set both men were obviously a little overawed by the general tension, and each started by losing their service. Vines was making many mistakes, but through his fierce deliveries was able to keep on level terms with Austin up till 3—all. Austin at this period drove down the centre with success. Then Vines braced, and put on the pressure heavily, forcing Austin to lose his services by driving wide of the lines.

The American had increased his lead to 5—3 on his service, and then, leading 5—4, after a long wait while he changed a shoe-lace, captured the valuable first set again serving splendidly. Up to now there had not been a great deal in it; a little luck and it might have gone Austin's way.

In the second set it was a case of the big man dominating the situation, and Vines looked a winner all the way through.

LUCK AGAINST AUSTIN.

The American was quickly 3—1 up, but Austin hung on grimly and reduced the lead. By terrific serving Vines was soon 4—2, and then Austin lost his service against the terrific corner shots of the American champion, who soon had this set also in his pocket at 6—2. It was Vines' set all the way.

The third set was merely a procession of points for Vines, who was by now hitting very clean and hard, and was right on top, and he took it to love. Austin made a fight of it to hold his service in the first and third games, but yielded up the latter on a double fault. Vines finished off the match with a characteristic cannon-ball right down the centre and rushed to shake hands with Austin. This young man from America had certainly scored a great triumph, and he was loudly cheered.

After the first set, which was won very easily by Borotra and Brugnon from Perry and Austin, the men's doubles was a brilliant affair, the result of which remained in the lap of the gods until the last stroke was played.

CRAWFORD BREAKS THE SPELL

By FRANK POXON
the " News-Chronicle " Tennis Expert

IN the most dramatic final seen at Wimbledon for many years Jack Crawford, of Australia, yesterday afternoon defeated Ellsworth Vines, America, at

4—6, 11—9, 6—2, 2—6, 6—4.

The Blue Riband of lawn tennis thus comes back to the British Empire for the first time since 1922, when Gerald Patterson, of Australia, won the men's singles championship for the second time—his first victory was in 1919. Since 1922, until yesterday, American and French players have " farmed " the championship.

Crawford is now the champion of Great Britain, France and Australia. He may go to America later in the year and win his fourth national championship in 12 months. A great player indeed.

" *The finest final I ever saw,*" said Henri Cochet, of France, to me after the match.

" *The finest final I ever saw,*" said H. Roper Barrett, echoing Cochet's words.

I saw both players afterwards.

Vines said :

" *On the day's play the better man won. It was a splendid match.*"

Crawford said :

" *I think I was a bit lucky to win. I never hope to play against a finer sportsman.*"

I think we might say : " Full marks both !"

CROWD'S UNFAIRNESS

But I can't say " Full marks " to the crowd. It was hysterical and—I hate to say so—unfair to Vines. They applauded his errors, which is the negation of sportsmanship.

They were right to applaud Crawford's good strokes ; they were utterly unfair and un-English to applaud Vines' bad ones. After all, there is such a thing as a square deal.

DOMINATED BY SERVICE

Crawford's Advantage in Winning Toss

The match was packed with unforgettable incidents.

It was certainly the finest final I ever saw, or probably ever shall see.

From first to last the match was dominated by the service. When Crawford won the toss for service, it may be that he won the match. For, as the games panned out, Crawford began each of the five sets on his own service. It was the deciding factor.

Each player had one pet stroke—the same one—a forehand drive to his rival's back-hand corner. It came off time after time.

In the first set Vines drew out to 3-1 and then 5-2. only for Crawford to win **two games in succession to reduce the lead of Vines to 5-4, the American then taking the set at 6-4**. It was early apparent that the crowd was pro-Crawford, but then the Wimbledon crowd always applauds the non-favourite.

AMAZING SECOND SET

I shall not soon forget the second set, nor will anybody else who saw it. Crawford started with the first service and for 19 games each man won his service in turn. It was wonderful " stuff " that was served up and the crowd was worked up to an extraordinary pitch of excitement.

At long last Crawford captured Vines' service in the twentieth game, to take the set at 11—9.

J. H. Crawford in play against Ellsworth Vines.

Vines struck a bad patch of wild hitting in the third set and Crawford, playing superbly, won it at 6—2 in quick time.

Vines won the fourth set at 6—2 just as easily as Crawford had won the third, and it seemed that the Australian was getting weary, but you can never tell with Jack Crawford ; he often looks languid when he is nothing of the kind. Vines also looked " fagged "—but he wasn't. The flame of inspiration to achieve victory was still burning brightly in that long, lean body.

Two sets all—one set to go—and Crawford still serving in the first game. Crawford served well, but Vines served like a super-man. I " clocked " one of his service games—15—0, 30—0, 40—0, 40—15. game. And the time was 40 seconds ! How to play lawn tennis !

A CHEERFUL LOSER

Crawford led at 3—2. 4—3. 5—4. Service for Vines. He faltered with the knowledge that only four points separated him from defeat. The steel went out of his racket, but he fought bravely, and yet without confidence.

Crawford. very weary, still kept on playing with classical artistry. He made no single mistake in this crucial tenth game.

The American netted the last two strokes and it was all over. Vines was a loser; he had lost the unofficial world's championship, but I never saw a more gallant loser. He was all smiles as his hand went out to his conqueror in a flash.

1933   News Chronicle

---

had been practising how to cope with his opponent's awesome power since their last meeting, and this proved worthwhile when he won the third set.

Vines showed true champion's quality in levelling the match but later, with the score at 5–4 to Crawford in the final set, the Australian broke Vines' cannonball service to win the Championship for the only time.

As Crawford acknowledged the applause from an ecstatic centre court crowd his wife, overcome by the drama and excitement, fainted in the stand.

Vivian McGrath never reached the highlights achieved by Crawford and Vines but, in 1933, he made history of his own on the centre court. The youngster from Sydney, Australia, introduced to world tennis the two-handed backhand, which has since been used with devastating effect by the five-times champion Bjorn Borg.

1934 Fred Perry
beat Jack Crawford
6–3 6–0 7–5

1935 Fred Perry
beat Gottfried von Cramm
6–2 6–4 6–4

1936 Fred Perry
beat Gottfried von Cramm
6–1 6–1 6–0

Fred Perry was born in 1909, the same year that Arthur Wentworth Gore won the Wimbledon men's singles title. A quarter of a century later, Perry succeeded Gore as the king of English, and world, tennis.

He did not take up the game until he was fourteen and he tried to emulate the all-round skills and courage of Henri Cochet. His father, a Labour Member of Parliament, would have preferred him to go into business but he let him persevere with lawn tennis especially as he won the world table tennis championship in 1929.

Perry had been making steady progress at Wimbledon and he started the 1934 Championship as both the United States and the Australian singles holder. To reach his first centre court final he had to win a tough five-set match against the 1931 champion Sidney Wood.

In the final he met the title holder and number one seed Jack Crawford. Perry lost three of the first four games but then, incredibly, won twelve successive games, and these helped him into a two-set lead. At 5–6 in the third set, the Australian double-faulted on match point to give the elated Perry the title he wanted more than any other.

It was a magnificent year for Perry and British tennis. He had won the Australian, United States and Wimbledon singles titles and victory in the French would have given him the Grand Slam – the four major championships in one year. But this was not to be. He won the French, however, in 1935 and became the first player to collect all the four major singles titles.

For the next two years at Wimbledon, Perry met the *(cont.)*

WIMBLEDON THRILLS TO PERRY'S MAGIC

NEW CHAMPION'S 12 GAMES
OFF REEL AGAINST THE OLD

Tennis the Centre Court Has Seldom Seen— How Crawford Sealed His Fate

By H. E. LAINSON WOOD

After a display of spell-binding tennis such as even Wimbledon has seldom seen, F. J. Perry yesterday won the men's singles championship by beating the Australian holder, Jack Crawford, in the final by 6—3, 6—0, 7—5.

Thus the supreme honour of the game returns to England after a lapse of twenty-five years—since A. W. Gore last won it in 1909, the year of Perry's birth.

Perry had already beaten Crawford in the final of the American and Australian championships, and his victory yesterday proves unquestionably that he is the greatest player in the world—and one of the greatest the game has ever known.

So complete was his mastery yesterday that at one stage he had won twelve games—virtually two love sets—off the reel.

In the final set Crawford made a gallant effort to retain a title that he won last year—only to lose it on a dramatic double fault.

The match began on a surprisingly low note. There was scarcely a volley in the first three games, but rally after rally of tentative driving from backhand to backhand.

These rallies ended generally on a mistake. Crawford, it appeared, was inviting a net raid by the shortness of his length, but Perry would not be tempted.

A prolonged first game went to the Australian on his service after deuce had been called six times.

Then Perry won a love game. Another long game resulted in Crawford retaining his service rather luckily, and then Perry was trailing at love—40.

The Englishman launched his first really sustained volleying campaign at this hazardous juncture and pulled up to deuce, but another fault gave Crawford the advantage and soon Perry was 1—3 down.

He replied by capturing Crawford's service to 15 and then his own to love, thus squaring this somewhat nervy and unenterprising set at 3—all.

Perry had by this time warmed up. Twice he advanced to the forecourt on a hard-struck forehand drive to Crawford's backhand, and each time the Australian's attempts to pass him found the net.

ELEGANT BACKHANDERS

Crawford now got more pace and length into his ground shots, especially those elegantly-produced backhanders, and he pulled up from 15—40 to deuce, but the game was Perry's for a 4—3 lead, soon to be increased to 5—3.

Perry completed a sequence of five games played with better concentration and greater certainty of touch to win a wholly comforting first set at 6—3.

Recollections of Crawford's similar bad start against Shields, the American, in the semi-finals, put a curb on early British enthusiasm. It might otherwise have broken all bounds, as Perry continued along a stronger and all-conquering path in the second set to lead 4—0.

He advanced on his service and behind drives of beautiful depth and pace

A LOVE SET !

It was Perry in his most decisive and unplayable form who transformed this great lead into a love set

Then there was a cheer—a real wave of patriotic fervour. Could Crawford stage another recovery against the stuff that our man was putting over?

When Perry won the opening game of the third set—to 30—he had actually won twelve games off the reel.

Think of it ! An equivalent of two love sets against the holder in the final—against Perry's only real rival in the race for the honour of being ranked as the world's best player.

That sort of thing could not last even against the spell-binding game Perry was playing.

Crawford held his service and won his first game since the fourth of the first set.

It imbued him with a little confidence. His drives came into length again. They widened and he shared the attack.

He came in, risking little, to snaffle a few points on the volley himself. He thus kept Perry away from the net for a while.

Crawford maintained his service games to 4—all, and the crowd began to sense a crisis.

They encouraged Crawford because it is the English instinct. They applauded the underdog.

Then came a game of breathless excitement. With Perry serving and Crawford showing more coolness and courage than he had previously done, making caution his watchword, the score ran 15—all and 30—all.

PERRY'S MISTAKE

Perry shot across a forehand for which Crawford had to sprint desperately. He could only lob the return high into the air.

Perry might have killed it—his strongest card was his overhead shot—but he allowed it to drop. It fell plumb on the sideline and Perry returned it meekly into the net.

Then Perry double-faulted and Crawford was ahead at last—5—4 and his service to follow.

This turn of fortune was not to Perry's liking and he showed how temporarily perturbed he was by netting a couple of fairly easy ones after he had reached 15—40 on Crawford's service.

Yet he won that game and the next, to take the lead at 6—5.

Crawford advanced to 40—love on his service. At the end of three fairly well-contested rallies he showed that he, too, had nerves by netting, and it was deuce.

Perry reached vantage with a lovely shot into Crawford's forehand corner, to which the Australian just got his racket, but he could not get the ball over. And then came catastrophe with a capital C.

Crawford was foot-faulted. His second service fell into the net. The great fight was over—ended tamely on a double fault.

One cannot dismiss Wimbledon on this great and glorious British day without a reference to those tennis-aged Frenchmen, Borotra and Brugnon, holders of the double championship. They defeated the last remaining British pair, I. G. Collins and F. H. D. Wilde, 7—5, 3—6, 6—2, 6—4, and to-day face the American heavy artillery of L. R. Stoefen and G. M. Lott.

A. W. Gore.

1934   Daily Mirror

MASTERLY PLAY

VON CRAMM FIGHTS IN VAIN

By ULYSS ROGERS

FRED PERRY wore his famous Cheshire cat mascot yesterday, but he had no need of it.

He defeated the German star, Gottfried von Cramm, in three straight sets, 6—2, 6—4, 6—4, and did it by playing masterly tennis that classed him with Tilden, Cochet, or Lacoste at their best.

He is the first man to win the Wimbledon championship two years in succession since in 1922 the law was instituted that champions must "play through."

Sixteen thousand eager spectators packed the Centre Court and watched every stroke of the match.

GRAND STYLE

The affair was made a kind of state function. The players were not permitted to carry their own rackets into court. A white-coated attendant carried them instead.

The royal box was packed with distinguished personages.

The peak of excitement in the whole match came when von Cramm, down 2-4 in the third set, plunged into the fight with the courage of despair.

He served with devil, half volleyed a beauty, ran like a deer, and made it 3—4. But he had not calculated on Perry's response.

HIGH SPEED PLAY.—Camera recorded rapid movement of Perry's racket, giving impression it was bent.

STROKE BY STROKE

In the next game von Cramm, storming the net, was passed by the wonder worker on the opposite side. Perry hit the line twice. He had the wizard touch and made it 5 3.

Yet again the fighting spirit of von Cramm showed itself. The pace became terrific in the ninth game. This is how it went:—

Von Cramm serving. Perry nets 15—0.

Von Cramm, crowding the net, volleys one that Perry fails to negotiate—30—0.

Perry passes von Cramm 30—15.

Von Cramm at net forces Perry to hit out—40—15.

Von Cramm, still pressing, muffs an easy volley—40—30.

Perry slams a wondrous backhand shot across von Cramm at the net—deuce.

Von Cramm, over-anxious, muffs another at net—vantage to Perry.

Perry hits out—deuce.

Von Cramm, with a service that almost baffled vision, aces Perry—vantage von Cramm. He had previously aced Perry three times in one game.

Another stinging service. Perry nets it. Game von Cramm.

It was Perry's service now, with the lead 5—4. Could von Cramm capture it, and gain another lease of life?

LAST SLAM

Alas for his hopes! The game went to 30—all. And then—

Von Cramm slams one over the base-line—40—30.

Perry, in sight of home, tamely nets—deuce.

And then von Cramm, in a last death agony, hits two more out and the heavens resound with the acclamations.

Just as Perry was leaving, Mlle. Suzanne Lenglen came along. She greeted him with a kiss on the cheek, and said: "You played some wonderful shots, Fred."

He did.

1935   Daily Express

German player Baron Gottfried von Cramm and won both finals in straight sets. A true stylist like Britain's Bunny Austin, von Cramm had to beat an up-and-coming 19-year-old Don Budge to reach the final in 1935.

In 1936 Perry faced Budge on the way to the final and the American was the only player to take a set from the champion in the whole fortnight. Unfortunately the final between Perry and von Cramm was something of an anticlimax as the German pulled a leg muscle and, despite his insistence to see out the match, he was unable to provide any real challenge.

Perry therefore joined the greats and, after the abolition of the Challenge Round, only he and, much later, Bjorn Borg were to achieve a hat-trick of Wimbledon men's singles titles. Later in 1936 Perry helped Great Britain win the Davis Cup for a fourth time before turning professional.

HUSHED CROWD SEES HIS HOLLOWEST-EVER TRIUMPH

White-Faced Von Cramm Battles in Anguish

By PETER WILSON

" I have been asked to announce that Baron von Cramm pulled a muscle in his thigh in his first service game, and he much regrets that he was not able to play better."

THAT was the announcement made by the umpire to a silent crowd of 15,000 people at the end of the match in which Fred Perry, for the third year in succession, won the men's singles at Wimbledon yesterday 6—1, 6—1, 6—0.

But although he won and so set up a record for the new Wimbledon Perry looked as unhappy as anyone else when he walked off the Centre Court for never has there been such a hollow victory.

The match had opened brilliantly and Perry was serving and both men, paler than usual with a strain of the final, were nevertheless producing glorious lawn-tennis.

Several times deuce was called before Perry, who had twice been beaten with net cord passing shots, won the game—also with a net-cord.

The tightly-wedged crowd had applauded every rally wildly. They would have been even more enthusiastic had they known that it was about the only real game they were to see.

Curiously enough, there was nothing noticeably wrong with Von Cramm in the second game, which he won with a terrific backhand.

As yet the crowd had no inkling of any disaster —although the damage was already done

Went to Pieces

Both men had been hitting the ball very hard off the ground with von Cramm slightly the more powerful, so that Perry had to go to the net whether he wanted to or not.

But in the fourth game von Cramm suddenly went to pieces. He was footfaulted in this game and at first I thought that had upset his concentration. But soon it was obvious that the trouble was more serious

The German's backhand strokes looked strangely tame, but it was not until the end of the set that it became quite obvious that von Cramm had injured himself.

By the second set Von Cramm had given up trying to return any ball for which he had to take more than one step, and a great hush had fallen over the crowd, who had ceased applauding even the most brilliant shots of Perry, who was playing some astonishing stuff.

At the end of the fourth game, when he was leading 3—1 Perry came to the net and spoke to his opponent, who waved him on to continue the game

What he said was inaudible, but the umpire, Mr. L. W. J. Newman, told me afterwards that Perry had asked Von Cramm if he wanted a masseur, and the German had replied that it was no good, and he must carry on

Getting Match Over

Perry won eleven games in a row against his crippled opponent, whose face was as white as the chalk on the court—doing quite the right thing in playing as well as he could so as to get this travesty of what might have been a great match over as quickly as possible.

I understand that Von Cramm will travel with the German Davis Cup team to Zagreb, where they will meet Yugoslavia in the final of the European Zone a week to-day.

Let us hope that the final of the women's singles to-day will not be afflicted by the bad luck which has dogged this year's championship.

It should be a great match, and steady as Mrs. Sperling is she can never have met anyone more determined to win than try-again Helen Jacobs

Great Britain is certain of winning at least one title to-day. For the first time since the war there is an all-British final in the men's doubles

---

Stepping out even faster than the ball flies. Fred Perry (Great Britain) in action against G. von Cramm (Germany) in the men's lawn tennis singles final at Wimbledon yesterday. Perry won 6—1, 6—1, 6—0.

"MY APOLOGIES" —VON CRAMM

" I can only express my regret to Perry, who, I know, would much have preferred a fight, and to the crowd who came to see the final in the hope of a keen contest."

Thus Von Cramm after that tragic final with Fred Perry at Wimbledon yesterday He continued:—

" Some time before play started I had a slight attack of cramp in the leg, but this was put right by massage.

" Then just as I was reaching up to strike the ball in my first service of the second game I felt a muscle go in my right thigh, and for the rest of the game I was practically a passenger."

As soon as her husband made his dramatic exit Baroness von Cramm hurried to his side and consoled him. " I am terribly disappointed my husband didn't win as this was his second final," she said.

Mrs. Perry (Miss Helen Vinson, the film actress) said: " I am glad that Fred has won the title for the third year, but I am extremely sorry that Von Cramm hurt his leg as this made such a difference."

The last player to win the title three times was Anthony Wilding, who lost his life in the Great War. He had four wins from 1910 to 1913 inclusive.

6-1, 6-1, 6-0

1936 Daily Mirror

Don Budge's reign as Wimbledon champion was phenomenal: whilst playing through to the finals two years in succession, he dropped only one set.

In 1937 he also triumphed in the men's doubles with Gene Mako and the mixed doubles with Alice Marble to become the first man to win all three events at one Championship. Twelve months later he repeated this achievement with the same partners and, even now, remains the only player to have been a triple champion two years running.

Budge, undefeated in major tournaments for two years, then became the first man to hold all four major championships – the Australian, French, American and English – at the same time. He did this in 1938; it wasn't until 1962 that Rod Laver became the second player to achieve a Grand Slam.

A tall Californian, Budge dwarfed most of his opponents and will always be remembered for his superb backhand. In his Wimbledon finals he met two of the game's most respected players in Baron Gottfried von Cramm and Bunny Austin but they were swept aside with ease by Budge.

After losing only four games in the final against Austin in 1938, he decided to follow Ellsworth Vines and Fred Perry by turning professional.

BUDGE ALL THE WAY IN ONE OF TAMEST WIMBLEDON FINALS

By PETER WILSON

IN one of the tamest Wimbledon finals I have ever seen, Donald Budge, the Californian red-head, disposed of Gottfried von Cramm, Germany's ace racketeer, in just three minutes over the hour. The score was 6—3, 6—4, 6—2.

Towards the end the crowd was amazingly silent as point after point flashed on the board after Budge's name, for in the final set von Cramm put up scarcely any fight until the last game of all and then it was more desperation than skill that enabled him to save two match points.

At first I thought we were in for a great struggle. Von Cramm's back hand was a far more penetrative shot than Budge's and he got a lower trajectory on the forehand, while the Californian was taking as long to put away his volleys as a man with false teeth and a mouthful of caramel.

Donald Budge in play against Von Cramm.

The Break-Through

The German broke through in the very first game and held his advantage up to 3—1, but with Budge settling down—although he was not yet at his best—von Cramm started to cross the lines with his drives more frequently than someone unsuccessfully taking an inebriation test.

As von Cramm's game fell away, so Budge's improved until, all of a sudden, he got his length under control and levelled the games at three-all and then proceeded to turn on the heat.

The German looked very uneasy towards the end of the set, and after Budge had captured his service for a 5—3 lead he put more things into the net than a butterfly hunter on a sunny day to lose five games in a row and the first set.

German's Rally

Budge continued his winning streak with another two games, and with Von Cramm snatching at his shots like a greedy child with a plate of eclairs in front of him—and making just as such of a mess—it looked as though the game would be a procession.

But after being 0—2 and 1—3 down Von Cramm rallied well. The rhythm returned to his racket, the length to his drive and the power to his attack.

Von Cramm actually led 4—3, but in spite of a double fault from Budge, which was as surprising as a hiccough from a teetotaller, the German's volleying, which throughout the match had been very unreliable, let him down badly, and they were on terms at 4—all.

The last hope of a German victory virtually vanished in the next game when, with Von Cramm covering the court from the net, Budge put up a shot which should have been killed quite comfortably. But as Von Cramm was moving to make the stroke, he slipped and Budge, encouraged by this piece of luck, broke through to lead 5—4.

Third Set Massacre

The third set was a massacre. Von Cramm was as stationary as a car with four flat tyres and no petrol and Budge blasted his way through his opponent's defence with his lofted forehand and lance-like backhand drives.

The American was playing really brilliant lawn tennis now, for he changed his game suddenly tempting the German into false positions and then passing him down the side-lines.

After making little attempt to win von Cramm's service at 5—1, Budge crowded on the pace in the eighth game. An ace, a volley and a smash, which was split by a netted forehand drive took Budge to 40—15 and two match points.

Courageously, von Cramm thumped home a perfect service return and came up to the net. Three times he had advantage points, and three times he lost them, until at last Budge, his red hair waving like a banner, charged in to the net and banged in a final decisive volley.

1937   **Daily Mirror**

BUDGE TOPS AUSTIN IN FINAL, 6-1, 6-0, 6-3

U. S. Ace Is Invincible as He Takes Only 66 Minutes for Defense of English Title

20,000 SEE HIM SCORE

'Never Played Better,' Don Says—American Sweep at Tennis Possible Today

WIMBLEDON, England, July 1.— Playing with precision and power that would not be denied, Don Budge today made doubly sure of his place among the immortals of tennis with a crushing victory over Henry W. (Bunny) Austin which gave the American the Wimbledon singles championship for the second year in succession.

The score of 6—1, 6—0, 6—3 was overwhelming but Budge's superiority was still more overwhelming. The three sets required only sixty-six minutes to play, and Budge, who had won fourteen games in a row, might have made it two love sets instead of one but for a slight lapse of concentration in the closing stages.

At it was, he allowed the Englishman only four games. In 1932 Ellsworth Vines defeated this same unfortunate Austin in straight sets with the loss of only ten games. Last year, in winning the title for the first time, Budge allowed Baron Gottfried von Cramm only nine.

Master of All Amateurs

But today will ever be memorable in the career of Budge, not because of comparative scores, but because it demonstrated he had attained his full stature in the game of which he is now the undisputed master— at least in amateur tennis.

Once he had conquered his early raggedness, which permitted Austin to hold his opening service for his only tally in the first set, Budge had every shot in his great collection working at its best.

Asked by this correspondent tonight to explain how it happened, Budge smiled and said, "It was just one of those things."

"I was right—I never played better," he continued before going on to praise Austin for carrying on throughout the tournament despite the strain of becoming a father for the first time.

Actually Austin, despite the arrival of his daughter and his 31 years, today played one of the best games of his career. Except for an unwise tendency to go to the net when the situation did not justify it—certainly not against Budge— Austin produced the same orthodox game that for years has kept him tantalizingly close to the heights.

Austin Sticks to Task

Even against a champion like Budge playing in today's form Austin never despaired. The moment Budge weakened Austin was quick as a flash to seize his opportunity— it was thus that he got his game in the first set and three in the third— and when Budge was content to stay on the baseline Austin most of the time held his own and occasionally even won a point with an untouchable placement.

Most of Austin's points, however, came from Budge's errors—which is by no means a contradiction of Budge's statement that he was "right" today. For he had to lose points now and then because there were so few winners from Austin that most of the games would otherwise have been decided at love.

Yet Austin started strongly. There was a most prolonged struggle over the first game, for Budge's first service was not functioning correctly and in unanswerable fashion. And since Budge took a certain amount of time to find his length, Austin held his own service at love.

But then Budge found his game and never looked back. It wasn't anything like blowing his opponent off the court, but a calm, cool application of irresistible pressure. A couple of times in the fourth game Austin, willing to try anything, hastened to the net only to despair at the passing shots that he could not get near.

Englishman Rallies

The first set thus went calmly and the second rapidly, although Austin managed to lead at 40—15 in the fifth game and even win an advantage after Budge had drawn level.

Now the spectacle was growing unbelievable for Austin, giving his best, like the plucky fighter that he is, was producing wonder shots that only elicited still greater shots in reply. Drop shots that other players would not have attempted drew Budge in from deep in the backcourt and he put them away. Passed at the net, caught on the wrong foot on the baseline, it was all one—

he gained in strength and precision as the games raced on.

Still without a sign of faltering, Budge went on through the first half of the third set, although Austin led at 40—15 in the third game. By this time it was obvious Budge was trying to close out the match with a run of seventeen games, which would have made history indeed, and the gallery applauded Austin every time he managed to save a point.

At this point the weather, which had been threatening throughout the match, produced a cold drizzle, and since it was obvious that the tournament officials hoped the match could be concluded without postponement, Budge redoubled his efforts to finish his opponent.

Budge's Service Broken

Austin, rising to the challenge, fought on all the harder and with his drives making up in precision their inferiority in power to Budge's swooping backhand, he broke Budge's service in the fourth.

A shout went up from every side of the center court stands in tribute to this effort and swelled to a roar as Austin, redoubling his efforts, took the next game at 15 and Budge was leading by only 3—2. The American came back to take the sixth at love, but Austin captured the next before a real downpour of rain forced the authorities to order an interval.

When they returned, Budge quickly annexed the eighth game, then, after falling in the ninth, proceeded to contradict the habits of ordinary mortals by taking the next three points for a 15—40 lead. A short rally and Budge missed his first match point, then another, and Austin put his forehand in the net to decide the match and the championship.

After such a glorious victory Budge could not resist the attendants who beleaguered him to get his signature on the balls used in this historic match. Then, while Austin, in token of his defeat, laughingly held an armful of Budge's rackets, the champion spoke in the rain to a British television audience.

Eden in Royal Box

From these activities Budge and Austin were summoned to the royal box, where the Californian received the congratulations of Queen Mary and the Duke and Duchess of Kent. Sitting in the back row, unnoticed by the crowd, was Anthony Eden, who has been playing tennis mainly since he left the Foreign Office.

1938   The New York Times

For the third successive year a male player triumphed in all three Wimbledon events. **Bobby Riggs** made the most of the absence of many of the top players by winning the triple crown in the year of his first championship.

With Vines, Perry and Budge now professionals and von Cramm not competing, Riggs beat his fellow American Elwood Cooke in a five-set final. It was rumoured that Riggs had placed a large bet on himself to win the singles Championship so he had to hold firm when Cooke took the lead with two sets to one. But Riggs won the next two sets and added the men's doubles with Cooke and the mixed with Alice Marble to his singles triumph.

In twenty years, since the end of the First World War, the Championship had witnessed the incredible skills and power of 'The Musketeers', as well as of Vines, Perry and Budge. The Second World War now brought about the end of this vintage period and the Wimbledon gates were closed once again, this time for seven years.

ROBERT L. RIGGS, 21-year-old Californian, won the men's singles championship at Wimbledon, beating another American, Elwood T. Cooke, 2—6, 8—6, 3—6, 6—3, 6—2, in a 130-minute final that was almost incredibly lacking in thrills.

Much of the tennis was academically perfect. There were Robot rallies containing so many perfect strokes that it seemed impossible for either player to make a mistake. But, from a box-office viewpoint, the men's singles final hit a new low level.

There were acres of space in the standing enclosures, which are usually crammed for the last-stage match. There were many empty seats. After two sets, there was a centre-court exodus the like of which has not been seen on a Wimbledon finals day for many a year.

Hundreds clambered noisily over the benches to depart while play was in progress. A colossal Wimbledon walk-out.

Not Easy

RIGGS and Cooke have clashed in their own country a dozen times—and Riggs has always won. He did not find winning an easy matter yesterday.

Cooke, aggressive from the start, was obviously out to break up the lethargic rhythm of his young opponent. Riggs had to counter.

He fell back on his precise driving to the lines—beautiful shots that checked the volleying ambitions of Cooke, and produced the long rallies I have already mentioned.

A "fencing" duel indeed. Each knows all there is to know about the other's play. Actually it was a brilliant clash of two top-class tennis brains.

Aggression

BUT one flash of court lightning will steal all the brainy player's thunder, where the crowd is concerned, and the customers were obviously disappointed at the absence of any such flash yesterday.

Cooke's campaign of aggression was very successful in the opening set. He volleyed magnificently at every opportunity, and only had one serious hold-up. That was in the third game, which he won to lead 3—0, after "deuce" had been called six times.

With Riggs a trifle jumpy on the forehand, Cooke went sailing away to a 4—1 lead in the second set. Then came a marathon sixth game which Riggs won after 12 deuces. Curiously enough, the next game was soon finished, Cooke winning it to love to establish a 5—2 lead.

Riggs Worried

RIGGS was obviously worried at this stage. Cooke had a set point at 40—30 in the next game, but Riggs volleyed him out of it, won the game and proceeded to collar Cooke's service in the next game for the first time in the match.

Riggs was now pulling out some really sensational back-hand passes that sizzled diagonally across the net and were absolutely unplayable. Quickly the tide turned.

At 6—5 it was Riggs' turn to drop a set point. He dropped three in all in this game, before Cooke finally clinched with a piece of acrobatics at the net that produced the first ripple of excitement among the silent onlookers.

Longest Rally

RIGGS was fighting. Helped by a double fault from Cooke, his first of the match, Riggs went to 7—6. Two more set points were desperately saved by Cooke before Riggs took the set at 8—6.

Cooke won the fifth game of the third set to lead 3—2 after the longest rally yet —fully 50 strokes with never a blunder by either player.

Cooke was still foiling Riggs' plan to keep him on the baseline. Grimly he volleyed to a 6—3 win.

Tiring

COOKE was plainly tiring when the fourth set opened and Riggs wisely started to pile on the pressure.

Now it was Riggs who came in to volley and smash at net. With shots to the corners Cooke didn't even see. Riggs raced (it was still slow, but racing pace compared to the previous stuff) to 4—0, 4—1, 4—2, 5—2, 5—3, 6—3.

Few could have had any doubt about the eventual result when Riggs took the first two games of the final set. Cooke made his last effort and gallantly levelled at 2—2, but Riggs still had quite a lot left.

Riggs' Best

HE pulled out a couple of service aces, crashed down glorious back-handers to the corners that only Budge could have equalled, and settled the affair in a manner which left not the slightest doubt of his superiority.

It was Riggs' best display in this country. He is a mystery-man no longer. The new champion is revealed as a truly great player, whose uncanny anticipation conserves his energy and whose wearing-down campaigns are brilliantly conceived and carried out.

Selectors' Shock

IF the Wightman Cup Selection Committee intended to play Miss K. Stammers and Mrs. Hammersley in the doubles at Forest Hills next month, having broken up the ready-made partnership of Miss Nina Brown and Miss Rita Jarvis, they must now be indulging in a spot of head-scratching.

Miss Stammers and Mrs. Hammersley failed in their women's doubles semi-final match yesterday, being beaten by Miss Alice Marble and Mrs. S. P. Fabyan.

Centre Court To-day

E. T. Cooke and Mrs. S. P. Fabyan v. F. H. D. Wilde and Miss N. B. Brown (semi-final);

Miss Alice Marble (U.S.A.) v. Miss K. Stammers (Great Britain);

C. E. Hare and F. H. D. Wilde v. E. T. Cooke and R. L. Riggs;

Mrs. Fabyan and Miss Marble v. Miss H. Jacobs and Miss A. M. Yorke;

R. L. Riggs and Miss Marble v. Wilde and Miss Brown or Cooke and Mrs. Fabyan.

1939   Daily Herald

Bobby Riggs. The triple Wimbledon champion leaps the net in a Daily Herald *picture after defeating Elmer Cooke in 1939. He turned professional two years later but it was in 1973 that he made worldwide news. At the age of fifty-five he played special challenge matches against Margaret Court and Billie-Jean King. Riggs beat Mrs Court but, in front of a record crowd of more than 30,000, he lost to Mrs King in the Houston Astrodome*

8 | The Great Americans

1946–55

In the first ten years after the Second World War, seven different Americans won the Wimbledon men's singles title. Jack Kramer was the 1947 champion and he signed up most of the subsequent holders for his professional circus before Wimbledon went 'open'.

Jack Kramer and Tom Brown. Brown watches his partner Kramer play an overhead shot on their way to winning the doubles title at Wimbledon in 1946. The two Americans contested the 1947 singles final

1946 Yvon Petra
beat Geoff Brown
6–2 6–4 7–9 5–7 6–4

1947 Jack Kramer
beat Tom Brown
6–1 6–3 6–2

When the Wimbledon Championships resumed in 1946 the centre court seating capacity had to be reduced by approximately 1,500 because of damage caused by a time bomb during the Second World War. This left a gaping hole in the stands and parts of the seating area had to be cordoned off. Otherwise everything was more or less the same as seven years before except that the men's singles champion, Bobby Riggs, had turned professional.

There had been no break in the United States championship and their title holder, Jack Kramer, came to Wimbledon as a hot favourite. The 25-year-old started well but then had a tremendous struggle in the fourth round against Jaroslav Drobny. Kramer was troubled by blisters on his racket hand and eventually lost in the deciding set after losing the all-important second 17–15. *(cont.)*

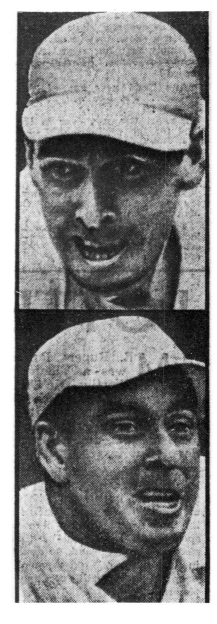

Yvon Petra. He defeated the Australian Geoff Brown to become the first post-war Wimbledon men's singles champion

YVON PETRA, champion of France, won the championship at Wimbledon yesterday. He beat Geoff Brown, the Australian with the two-handed grip, by 6—2, 6—4, 7—9, 5—7, 6—4 in one of the most thrilling finals ever seen at Wimbledon. The biggest crowd ever was kept on tip-toe with excitement till the last stroke.

Petra is the first Frenchman to win the championship since Henri Cochet in 1929.

I do not know whom to admire the more. Both fought with grand courage.

Petra faced the keenest discouragement when victory was snatched from him in the third set. He led at 6—5, and lost his own service, for the first time in that set.

In the fourth set Petra had a match point in the ninth game and two more on his own service (he led by 40—15) in the tenth game, and again he lost the set. Yet, unperturbed by those reverses, he won the final set. Brown fought his up-hill battle all through the match with the finest tenacity and pluck.

Seven pounds lost

When Petra, who played with the greatest confidence, had won the first two sets rather easily — Brown was uncertain—it looked to be a one-sided final. Few of us gauged the resourcefulness of the Australian, who looked a pigmy beside the giant Frenchman. (Brown was 10st. 8lb. in weight when the tournament began; he entered the court yesterday 7lb lighter.)

Petra began to show signs of anxiety when, leading by 6—5 in the third set, he crossed over to serve what everybody thought would be the last game. The aces which had flowed from his racket in former games deserted him.

This gave Brown his long-awaited opportunity to break through and level the set at six games all. He followed up by taking the following game to 0, serving three balls to which Petra did not get his racket.

Still Petra held on, making the score seven all. But Brown dominated the next game and then, amid cheers, took Petra's service for the set.

The fourth set ran a somewhat similar course. Petra gained the lead in the third game, led at 5—3, and got to match point on Brown's service. But Brown paused, poised for a mighty delivery, and twice served aces. Then he clipped the line with a grand return and again robbed Petra of victory.

In the next game Petra reached 40—15 (two more match points). Surely he must win now! Drawing himself up to his full height he sent in his fiercest service. Brown miraculously returned it—much too fast for Petra. Another terrific delivery and again Brown scored.

That settled the set. Brown, now playing as never before, took the next two games and the match was level at two sets all.

Few in the crowd can have expected Petra to win now. But the Frenchman amazingly recaptured his poise and his first-set steadiness. I never have before seen so many returns in which the ball hit the lines. The linesmen had a busy day and did their task well.

Rallies were brilliant in this last stage. But Petra, having broken through Brown's service in the first game of this set, had merely to hold his own service to win the match. This he did, though he had many anxious moments. When he came to the last game he served himself out to 0—a brilliant ending to a magnificent match

MEN'S SINGLES.—Final Round: Y. Petra (France) bt G E Brown (Australia) 6—2, 6—4, 7—9, 5—7, 6—4
WOMEN'S DOUBLES.—Semi-final Round: Miss L. Brough and Miss M. E. Osborne (U.S.) bt Mrs. P. C. Todd and Miss D. Bundy (U S) 6—4, 6—2. Miss P Betz and Miss D. Hart (U.S.) bt Mrs E. W. A. Bostock and Mrs. M. Menzies (G.B) 3—6, 6—3, 6—4.
MIXED DOUBLES.—Semi-Final Round: T. Brown and Miss L. Brough (U.S.) bt H. C. Hopman (Australia) and Miss M. E. Osborne (U.S.), 6—3, 6—3; G. E. Brown (Australia) and Miss D Bundy (U.S.) bt B Patty and Miss P. Betz (U.S), 12—10, 6—2.

1946 Daily Mail

Drobny, who became one of Wimbledon's all-time favourites, was beaten in the semi-finals by Geoff Brown. This Australian's powerful serve had earlier accounted for the number eight seed Lennart Berglin – the Swede who was later to guide Bjorn Borg to five successive Championships (from 1976 to 1980).

In the other half of the draw the top seeded Dinny Pails of Australia went out in the quarter-finals to **Yvon Petra**. Pails' defeat certainly had something to do with the fact that he got lost on the London underground on his way to Wimbledon for the match. He arrived on court twenty minutes late to find that Queen Mary was among the spectators he had kept waiting. His nerve went and he lost in four sets to Petra.

Petra went on to gain a final place against Brown and, in a variable five-set match, he became the first post-war Wimbledon men's singles champion. Both players hit the ball very hard on serve and groundstrokes although Brown – at 5 ft 7 in. – was some eight inches smaller than his opponent.

After his victory Petra, a Frenchman born in Indo-China, attributed his success to a German surgeon who had saved his leg from being amputated while he was a prisoner of war.

In 1947 **Kramer** made no mistakes and cruised to the title for the loss of only one set. He defeated his fellow countryman Tom Brown in a very one-sided final. A true all-American boy, the short-haired, clean-cut Kramer had a fine all-round game and would figure in many people's top six list of players.

Kramer, who had retained his US title, then turned professional and started his own successful international tennis circus.

Jack Kramer. A leading promoter of the professional game, he now commentates on the Wimbledon Championship for BBC-TV

Kramer Beats Brown in Final at Wimbledon

BY KERMIT HOLT
[Chicago Tribune Press Service]

LONDON, July 4—The king of England delayed Jack Kramer's Fourth of July celebration today, but the Los Angeles tennis star overcame the resulting attack of nerves and made short work of his fellow American, Tom Brown, to win his first Wimbledon championship.

Kramer's straight set victory took only 45 minutes from start to finish. The scores were 6-1, 6-3, 6-2.

Both Kramer and Brown were visibly affected by the half hour delay in starting the match—all because the king, a former so-so Wimbledon doubles player himself, and his wife and younger daughter exercised their royal prerogative of being late.

The King Arrives

Itching to get on the court and get the match over with, the American players paced the floor in their dressing room and worked up a nervous sweat as the minutes ticked by. Both were trembling when the royal party finally arrived.

After the game, Kramer went to the royal box where the king presented him with the challenge cup, which he will take back to Los Angeles to decorate the new apartment he and his wife have just found. Kramer will fly back to the United States Sunday. The new Wimbledon champion had little to say about the royal family except to comment:

"Princess Margaret—boy, is she beautiful!"

He'll Stay Amateur

Asked about the reports he intended to turn pro immediately, Kramer replied: "I am an amateur player, and that is the truth. All I am interested in is helping my country hold the Davis cup and win the amateur championship. I don't think I'd be interested if they offered me some phenomenal sum—which they haven't."

The Wimbledon championships will end tomorrow with the finals in the women's singles, the women's doubles, men's doubles, and mixed doubles.

1947   Chicago Tribune

1948 Bob Falkenburg
beat John Bromwich
7–5 0–6 6–2 3–6 7–5

1949 Ted Schroeder
beat Jaroslav Drobny
3–6 6–0 6–3 4–6 6–4

1950 Budge Patty
beat Frank Sedgman
6–1 8–10 6–2 6–3

1951 Dick Savitt
beat Ken McGregor
6–4 6–4 6–4

Following Kramer's victory, four more Americans were to become Wimbledon men's singles champions from 1948 to 1951.

First, the 6 ft 3 in. **Bob Falkenburg** saved three match points in the 1948 final against John Bromwich. He was not a popular winner with the Wimbledon crowd as he used stalling tactics to upset Bromwich's rhythm. However, it transpired that Falkenburg had suffered a thyroid complaint throughout his career and, in several matches, he gave away sets to conserve his energy.

A year later Bromwich gained revenge over Falkenburg but was crushed in the semi-finals by Jaroslav Drobny. In the other half of the draw the number one seed **Ted Schroeder** was taken to five sets three times before reaching the final. It was almost inevitable that the Schroeder–Drobny encounter would go into a deciding set and at 5–4 in the fifth the American served a love game to make his only Wimbledon appearance a successful one. He played a lot of hit-or-miss shots, usually gambling on big points, and this earned him the nickname 'Lucky Ted'.

A postscript to the 1949 Championship was the appearance of Ricardo 'Pancho' Gonzales from Argentina. Seeded two, he lost in the fourth round of the singles to the 1946 runner-up Geoff Brown but won the men's doubles with Frank Parker. He then joined Jack Kramer's circus and was ranked the number one professional player for nine years from 1951 to 1960. *(cont.)*

FALKENBURG LAY DOWN AGAIN BUT SNATCHED THE TITLE

The new singles champion, Robert Falkenburg, down on the Centre Court during yesterday's final.

Bromwich, sportsman to the end

By LAURIE PIGNON

ROBERT FALKENBURG, 22-year-old Californian, won the Wimbledon crown by defeating John Bromwich, of Sydney, 7–5, 0–6, 6–2, 3–6, 7–5, after having three match points against him when he was 5—3 down in the final set and suffering from cramp in his right hand.

"Cramp beat me last year," he told me after the match. "When I felt it coming on in the third set I said to myself I'll win if it kills me."

He added: "I gave the second set away to rest. Why should I tire myself after Bromwich had broken my service twice."

Bromwich, a sportsman to the end, made no excuses. His comments were: "If a man hasn't the nerve to go for his shots he doesn't deserve the title."

For a final the tennis was disappointing. Falkenburg certainly looked to be playing for time, and was asked twice by the umpire to get on with the game when he was sitting on the court.

The first four games went quite naturally with the service, but Bromwich failed to hold his delivery in the sixth game, but pulled up level to four all.

Up to now Bromwich had shaken the American by returning winners from his cannonball services—what a pity he couldn't follow this advantage by putting his smashes away with the same confidence.

Set given away

For it was this failure which cost him the set and probably the match, for Falkenburg is a bad recoverer. Bromwich was 5–4 and 40—15 up (three set points), when his service failed him.

The Australian began the second set by breaking the service. Falkenburg, dumbfounded the Centre Court galleries by giving the whole set away. Bromwich went into full-blooded attack. Even so the first four games were against the service, Bromwich having four points for a 3–1 lead.

The fourth set was all Bromwich. Indeed the match looked all over when the Australian led 4–2 in the final.

Then for the first time Falkenburg began to show signs of cramp, although it must be reported that he still produced ace services. Bromwich held his lead to 5–2, but double-faulted when he was within two points of match. At 5–4 Bromwich failed on three match points. His nerve had cracked.

Men's Singles—Final
R. Falkenburg bt. J. Bromwich 7–5, 0–6, 6–2, 3–6, 7–5.

Men's Doubles—Semi-Final
T. Brown and G. Mulloy bt L. Bergelin and J. Harper 1–6, 6–3, 4–6, 6–4, 8–6.

Women's Doubles—Semi-Final
Miss L. Brough and Mrs. W. du Pont bt Mrs. H. P. Rihbany and Miss B. Scofield 7–5. 6–0; Miss D. Hart and Mrs. P. C. Todd (holders) bt. Mrs. E. W. A. Bostock and Mrs. N. W. Blair 6–4, 8–6.

Still smiling confidently, John Bromwich falls backwards during a fierce exchange with Falkenburg.

The camera has caught the British doubles pair, Mrs Bostock and Mrs Blair, in tense action in their semi-final match against Miss Hart and Mrs Todd (holders) of America. Mrs Blair smashes home a shot, with her partner spring-heeling for the return. The English girls lost 4–6, 6–8. They led 3–1 in the first set, but gave the opposition too much liberty at the net. Mrs Blair was the better of the home pair.

1948 Daily Graphic

SCHROEDER WINS AT WIMBLEDON

The five-set match in progress on the Centre Court at Wimbledon yesterday, when F. R. Schroeder (U.S.), who was seeded No. 1 in the men's lawn tennis championship, beat J. Drobny (Czechoslovakia), nearer the camera. The score was 3-6, 6-0, 6-3, 4-6, 6-4. In the royal box watching the match were Queen Mary, Princess Margaret, and the Duchess of Kent.

Sporting News

LAWN TENNIS

SCHROEDER THE CHAMPION

DROBNY'S GREAT FIGHT

FROM OUR LAWN TENNIS CORRESPONDENT

Queen Mary, Princess Margaret, the Duke of Edinburgh, and the Duchess of Kent were present at Wimbledon yesterday to watch the final of the singles, in which F. R. Schroeder, of the United States, beat J. Drobny, of Czechoslovakia, by 3—6, 6—0, 6—3, 4—6, 6—4.

It was a match that will be long remembered by all who saw it, not merely for the standard of play, high though that was, but more for the character of the two finalists. Schroeder, the new champion, 29 years old, is as worthy of the title as any were before him, not only for his all-round skill, which goes without saying—for no one can win at Wimbledon without that—but for his determination. He had to play four matches of five sets to do it, and if he will not quite be pigeon-holed among the highest—Tilden, Lacoste, Perry, Budge, or what you will—he will at least be thought of as one of the best match players of all time.

Previously, against F. Sedgman, twice did one perilous point separate Schroeder from defeat, but fortune favoured the brave; and again yesterday when put to the real test he was able to achieve mastery. It seems that he can rise to any height when the moment comes. In a fine tactical contest his fleetness of foot in making almost impossible recoveries, and his flair for guessing rightly where his opponent is, thereby to find an empty court, come most readily to mind. A man who volleys so well and so often must be also good on the half-volley in this class, and he is the master of that most difficult stroke. Nor must his top-spin lob be forgotten. His return of Drobny's service went a long way towards his winning this match, for his own service was sound all through.

Drobny, one is inclined to think, has seldom played better, if his missed smashes when under pressure are excepted. His left-hand spin without doubt worried Schroeder for a time, and he is a better player off the ground than ever he was before, especially from the backhand. His stop volleys, too, were often perfection. As can be imagined by those who know Drobny, the contest was not a long one as five-set matches go, but for four sets it was fast, tense, and exciting.

In spite of two double faults Drobny, serving from the Royal Box end, won the first game. Schroeder more surely drew level, but Drobny with his fastest service took the lead with a love game. Clearly it was going to be a game of service, and at once we knew what Schroeder could do in that way to make sure of drawing level. But in the sixth game a very clever return of service beat the American, coming in to volley, and when Schroeder hit an easy volley beyond the base line Drobny was 4—2. At 5—3 Schroeder saved a set point with a clever top-spin lob, but another came and this time Drobny was home with the neatest of cross-court volleys.

THE LOAN CALLED IN

A halt was called to repair the belt in the middle of the net, damaged doubtless by

Drobny, and then Schroeder served first in the second set. He saved a game point when Drobny seemed to have him at his mercy, and after further effort was 1—0. A whipped top-spin forehand drive then brought Schroeder to game point. Drobny was equal to the occasion, but two more similar, but faster, forehands hit either side line and Schroeder had at last broken through. Drobny then spent the rest of this set looking at his opponent through his spectacles, as he once did at Kramer, like a bank manager would do wondering what overdraft to allow. If this second set can be so described, in the third Drobny was quick to call in the loan.

But Schroeder served first, which in this kind of match is worth a bisque; for it is almost probable that the other man will have the strain of having to save the set. At 3—4 down Drobny, serving, made mistakes, one of them overhead, and was 0—40. At 15—40 he made a perfect drop shot. How Schroeder got it only he will know. But he did, covering six yards in less than a second. His answering stroke hit the net cord but it beat Drobny, and it won him this absolutely vital game for 5—3. Not unnaturally Schroeder then rubbed it in with a love game to lead now by two sets to one.

But Drobny now served first. At 2—1 to him, Schroeder made his first major mistake, an easy smash going beyond the side line. Another half-paced stroke was hit too wide and Drobny reached 3—1. But Schroeder gathered himself together as he so often does and won Drobny's service with a fine attack. At 3—all Drobny, serving, was 40—0, but Schroeder, fighting back, got to advantage with the fastest backhand drive of the fortnight, across the court. Four times he was within a point of the game, which could almost have meant the match. But Drobny performed prodigies of valour to save them and it was 4—3 to him.

The American easily drew level, and was 30—0 in the next game but Drobny, again equal to the task, reached 5—4. Then it was Drobny who reached set point, and Schroeder after just failing with a lightning service, hit the top of the net with his second and it was two sets all.

A beautifully checked volley won Drobny the first game of the final set. A remarkable smash from baseline to baseline was among the winners with which Schroeder drew level. At 3-all he reached the same position as he had done in the fourth set, by great returns of good services. This time Schroeder brought it off with a backhand down the side, 4—3, and he served and won his way decisively to 5—3. He was 30—15 in the next game, but Drobny, though clearly feeling the strain, made a great effort and saved it, 4—5. But Schroeder then served for the match. Calmly and decisively he won every single one of the four points against his gallant and wearied opponent. It was a typical Schroeder finish.

This has been inevitably written from the new champion's point of view, for he has been the figure of the year. But a word should be added about Drobny, with his terrific left-hand service. He has never failed to give a great deal of pleasure to a great many people at Wimbledon. And he always will.

The doubles semi-final which followed looked for a time one-sided, but in the end it was only by 7—5 in the fifth set that R. Gonzales and F. Parker beat the very good scratch pair of E. W. Sturgess and B. Patty. When the American pair were two sets to one and leading by 5—4 and 40—30 it was nearly over. But Patty saved the set against his fellow-countrymen and he and his partner played their best together to square the match at 7—5.

They were level all the way in the final set until Sturgess lost his service for the match.

HE GAVE RIGHT ANSWER

Budge Patty cuts off a return by Frank Sedgman as they battle for the Wimbledon championship yesterday. Shots like this paved the way to brilliant victory for Patty. And at the end he was so tired that he could not jump the net in the traditional style—he put one leg over and wearily drew the other after it

Patty won in the style of Perry

By GERARD WALTER

BUDGE PATTY, former American G.I., won the Wimbledon singles title yesterday in one hour, defeating the favourite, Frank Sedgman, by 6—1, 8—10, 6—2, 6—3.

It was a great victory for a man who has had to conquer physical disability in the form of low blood pressure and who, till he won the French championship recently, was not considered capable of long sustained effort.

Patty beat Sedgman by using the tactics which Fred Perry employed in his three pre-war triumphs at Wimbledon.

Winning attack

Perry was in the stand to see Patty, leaping upon the short return and stabbing it deep to his opponent's backhand corner, come up in full cry for the point winning volley.

Time after time he tore gaps in Sedgman's defences with this stroke.

This plan of campaign was backed by an armoury of service returns and smashes that Sedgman never matched. On top of that the American's footwork was so much better. Rarely was he wrong-footed and even on the run he could, and did, score with a backhand passing shot that was a jewel of precise placing.

There were three occasions upon which Sedgman afforded his friends a glimmer of hope.

In the second set, in spite of indifferent smashing, he broke through for 8—all, held his service for the seventeenth game and captured Patty's to advantage when the American double-faulted at 40—15.

Hope faded out

Again in the fourth set Sedgman, love—3, captured the fourth game in which Patty, with the service, had a point for four—love.

The crowd, who obviously wanted a Sedgman victory, had their hopes raised when the Australian won the long fifth game also to advantage after many deuces.

The glimmer, however, faded and died out. Sedgman, who never really attained his best form and was the victim as much of his own bad shots as of Patty's good ones, held his service with difficulty in the seventh.

Then Patty, lobbing his opponent out of the forecourt, sailed to victory.

His second visit to Wimbledon was at the age of forty when the tournament became open in 1968.

Budge Patty, born in Arkansas, brought up in California and based in Paris, was an artistic player and his men's singles final against Frank Sedgman in 1950 was a classic match. Sixteen seeds were nominated as an experiment and Patty – the number five – upset the odds by defeating the number one Sedgman.

The committee decided to cut the seeds back to ten for the 1951 Championship and again Sedgman was at the top of the men's list. This time he was beaten in a five-set quarter-final by Herbie Flam, who was playing in his first Wimbledon.

However, it was another Championship debutant – **Dick Savitt** – who was to take the title beating Flam in the semi-final and Australian Ken McGregor in the final. Savitt, a good server and volleyer with a classic backhand, out-hit his opponent to win in straight sets.

The match of the year was a third-round game featuring Britain's Tony Mottram and Drobny. Mottram, a bomber pilot in the war, upset the number two seed by recording the most satisfying win of his career, 8–6 in the final set.

AMERICAN SWEEPS 63-MINUTE MATCH

Savitt Wins, 6-4, 6-4, 6-4, to Become 5th U. S. Player In Row to Take Title

---

M'GREGOR'S SERVICE FAILS

Australian Double-Faults 5 Times at Wimbledon Net— Richardson-Patty Bow

---

WIMBLEDON, England, July 6 (UP)—Dick Savitt of Orange, N. J., who never took a tennis lesson, established himself as the world's No. 1 amateur player today when he won the Wimbledon men's singles title by defeating Ken McGregor of Australia in one of the shortest finals ever played on the center court.

Savitt beat the Australian Davis Cup player, 6—4, 6—4, 6—4, in 63 minutes before a standing-room crowd of 15,000. The 24-year-old American culminated his first foreign tour and his initial Wimbledon appearance with the finest array of volleys and passing shots seen in this 65th staging of the game's best-known tournament.

Savitt became the fifth straight American to win the men's crown as he repeated the triumph he had scored over 22-year-old McGregor in the Australian final last January. He also became the first player to sweep the Australian and Wimbledon titles in one season since Don Budge in 1938.

Victor Over Larsen

Savitt had defeated Jack Bromwich, Frank Sedgman and McGregor—the craftiest and youngest of the Australian Davis Cup players — to win Australian title. To gain the gold Wimbledon trophies he received from the Duchess of Kent, he eliminated seven players, including the United States champion, Art Larson, in the quarter-finals and Herb Flam, America's second-ranked player, in the semi-finals.

Awake Since 5 A. M.

Savitt was nervous when he began the most important match of his career. Unable to sleep, he had been up since 5 A. M., pacing the floor of his London hotel room. The tension showed in the first few games but after that his booming service and forehand and the most devastating backhand he ever has shown proved too much for McGregor.

The 6-foot 3-inch Savitt broke McGregor's service — his best weapon—five times. The American's attack so unnerved the Empire hope that McGregor double-faulted five times and his first serve missed often after the first set.

Savitt began cautiously and finished with sharp backhand cross-court shots which upset the Australian's net game. The end came with the 6-foot 5-inch McGregor lying flat, his drawn face buried in the carefully manicured grass. He had dived desperately but missed the title-winner, a sizzling forehand drive, by inches. The ball barely skimmed the net and rocketed past the Australian to land well inside the alley sideline.

As McGregor rushed to the net to congratulate Savitt, the happy American tossed his racquet high in the air and let go a shout of triumph that echoed above the applause.

Hopes to Defend Crown

"I will fly home on Sunday night," Savitt said after the match. "I may play in the clay-court championship at Chicago next week. At the moment, I am not sure."

Savitt said he hoped to defend his crown in 1952.

He hopes to make the United States Davis Cup team and play in Australia again.

"I thought the reaction of the Wimbledon fans was first rate," Savitt said. "They were not partisan in any way. They cheered my shots just as much as they applauded McGregor's."

The Americans also have a chance to win a share of the mixed doubles title tomorrow when Miss Hart teams with Sedgman against Mervyn Rose and Mrs. Nancye Bolton of Australia. Rose and Mrs. Bolton upset the top-seeded team of Miss Brough and Sturgess in today's semi-final, 7—5, 6—2. Miss Hart and Sedgman had reached the final yesterday.

Skaff Quits Baltimore Post

BALTIMORE, July 6 (AP)—Baltimore University today announced the resignation of Frank Skaff as athletic director and basketball coach.

1952   Frank Sedgman
beat Jaroslav Drobny
4–6 6–2 6–3 6–2

1953   Vic Seixas
beat Kurt Nielsen
9–7 6–3 6–4

The Australian **Frank Sedgman** temporarily broke the monotony of the American wins at Wimbledon when he won the title by beating Jaroslav Drobny in 1952. A few weeks earlier Drobny had beaten Sedgman in the French championship playing on hard court but the Australian was at his best on the fast grass courts. There was little to choose between the players' serving abilities but Sedgman, with his lightning reflexes, was the more dominant at the net.

It proved to be a great year for Sedgman as, with Ken McGregor he won the men's doubles and with Doris Hart the mixed doubles to become a triple Wimbledon champion. He was the third man to achieve this feat. Then, like his two predecessors Don Budge and Bobby Riggs, he turned professional while he was Wimbledon champion.

The illustrious names of Ken Rosewall and Lew Hoad appeared in the Wimbledon draw for the first time in 1952. A year later Rosewall, at the age of 18, was seeded number one to win the Championship, having won the Australian and French championships. However, he was knocked out sooner than expected, by the unseeded Dane, Kurt Nielsen, in the quarter-finals.

In the semi-final, Nielsen then beat the crowd's favourite, Jaroslav Drobny. This victory would have been a greater surprise had Drobny not been suffering from a ruptured blood vessel in his leg and blistered hands – the price of his victory against Budge Patty in the third round 8–6 16–18 3–6 8–6 12–10.

This epic match had begun at five in the afternoon and was still in progress more than four hours later. At 10–10 in the deciding set the referee Colonel John Lugg informed the players that because of

H.R.H the Duchess of Kent presents the Cup to Frank Sedgman, of Australia, after he had beaten Jaroslav Drobny 4—6, 6—2, 6—3, 6—2, in the Men's Singles final at Wimbledon yesterday.

SEDGMAN JUSTIFIED HIS SEEDING AT THIRD ATTEMPT

By JOE BROMLEY

FRANK SEDGMAN, 25-year-old stockily-built Australian, won the men's singles championship at Wimbledon yesterday, beating the bespectacled left-hander, Jaroslav Drobny, formerly of Czechoslovakia, who is five years his senior, 4—6, 6—2, 6—3, 6—2 in the final on the centre court.

Thus Sedgman, at the third attempt, justified his successive pre-tournament selection as No. 1 " seed," but there were moments in the 80 minutes battle when it looked as though Drobny's ninth annual appearance at the All-England club would be crowned by the glory he has striven so hard to attain over the years.

A DECIDER

It was the fifth time the pair had met in various parts of the world this year, but only the first on which they had clashed on grass, and they entered the arena with honours even, each having won twice.

Following the previous day's complete wash-out the crowd had gathered prepared for the worst so far as weather was concerned and they lacked that bright and gay appearance which had presented so memorable a picture in the earlier stages of the tournament.

Neither were the onlookers in a volatile mood   They sensed the drama of the occasion even before a ball was hit, and it took them a long time to warm up to their normal vociferousness.

There seemed to be more sympathy and encouragement for Drobny at the outset, but later, there was a wider general appreciation of the merit of Sedgman's play.

MANY MISTAKES

It was by no means the most thrilling final I have seen, but guile on both sides of the net made up for the unexpectedly high percentage of errors and the manner in which Sedgman corrected his faults, even when under sustained pressure, made the match noteworthy.

The Australian, faced with a heavy programme of three important clashes during the day, began the final at high speed, but Drobny met him half-way and the first service break did not arrive until the ninth game, which went to the left-hander.

Sedgman had been following up fast on service and found himself passed by some beautiful straight returns down the lines, but he won the second set more easily than the deliberate Drobny had taken the first.

Still it was anybody's match, and with Sedgman having difficulty with his first service and faltering in his overhead play, Drobny looked likely to seize the initiative and hold it.

Four successive service breaks characterised the opening of the third set and then Sedgman who had been behind at 1—2, took the lead for 3—2 and 4—3.

In the eighth game, Drobny served a double-fault and dropped another point when, after a long rally full of guileful drop-shots and angled volleys, Sedgman outmanoeuvred him.

That was the turning point of the match, for the left-hander lost the game to love, and Sedgman went on to rejoice in a new-found confidence.

He took the next five games in a row, to lead 4—0 in the fourth set, and this turn of the tide so decisively in his favour was due to his great mobility and the fact that he had now regained control of both his first service and his effective volleying.

Drobny's general play had fallen away considerably, and the Australian went into a 5—1 lead on a love game.

He was hard pressed by a desperate Drobny in the seventh, and survived several temporary setbacks to win on his first match-point at advantage.

The Duchess of Kent left the Royal Box to present the trophies on court.

1952   The Sporting Life

It was not a great final—Seixas

First the Cup, then the kiss

By LAURIE PIGNON

VICTOR ELIAS SEIXAS, who as a little boy of five preferred playing lawn tennis to cowboys and Indians, had all his young dreams and wildest aspirations answered in a gentle handshake yesterday.

It was the congratulating hand of the Duchess of Kent, presiding over her own club at Wimbledon, that meant so much to this 29-year-old American, who had just defeated Kurt Nielsen, the unseeded Dane, 9—7, 6—3, 6—4, to become world champion.

Easiest of all

It was not a great or stirring final. In fact it was Seixas's easiest match of Wimbledon's second week, and it lasted only 90 minutes — not a great reward for the hundreds who had braved the cold night to get a place on the Centre Court.

Nielsen, the man with many plans, who upset world form by beating Gardnar Mulloy, the American No. 1, Ken Rosewall, Australian official favourite, and Jaroslav Drobny (all of whom were unfit, particularly the last named), had no real answer to the power, pace and accuracy of his rival finalist yesterday. As often befalls the man who is hard-pressed his own game let him down. The big serves of this 22-year-old Dane were punctuated with double faults, his powerful volleying, which in earlier

Dane's errors

Had he continued to hit the ball with everything he had instead of trying to play Seixas, which was about as useless as trying to play a river pike with a bent pin, he might have done a lot better. But he pushed his volleys instead of hitting them, and gave the American chances to recover from what should have been impossible positions.

Thus the remaining sets were merely a matter of course and

rounds were guided missiles that destroyed all - comers, were only push-backs.

The almost uncanny anticipation of Seixas made Nielsen look worse than he really was.

"I did not feel nervous in myself, but I guess I must have been to have double faulted like that." said the disappointed Dane with an American accent.

Seixas began as if he wanted to be back in Philadelphia in the morning — he lives there. Before he could say "Goodness gracious, Mr. Seixas," for he is still an amateur in spite of having done nothing else for 18 months but play tennis, the American was leading four games to one. Indeed, he had points for a 5—1 lead before Nielsen won his service game.

The young Copenhagen jazz club owner then changed his tune, and for the first time produced his "hit or miss" policy which paid such unexpected dividends in the earlier rounds.

time, both of which the young Dane helped along with his own errors while Seixas merely played his normal hard-serving, net - attacking game.

"I didn't have to change my usual game as I seemed to be doing all right. It was an easier final than I expected, for if Drobny had been fit I'm sure it would have been a really tough fight," Seixas told me afterwards.

Terrified

Britain's No. 1 Wightman Cup pair, Helen Fletcher and Jean Rinkel, were terrified into a state of tennis immobility when they met Doris Hart and Shirley Fry in the semi-final of the women's doubles. They lost without winning a game—without ever looking like winning a game.

And just to prove how useless is the Wightman Cup Britain's second pair, Angela Mortimer and Ann Shilcock, were beaten 6-2, 6-2 by Maureen Connolly and Julie Sampson, who are not a good partnership.

First match to-day is the women's final, in which Maureen Connolly meets Doris Hart for the third time this season. My money goes on "Mo."

England beat Scotland

England were much more consistent in the second match of the national speedway series at Leicester last night and beat Scotland by 66 pts. to 42.

National Trophy: Bristol 65 pts., Bradford 42.
Challenge Match: Wolverhampton 59 pts., Southern League Stars 4½.

FOR DOUBLES OR TREBLES

★★★ Nourreddin
A.P., 3.0
★★ Ballylinan
A.P., 3.30
★ Melinda
A.P., 2.0
Joyful Christine
Haydock, 4.0

System horse
Wyandank, Haydock, 3.30

Ladies' luck

DIANA'S CHOICE
in the 2.30 race at Alexandra Park.

RESULTS

MEN'S SINGLES (final)
V Seixas (U S A) bt K Nielsen (Denmark) 9-7 6-3 6-4

WOMEN'S DOUBLES (semi-final)
Miss D Hart and Miss S Fry (U.S.A.) bt Miss H M Fletcher and Miss J Rinkel (G.B.) 6-0, 6-0
Miss M Connolly and Miss J Sampson (U.S.) bt Miss A Mortimer and Miss A Shilcock (G.B.) 6-2, 6-3

MIXED DOUBLES (semi-final)
E Morea and Miss S Fry bt O A Worthington and Miss P k Ward 6-2, 6-4
V Seixas and Miss D Hart bt L A Hoad and Miss J Sampson 6-3, 7-5

Haydock runners

2.15—WINWICK PLATE. 3y., 1m.
21 Tearaway 7-7 ...... J Sime
250 Pickering Vale 9-0 ...... W Carr
010 London Town 9-0 ...... P Crawley
245 ROYAL LADY 8-11 ... D Smith
11-10 Royal Lady, 15-8 Tearaway, 5-1 Pickering Vale.

2.45—SATURDAY S. PLATE. 3y., 11m.
105 Pretty Fair 9-0 ...... W H Carr
001 CLOVER 9-0 ...... V Mitchell
001 Headmist 9-0 ...... J Wright
004 Jalamayoor 8-9 ...... A Breasley
15-8 Jalamayoor, 2-1 Headmist, 7-2 Clover, 5-1 Pretty Fair.

3.30—OLD NEWTON CUP H'CAP. 11m.
020 Calistan 8-13 ...... T Gosling
100 Summer Rain 4-8-2 W Rickaby
132 WYANDANK 4-9-1 ... A Breasley
110 Rass Castle 4-8-2 ...... J Sime
010 Merving 5-8-0 ...... E Mercer
201 Bold Tudor 4-8-0 ...... W Elliott
241 Sleeping Warrior 4-7-13 D Smith
142 Wellington Castle 4-7-9 R Clayton
010 Golden Test 3-7-8 ... P Povall
015 Gratiano ......
014 Alleslanne 4-7-4 ...... J Mahon
4-1 Sleeping Warrior, 5-1 Calistan, 13-2 Wyandank, 8-1 Allesianne, Wellington Castle, 10-1 Summer Rain.

4.0—PADDOCK HANDICAP. 11m.
114 Wyedale 6-7-11 ...... J Fordyce
151 JOYFUL CHRISTINE 4-7-12 ... T Mahon

Selections

GIMCRACK	BART
2.15 Royal Lady	Pickering Vale
2.45 Clover	Jalamayoor
3.30 Wyandank	Wellington Castle
4.0 Joyful Christine	Wyedale
4.30 Rowston Manor	Rowston Manor
5.0 Man About Town	Man About Town

120 Beckford 4-7-11 ...... S Clayton
3.00 Penny Orange 3-7-10 A Breasley
711 Toren Singer 4-7-10 ... J Wright
132 Bunker II 9-7 ...... W R Eady
0312 Daytona 5-7-5 ...... J Caldwell
05 Pluvious II 4-6-12 D Greening
4 Teen Singer, 100-30 Daytona
6-2 Joyful Christine, 6-1 Wyedale, 10-1 Beckford

4.30—BETTISFIELD PLATE. 2y., 6f.
0 Master Tommy 8-12 R Cartwright
Blakemere 8-7 ...... W R Wenson
55 ROWSTON MANOR 8-12 D Smith
Prescription 8-12 ...... W R Eady
00 Winay 8-9 ...... J Caldwell
200 Black Vein 8-9 ...... A Roberts
1-3 Rowston Manor, 7-2 Prescription

5.0—EAST LANCASHIRE STKS. 2y., 5f.

Victor Seixas, Wimbledon men's singles champion receives the trophy from the Duchess of Kent (top picture) and then gets his second reward—a kiss from his wife. He had an easy win in the final.

1953   Daily Sketch

---

deteriorating light only two more games could be played that evening. The bespectacled Drobny, having already saved six match points, summoned up every ounce of willpower to take the next two games and win what was then the longest match in Wimbledon's history. Both players were presented with engraved cigarette

cases by Princess Marina to mark their memorable duel.

So Nielsen reached the 1953 men's singles final and, as an unseeded player, equalled the feat of Wilmer Allison in 1930. He put up a brave fight but was beaten in three sets by **Vic Seixas** who restored America's grip on the title.

Seixas had, at last, won his first

major singles event at the age of 29. Unlike many champions before him, he decided to remain an amateur and represent his country in the Davis Cup. A superb doubles player, he won four successive Wimbledon mixed titles (with Doris Hart from 1953 to 1955 and with Shirley Fry in 1956).

1954   Jaroslav Drobny
beat Ken Rosewall
13–11 4–6 6–2 9–7

1955   Tony Trabert
beat Kurt Nielsen
6–3 7–5 6–1

Jaroslav Drobny, a refugee from Czechoslovakia exiled in Egypt and awaiting British citizenship, became one of the most popular men's singles champions in 1954.

The 32-year-old left-hander had been playing at Wimbledon since before the war and time was running out. With this in mind the centre court crowd was totally one-sided, believing that his young Australian opponent, Ken Rosewall, would win the title in the future. Little did they realize that, despite playing in four finals between 1954 and 1974, the Wimbledon singles was to be the one major event to elude 'Muscles'.

The Drobny–Rosewall match was a classic encounter and, as tie breaks were not introduced until 1971, the marathon of fifty-eight games is likely to remain the longest final in Wimbledon's singles history.

Drobny, who had more success on the slow hard courts, was seeded sixth in 1955. He reached his place in the quarter-finals but was then beaten by the eventual winner, **Tony Trabert**. A former US Marine, Trabert was playing at his second Wimbledon and he equalled Don Budge's achievement (since the abolition of the Challenge Round) in winning the title without dropping a set.

Kurt Nielsen, his final opponent, came through as an unseeded player for the second time, having been runner-up to Vic Seixas in 1953.

Trabert's victory meant that the men's singles title had been won by seven different Americans in a decade since the Second World War. With Louise Brough, Maureen Connolly, Doris Hart, Pauline Betz and Margaret Osborne winning the ten ladies finals between them, America dominated this period at Wimbledon.

DROBNY PULLS IT OFF WITH A FREAK SHOT

By Tom Phillips

ONE moment in Jaroslav Drobny's pulsating, all-action Wimbledon triumph will live in my memory.

Hushed is the jam-packed Centre Court crowd. The match is in the melting pot. The "Old Maestro," 32-year-old Drobny, is leading by two sets to one—13-11, 4-6, 6-2—against the boy Australian, 5ft. 7in. terrier-like Ken Rosewall, 19. They are seven-all in the 15th game of the 4th set.

Fighting grimly, desperately, to stop Drobny breaking through his service, Rosewall stands poised a few feet from the net, waiting to put away a short lob return from his wily opponent.

And the tension is all the greater because "Droh" wants just one point to clinch the game, with his service to follow.

Then comes a once-in-a-million freak shot.

Stunned

Rosewall stands stunned, petrified, as the ball lands softly on the net cord, almost sits there, then drops plop! plumb-dead down on Rosewall's side, tantalisingly out of his reach.

Impetuously Rosewall, who still has a ball in his hand ready for his next service, draws his hand back as if to throw it at his opponent.

But his good sportsmanship prevails, checks him in time. And Drobny throws his arms in the air in a gesture which seems to say, "It's all in the game, son!" So Drobny leads 8-7. But it isn't all over yet.

Rosewall, with all the grim determination of the fighting Aussie, strives every sinew to even the score by breaking Drobny's service.

All through the tournament he has amazed the crowd with his miraculous returns, leaping from nowhere to retrieve what looks like a hopelessly lost ball to send it back a winner.

Now he does it again. Drobny smashes an angled drive near the far corner of Rosewall's forehand. What is Rosewall? An acrobatic magician of tennis?

One prodigious leap, ending in a ten-foot slide, and the ball flashes, like lightning, past Drobny, who has come to the net for a kill just in case.

In his amazement Drobny falls flat on his face—and the crowd gasps Ooh! and cheers Rosewall to the echo.

So Rosewall fights back, leading 40-15. One more point and he will even the score and may yet go on to snatch victory.

But Drobny feels that the triumph he has striven for so long is in his grasp. He keys himself up. Now his service, which has been so mediocre throughout the match, is at its best — and he marches on to victory. Last shot of all—Rosewall hits the net on the return, his one big fault.

All over

And so it is all over, two hours and 38 minutes of breath-taking tennis, inspiring to watch.

Drobny, sly old fox, says when it is finished: "I knew if I could lure him into lobbing to me, I could kill those returns with my smashes.

"The first couple of times I did this I saw he was shaken. From then on I was confident I would win."

Never will he have a greater victory. Never will Rosewall be more magnificent in defeat.

—HOW THEY ENDED—

MEN'S SINGLES

FINAL.—J. Drobny bt K. R. Rosewall 13-11, 4-6, 6-2, 9-7.

WOMEN'S DOUBLES

SEMI-FINALS. — *S. Fry and D. Hart, holders, bt *A. Mortimer and J. A. Shilcock 6-2, 6-1; *L. Brough and Mrs. W. Dupont bt Mrs. W. Brewer and K. Hubbell 6-1, 6-1.

MIXED DOUBLES

FIFTH ROUND.—M. A. Otway & Miss J. S. Burke bt *R. N. Hartwig & Mrs. C. Pratt 7-5, 6-3.

SEMI-FINALS.—*K. R. Rosewall and Mrs. W. Dupont bt *L. A. Hoad and Miss M. Connolly 6-8, 6-4, 6-4; *V. Seixas and Miss D. Hart, holders, bt Otway and Miss Burke 6-4, 6-1.

*Seeded players.

Whack! Just one of those Drobny smashes that helped to carry him to his first Wimbledon triumph.

1954   Daily Herald

TRABERT EQUALS FEAT OF DONALD BUDGE

◆

Women's Doubles Final Will Be All-British Battle

From LANCE TINGAY
WIMBLEDON, Friday.

A RELENTLESS power player, who scarcely made a loose or thoughtless stroke from the start of things last Monday week, became men's singles champion here this afternoon. Tony Trabert, as expected, was the winner, the 12th American to take the crown, and in the final, watched by Princess Margaret and the Duchess of Kent, he overwhelmed Kurt Nielsen 6-3, 7-5, 6-1.

Great Britain have not, however, come so badly out of the Lawn Tennis Championships after all. The women's doubles final to-morrow will be entirely British, Miss S. Bloomer and Miss P. E. Ward against Miss A. Mortimer and Miss J. A. Shilcock.

A Wimbledon title has not been wholly British since 1937. The last all-British final was the men's doubles in 1936 and the last women's doubles exclusively British was 1929.

To bring about this happy state of affairs Miss Bloomer and Miss Ward, in the semi-final to-day, reversed the result of the French Championship final by beating the Americans, Mrs. Beverly Fleitz and Miss Darlene Hard, 6-3, 9-7. Earlier, in the curtain-raiser of the day, Miss Mortimer and Miss Shilcock beat the Australians, Miss F. Muller and Mrs. L. A. Hoad, 6-2, 6-1.

REAL CHAMPION
Hallmark of Calibre

It is a matter of record that, since the abolition of the challenge round in 1922, only one man, Donald Budge, had become champion without losing a set. Trabert has equalled this feat. Not only did he not concede a set but he scarcely ever looked like doing so.

Trabert has become Wimbledon singles champion in about eight hours' total playing time. With Budge and Jack Kramer and Frank Sedgman it was much the same. They chopped down all opposition with the precision and vigour that is the hallmark of a real champion's calibre.

Trabert took 73 minutes on the Centre Court to-day to make himself the champion. There have been more adventurous finals both here and its excitement as a contest with uncertain issue was fleeting.

The winner was too good. Nielsen, who drew inspiration from the distinguished setting to bring Ken Rosewall down in the semi-final, was less inspired to-day. Even if he had been in better form I doubt whether Trabert would have been unduly troubled.

Surging Tide

His game, from start to finish, was like the surging of the tide. In attack he went on and on, always pressing netwards. In recoiling against Nielsen's pressure weapons the sharp counter-thrust was always ready and even when such was obviously impossible he scampered to retrieve.

His precision and unity of purpose, his freedom from error, his lack of weakness (unless the common vulnerability to a lob over the backhand shoulder be reckoned as such) made him, so far as Nielsen was concerned, like a rock.

It was essentially a power game, though some of his most damaging guns were muffled rather than loud. His service, for instance, was the kicking ball. Nielsen took one set and a half to get hold of this and always it gave Trabert time to stand dominantly at the net.

His backhand rolled out winning shots magnificently, but he was not without the gentler touch. The final

E. W. SWANTON
(University match prospects) and other Cricket, B. C. JOHN-STONE (Henley)—P3

winning shot was a lob, as good a hoisted ball that ever was, for it pitched within an inch of the baseline and had Nielsen entirely beaten.

NIELSEN'S WEAKNESS
Ineffective Volley

As for Nielsen, he can hardly be called a failure. It is true his service worked less well than sometimes and of the many points he gave away a high proportion came from an ineffective stroke with a forehand volley that was more than waist high.

He was, however, under such constant pressure that it is small wonder that he cracked. His purely defensive equipment was not adequate to cope with Trabert's guns and he did not try.

His counter-attack, with which he constantly persisted, proved ineffective. Trabert was always moving towards the ball and the general pattern of the contest was of both men coming in towards the net. More volleys were played than ground shots.

Where Trabert had marked superiority was in quality of service return. This factor alone marked him out among the majority of challengers at Wimbledon this year. It required a delivery of special quality to induce a reply that lacked sting.

Early Punches

Relatively one-sided though it was there have been many worse finals. The first game went off in crackerjack fashion, Nielsen in the forecourt with Trabert performing marvels of intelligence and precise retrieving, and armed always to make the counter-blow.

Many hard punches were given and taken in these opening rallies and Nielsen was the first to recoil. His service was taken in the third game and he helped his own undoing with a double fault.

Nielsen did not come near to saving the set that had early turned against him. Not once did he get even within one point of taking a service game from Trabert, and in the ninth game his own delivery once more failed him. He fought frantically to hold it, saved four set balls valiantly, but it was a lob that eventually proved his undoing.

The Dane handled service much better in the second set and here he had the only chance that came to him. The fifth game was the critical one for Trabert when, for the first and only time, he lost his service.

Some lobs over his left shoulder had him scampering, and if ever he wavered throughout the match it was here.

Nielsen increased his lead to 4-2, though not before Trabert was well back in the fight with four chances to level at 3-3. The Dane, now within sight of the set, could not stop Trabert reducing his lead to 4-3, and he only required to win on his own delivery to be in front 5-3.

He had the advantage of serving with new balls, but in this crisis Nielsen allowed himself to be distracted. The clicking of photographers worried him. With more even temperament and better concentration Trabert gave such matters no concern. A missed smash and yet another winning lob by Trabert brought disaster to Nielsen.

Trabert was level at four games all and I think "fair to say Nielsen was not afterwards truly in the match. The Dane, saving a set point in the 10th game, kept level at 5-5 but in the 12th game he dropped his service to love.

That was Trabert two sets up and the outcome now a mere formality. Nielsen, seeing the inevitable, became relaxed and almost carefree. Trabert continued as precise of purpose as ever. He won the next set 6-1 and was Champion of Wimbledon.

Ball Touches Hand

One small incident during the match gave the lawn tennis lawyers a talking point. In the fourth game of the first set Nielsen made a sweeping forehand passing shot that apparently touched the top of the post and was deflected into court.

A seeming winner was given Nielsen when the net-cord judge pointed out the ball had touched his hand. No one would dispute the legal ruling, but Nielsen might well have asked what business the net-cord man had in not withdrawing his hand long before.

Much Better Pair

Of the first women's doubles success I need merely say that the British girls were much better than the Australians, Miss Muller and Mrs. Hoad, who, in fact, were not themselves the brightest of pairs.

Miss Bloomer and Miss Ward, who cast away a French doubles title that was almost in their pockets by the indecision of Mrs Ward, made amends to-day. This time there was no "elbow" by Miss Ward when it came to the crisis, and with this defeat of Mrs. Fleitz and Miss Hard the prospects of Britain in the Wightman Cup have become brighter.

THE CHAMPION.—Tony Trabert playing against Kurt Nielsen at Wimbledon yesterday, when he won the Men's Lawn Tennis Championship. Trabert is the 12th American to win the title.

YOUNG PLAYERS IN DAVIS CUP

◆

MOTTRAM & PAISH LEFT OUT

R. Becker, W. A. Knight, R. K. Wilson and M. Davies, with H. F. David as non-playing captain, have been nominated as Britain's Davis Cup team against Italy at Edgbaston on July 14, 15 and 16, writes Lance Tingay.

A page in the history of British lawn tennis has turned. After nine years' continuous service, longer than any before, Tony Mottram and Geoff Paish have been dropped.

It was, sooner or later, inevitable, and as a new young side takes over one can only look back on the years from 1947 until now with high appreciation for the way Mottram and Paish have done noble lawn tennis duty. Much will now depend on Becker, the only man of real experience in the side.

Knight and Wilson have both been in the side before, but only as reserves. Davies is a newcomer. Becker is 21 and the others all 19.

Becker, it goes without saying, will be the top singles man. As to his support, that is a pretty problem for Capt. David, since all three could stake claims for a place.

ITALIANS DROP MERLO

It was also announced yesterday that Giuseppe Merlo, who retired during his fourth round men's singles match at Wimbledon against Ken Rosewall, is to be replaced by Nicola Pietrangeli in the Italian team. Merlo has returned to Italy because of ill health.

Pietrangeli, who beat A. J. Mottram in the second round at Wimbledon, reached the men's singles semi-final before being beaten by Kurt Nielsen, of Denmark.

9 | The Great Australians

1956–67

The American domination was followed by an era that saw the great Australians Lew Hoad, Rod Laver, Neale Fraser, Ashley Cooper, Roy Emerson and John Newcombe become champions. However, the title evaded the incredible Ken Rosewall (four times a runner-up) and Fred Stolle (three times).

Roy Emerson and Fred Stolle. Emerson jumps the net following his victory over Stolle in the 1964 men's singles final in this Daily Mail *photograph*

1956   Lew Hoad
beat Ken Rosewall
6–2 4–6 7–5 6–4

1957   Lew Hoad
beat Ashley Cooper
6–2 6–1 6–2

Lew Hoad became the first player since Don Budge (who won in 1937 and 1938) to win the Wimbledon men's singles title in successive years. His first victory, in 1956, was against his 'tennis twin' Ken Rosewall. The two players were both aged twenty-one, with Rosewall the senior by 21 days. Hoad's four-set win gave him his third major championship title that year. A fourth in America would have meant the Grand Slam, but Rosewall gained revenge for his Wimbledon defeat before turning professional.

In their careers Hoad never won the US title and Rosewall was unable to gain Wimbledon final success. Together, they won the men's doubles title at Wimbledon in 1953 and 1956.

Hoad was many people's idea of the greatest player ever and his strength and precision with all shots was outstanding. On the other hand, Rosewall had to make up for his lack of power on serve and volley with excellent groundstrokes.

In the 1957 final Hoad had an easy victory against Ashley Cooper. His form was invincible as he destroyed his 20-year-old fellow-countryman in just under an hour for the loss of only five games.

During Hoad's reign there had been some encouraging British performances. Bobby Wilson, who played in twenty successive Wimbledon Championships, beat the former champion and number four seed Budge Patty in 1956. A year later he reached the last sixteen along with the left-hander Billy Knight, who had done particularly well considering his game was more suited to hard courts.

1956   Melbourne Herald

LONDON, Friday. — Today's Wimbledon triumph for Lew Hoad over Ken Rosewall was not the best of the clashes between the tennis "twins" but it brought into the game such a wide variety of tactics and strokes that it delighted most, although it lacked the "electric" tension.

I thought there were too many mistakes to call the match great, but I don't agree with many internationals, including Sven Davidson, Jaro Drobny and Vic Seixas, that it was poor.

It might have been erratic but there were many brilliant patches which more than made amends for the mistakes. The match greatly enhanced Australia's reputation.

There were no smiles—as some of the critics appear to want every time a player steps on a court — but it was such a keenly-contested fight that it kept the gallery's concentrated attention throughout.

Both players showed excellent demeanor, although one or two who did not understand the situation might have thought them a little too grim.

Any Rosewall-Hoad meeting nowadays must be different to the days when they were youngsters.

Now they are battling for top world or top international honors, and the history of the international play proves that such occasions cannot help being grim.

Service was feature

The feature of the play, in relation to Hoad's win, was that Hoad had greater power of service, and could attack Rosewall's service often; Rosewall was unable to attack Hoad's service, whether it was the first, and fast one, or the slower, kicking delivery.

Over the concluding stages, Hoad's service, and especially his big one down the centre into the second court, was a telling factor.

Hoad finished the day with a bad back, but heat treatment at the courts, and later tonight, might mend it for the doubles final tomorrow.

Hoad has been troubled by back soreness, on and off, for the past month, but it was not serious until he went on the court for the doubles semi-final against Howe and Larsen.

Then it was evident he was worried.

No doubt the long delay in being televised and interviewed after the singles final while still in his wet shirt, led to the trouble.

Hoad celebrated his win at his hotel tonight with many friends.

Not turning pro. yet

He has no intention of considering professional offers. If any are received. None has arrived so far.

He is keen now to try to equal Don Budge's "grand slam" of 1938, but it won't alter his plans to remain in Europe until just before the American National doubles at Boston about the middle of August.

With Hoad and Rosewall in the final and these two in the doubles final as well as Daphne Seeney and Fay Muller in the women's doubles final, Thelma Long in the final of the Women's Plate and Rod Laver in the final of the junior boys' singles, it is truly an Australian Wimbledon.

Laver is to meet top American junior Ron Holmberg whose big-hitting game appears to hold too much power for the Rockhampton lad.

Lew Hoad. Wimbledon men's singles champion in 1956 and 1957

HOAD'S AMAZING POWER DISPLAY CRUSHES COOPER

ROY McKELVIE on WIMBLEDON

L EW HOAD gave a wonderful display of top-speed power tennis, to beat his compatriot, the Australian champion, Ashley Cooper, by 6—2, 6—1, 6—2, in Wimbledon's men's final yesterday. It was all over in 56 minutes, the shortest final since 1932, when Ellsworth Vines slaughtered Bunny Austin in 48 minutes. And Hoad, in yesterday's form, is a better player than Vines ever was.

An unruffled Hoad, showing no hint of temperament, even when hair kept on getting into an eye, produced his greatest for the first time since last year's final.

Hoad, first man since the war to win the Wimbledon singles title twice, agreed that he had rarely played better. Perhaps, he thought, in beating Rosewall in last year's final, and more certainly when he beat Tony Trabert at Forest Hills in the 1955 Davis Cup challenge round.

When Hoad is in such form as he showed yesterday no player in the amateur ranks is in his class. Cooper, poor fellow, looked almost a hack, which he certainly is not.

His three gifts

Three things give Hoad this vast superiority over his fellows.

First, his amazingly fast reflexes. He seizes the ball faster than any other. There was one occasion, near the end of the match, when he sprinted across court to cover a drop shot and made a winner off it.

Second, Hoad and his racket are one. As a fast-moving boxer darts out his lightning thrusts, so Hoad and racket dart on to the ball, taking it as early as any man since the war.

Third, Hoad has such superb wrist power that he has only to flick the ball and it is gone. Opponents either fail to spot the direction or it goes too fast for them.

Infinite variety

Repeatedly Cooper's hoped-for winners or opening shots came back with dividends attached. Hoad has an infinite variety of shot and spin, and his game has no set pattern.

It was surprising that he should suddenly reach this peak. His recent performances have been erratic, untidy.

Perhaps he had saved himself for this moment.

On Thursday evening, after a long doubles match, Hoad played two fast sets on an outside court with Gil Shea, "just to get the feel of a singles court again."

This extended effort caused some soreness in a thigh muscle and Hoad had to be massaged. Then yesterday morning, when Hoad was knocking-up, a string broke in his favourite racket.

Helpless

His wife, Jenny, dashed to a sports shop, had the racket repaired, and sent it on to court at the end of the first set. Hoad used it for the third set.

These things, however, are extraneous, and only background to a magnificent performance of speed-play. Cooper, as strong, as fit, and as fast as any other amateur in the game, was helpless against it.

No more than half a crack ever appeared in Hoad's game.

He lost his service at 4—1 in the first set, and he served two double faults in the third game of the third set.

Rare errors

Those were the only occasions Hoad lost his service, and the total number of his errors did not exceed half a dozen.

In the first set, Hoad was too far ahead and too dominating to let that service loss affect him. For a few rallies he let Cooper make the running and the pace, but in the next game he was dominant again.

In the third set, having lost the service, Hoad came back with a series of ripostes that rocked Cooper and made it two-all.

The Duke of Edinburgh hands back the Men's Singles Cup to Lew Hoad, first player for 19 years to win the Wimbledon title in successive seasons.

1957   Daily Mail

1958 Ashley Cooper
beat Neale Fraser
3–6 6–3 6–4 13–11

1959 Alex Olmedo
beat Rod Laver
6–4 6–3 6–4

1960 Neale Fraser
beat Rod Laver
6–4 3–6 9–7 7–5

Ashley Cooper recovered from his crushing defeat by Lew Hoad to reach the Wimbledon men's singles final again in 1958. He had played some close matches on his way to meeting the left-handed Australian Neale Fraser, needing five sets to overcome Bobby Wilson – and the patriotic crowd – in the quarter-finals.

In his second final, Cooper led two sets to one and won the long fourth 13–11 to win the Wimbledon title at the age of twenty-one. Then Cooper turned professional and did not compete in 1959 when a 20-year-old from Queensland began to make his indelible mark on the Championships. Rod Laver was his name; he became the third man to reach a singles final unseeded (after Wilmer Allison in 1930, and Kurt Nielsen in 1953 and 1955). (cont.)

Ashley Cooper. 1958 champion

YAWN TENNIS!

A SHLEY COOPER, the twenty-one-year-old from Melbourne, beat Neale Fraser, the twenty-four-year-old left-hander, also from Melbourne, 3—6, 6—3, 6—4, 13—11, in the final of the men's singles, at Wimbledon yesterday.

It would 'be unfair to say that this was the worst Wimbledon Final ever. It would not be untrue to say that it was one of the dullest.

There's an old saying "Difference of opinion is what makes horse-racing."

The one kiss of death on any sport is when a result becomes inevitable As early as the fourth game of the first set—the only time when Cooper dropped his service—you knew that he was LIKELY to lose that set, but CERTAIN to win the match.

The sad thing was that the match had to go on until one man had won three sets.

Frankly, I think boxing, for instance, does this kind of thing better, for a referee can always stop a contest when it has become outrageously one-sided.

And in cricket, when you are leading by 300 or 400 runs, you can declare.

VICIOUS

Fraser — let's be honest about this — was never in the match with a chance ...EXCEPT THE CHANCE OF LOSING.

He "lived" on his service, which is vicious, hard to anticipate and remarkably free from the blemishing of double faults.

Early in the match he brought off some wonderful whiplash passing shots, and he always volleyed well. Against a Cooper, who far too often lobbed short, Fraser's overhead was devastating

But I doubt if a man has ever got to the final of Wimbledon with such an apology for a backhand

WHAT A "PARDON ME" STROKE THIS ONE OF FRASER'S IS.

Often you had the ludicrous spectacle of the man who is supposed to be the

CENTRE COURT TODAY

A. Mortimer (G B.) v. A. Gibson (U S.)

S Davidson, U Schmidt v. A. Cooper, N Fraser.

Mrs. W. Du Pont, M Varner v. Gibson. M. Bueno.

R. Howe, L. Coghlan v. K Nielsen Gibson.

* Seed

second best amateur in the world, running round shots directed to this wing.

Once he did it so obviously that Cooper, who had already started his service swing, was able to change the direction of the shot and beat Fraser by three-quarters of the width of the service court.

Curiously enough, the match only really came alive in the final game.

BUTTERFLIES

Cooper, who had never tried to pull out "cannon balls" on his service, got to 40—0 after a couple of net cords.

Then with Cooper playing as though he had butterflies in his racket. Fraser made a backhand passing shot. One match point gone.

At 40—15 Cooper served a double fault, which is the equivalent of committing hara-kiri when you've won a battle 40—30.

The crowd were now in a state of suspended animation ... with hands ready to clap or prepared to be thrown in the air with horror.

Cooper serves, the return is weak, he advances effortlessly to the net, where Fraser tosses up a short lob.

The dark, handsome, twenty-one-year-old, looking taller than the Eddystone Lighthouse, is dominating the court. HE MUST BE THE WINNER NOW.

And then he plays one of the worst smashes I have ever seen in a final—right off the maker's name on the racket

A CHANCE

By gosh it's deuce and Fraser is still in there with a chance.

From there let Cooper take over the story After-wards he told me:

"At 40—0 I thought Only one more point and I've won Wimbledon.' After that I never saw the ball until deuce was called."

But then there was no further argument A smash from Cooper - and he had his fourth match point.

He finished off the match with a shot of a real champion - a stop volley which had hydraulic brakes.

And Cooper now played

PETER WILSON —at Wimbledon

the most joyous " shot of the match. He banged towards the clouds the ball which he still held in his hand.

It went so high that it did not come down again until the two " Cobbers " who share a hotel room who breakfasted together who travelled to Wimbledon together but who never talked about the match, shook hands at the net.

Afterwards Cooper didn't want to discuss his possible future as a professional.

But he said that he would still be available as an amateur for the Challenge Round of the Davis Cup when Australia will be defending the trophy at the end of the year.

But even before his country calls on him, Ashley will be making one call on his own to Tinaroo Falls, a tiny village in the Australian "Outback" — where beauty queen Miss Helen Wood is staying.

For Helen, Miss Australia of 1957, is the girl who might one day be Mrs. Cooper.

After a series of letters which got no one anywhere, they had a long-distance phone conversation.

It so settled Cooper that he was afterwards able to play relaxed tennis which made him champion.

A DOUBLE

Cooper and Fraser reached the doubles final when they beat Barry MacKay and Mervyn Rose 3—6, 8—6, 7—5, 7—5. They meet Sven Davidson and Ulf Schmidt, Sweden, who beat the Italians, Orlando Sirola and Nicole Pietrangeli, 8—6, 3—6, 6—3, 7—5.

1958 Daily Mirror

I NAME CHAMP ALEX 'SENOR QUICKSILVER'

ALEX OLMEDO, Peru's 23-year-old sports idol, put his name among the great Wimbledon champions in a 72-minute victory over Rod Laver, Australia's unseeded 20-year-old, yesterday. The score was 6—4, 6—3, 6—4, and the match just as clear-cut as those bold figures show.

It Olmedo, 2—1 favourite for the title, did not win the final in a canter he at least won as he had in all the five rounds that preceded it—without involving himself in any sort of a crisis, or giving his backers any anxiety.

The strong-serving, agile Peruvian, fluid as Black Velvet in the way he glided around the court, was much too fast for the younger Aussie, a lean and muscular athlete who is no slouch himself.

LAVER: HE'S SO FAST

Just as Olmedo had outpaced all his other rivals since he struck his first ball last Monday week, he outpaced Laver from start to finish yesterday.

Only once was the poker-faced Queenslander in front. Just briefly, when he led 3—2 in the second set—and that was a routine service lead.

Even his mentor, Harry Hopman, who brought Laver to Wimbledon four years ago as a colt on a "scholarship" trip, paid for by Arthur Drysdale, Tasmanian lottery promoter, could have had no more than a prayer that he would keep that lead.

Laver, who curiously was not nervous, in contrast to the scared Olmedo, confessed to me afterwards: "It was speed that did it. Mackay attacked me like that with serve-and-volley in the semi-final, but this bloke is so terribly fast about the court too."

I name Olmedo henceforth "Senor Quicksilver." But crafty Olmedo has more to back his championship qualifications than that speed.

He has a machine service-and-

By FRANK ROSTRON

volley routine which became almost boring because it was so mechanically successful. He is a sound ground-stroke player, and a fearless smasher. And he is a dusky witch doctor with his mastery of pace and length.

Several times, when "Rocket" Rod raced helter skelter to the net Olmedo lobbed past him with a lazy delicacy of touch that was as phenomenal as his full-hit drives and volleys.

It was not a great final, because the further it went the clearer it became that the complete summary of the match was: "Anything Rod can do, Alex can do better—and faster."

How does Olmedo compare with previous champions? Perhaps he is not quite up with Kramer, Budge, Perry and Co.—yet. But he is mighty near them.

COOPER: HE'S GOOD

Said last year's champion Ashley Cooper, who flew in from Memphis, Tennessee, to watch: "He's a real good one."

Said Baron Gottfried von Cramm, three times a finalist: "What a player! I'd like to see him in an Open Wimbledon against all the top pros. That would be great."

Last word by Wimbledon's Grand Old Man, 45-year-old Gardnar Mulloy: "It was tough on Rod. Olmedo had it easy because Barry Mackay softened

CHAMPION

Olmedo—and trophy

Laver up in that three and three-quarter hour semi-final. That was what really killed Laver."

1959   Daily Express

To achieve this, Laver had to win a marathon semi-final against the number five seed Barry Mackay (11–13 11–9 10–8 7–9 6–3). In the quarter-finals he had beaten Alan Mills, now the Championship referee, who had caused a major upset in the first round by knocking out the 1954 champion Jaroslav Drobny 14–12 3–6 10–8 8–6.

Alex Olmedo, born in Peru but a member of the United States Davis Cup team, came through as the number one seed in the other half of the draw to meet Laver in the final.

He had a much easier task in his semi-final, beating the Australian, Roy Emerson, in straight sets, and went on to record the same margin of victory against Laver.

Olmedo won the Australian singles championship before joining most of the previous men's singles champions on the professional circuit.

In 1960 **Neale Fraser** became the sixth successive number one seed to win the Wimbledon men's singles title. In the battle of the left-handed Australians, he beat Laver in four

close sets.

Once again Laver had had a gruelling semi-final match while his opponent's passage to the final had been trouble free. This time he was taken to five sets by the magnificent strokeplay of the Italian Nicola Pietrangeli.

Fraser resisted offers to turn professional and continued to have success at Wimbledon in the doubles events. In 1969 he became the team manager of the Australian Davis Cup side.

FRASER ENDS 7 LEAN YEARS

Britons in doubles final for first time since 1939

THE seven lean Wimbledon years which began in 1954 ended for Neale Fraser yesterday on a packed centre court in front of what I can only describe as "a Royal Flush"—so crammed with dignitaries was the Royal Box.

Fraser beat his fellow Australian—and fellow left-hander—Rod Laver 6—4, 3—6, 9—7, 7—5. And let it be said at once, he thoroughly deserved his victory.

It was not until rain interrupted play in the ninth game of the third set, a wildly-exciting game. Indeed, with both men left-handers and both exponents of the "big" game of cannonading services and net-storming, it was rather like a man playing himself in the mirror.

The first set, which went to Fraser and in which there was not a rally of five strokes, was in fact decided by one shot—a perfect lob from Fraser which gave him the solitary service break and a lead of 5—4.

In the second set there were three service breaks, Laver leading 3—love and 4—1, and then being hauled back to 4—3 with another of those high tosses.

Then it was the red-head's turn to pull out something special, and he did so with a short back-hand pass that was like a stab from a clasp-knife.

Then came a long raking shot down the line of the same wing, like a rapier being rasped out of its scabbard.

No Mistake

He made no mistake about holding his service to take the second set and level the match.

In the third set, Laver's great chance came in the fifth game.

He made four such superb back-hand returns of service that Fraser could not touch one of them—and "the quick brown fox" had got his nose in front.

And then, unaccountably and inexplicably, he cracked. He made one of the weakest volleys I have seen from him, fluked a half-volley, and then, suddenly leaden-footed and lacking in all anticipation, he volleyed clumsily for Fraser to break back at 3—all.

His slump continued, and now Fraser with greater weight of stroke, and considerably more venom in his service, looked in full cry for the set.

Just to add to the general excitement, at the end of the eighth game, with Fraser leading 5—3, the Duke of Edinburgh arrived by helicopter with Princess Anne.

And with Princess Margaret, the Duchess of Kent and other members of the elite already present, we had a "Royal Full House."

And then — dammit — if the rain didn't put in its clammy spoke.

Fraser was serving to clinch the set, but at deuce the players had to retire to the dressing-room.

PETER WILSON at Wimbledon

When they resumed some fifty-five minutes later it was Laver who "trapped" fastest, winning the first five points before Fraser got his joints greased again with the honest oil of perspiration—and they were level at 5 all.

Crisis came to Laver in the sixteenth. He was love-40 down on his service with three set points to save. He saved one with a service. He saved a second likewise—Fraser's return dropping just out.

A cracking net rally followed, with Fraser putting a forehand out.

Pressure Off

With the pressure temporarily off, Laver netted a back-hand volley to make it set point for the fourth time.

And then, driven back, Fraser fell, his racket jinked out of his hand, he was sprawled helplessly on the grass. . . .

When he looked up, the ball was in the net on Laver's side of the court, for he had fluffed an easy back-hand volley.

Now it was the fourth set, and game after game was going with the service.

Laver was crowding and ever-crowding the net, but the forecourt was a mine-field for him, because when he got too close Fraser would wrench him backwards with lobs.

At last in the twelfth game one of these sent Laver scampering back, and his return lob fell out. Match point.

A truly great and courageous rally followed, with Laver finally gaining another breath with an incredible net-cord volley.

Then Fraser showed a touch of genius by running round his back-hand at the last possible moment and cracking in an untouchable return.

And then—Bingo! Down the line went the passing shot which crowned Fraser.

And the man who in 1956 had been persuaded only by his parents to stay in the game overshadowed by Hoad and Rosewall, and was suffering from varicose veins, was a worthy champion.

I liked his remark afterwards when he was asked what he thought about an "open Wimbledon" and replied: "They can do what they like—NOW!"

But, considering the quality of the professionals, I thought it was only honest when he added: "I think they should leave it as it is."

Comfortable

For the first time since 1939, when Charles Hare and Frank Wilde got there, Great Britain has a pair in the final of the men's doubles.

Yesterday, Mike Davies and Bobby Wilson scored a fairly comfortable four-set victory over the young Australians Bob Hewitt and Martin Mulligan, winning 3—6, 6—3, 6—2, 6—4.

The sometime stormy petrels have now settled down into a very reasonable combination, with Wilson producing the flashing, crowd-delighting clinching shots but Davies "grafting" away solidly.

Today they meet the American-Mexican combination of Dennis Ralston and Rafael Osuna.

Neale Fraser, the new champion, scored most of his points with his forehand drive, which he has just completed in this picture from The Sporting Life

1960   Daily Mirror

1961 Rod Laver
beat Chuck McKinley
6–3 6–1 6–4

1962 Rod Laver
beat Marty Mulligan
6–2 6–2 6–1

Rod Laver, the 22-year-old Australian, fulfilled the promise of his talent and skill when he lifted the Wimbledon men's singles trophy in two successive years. Twice a beaten finalist, it was third time lucky for Laver in 1961 as he defeated American Chuck McKinley in straight sets for the loss of only eight games.

A year later he won another one-sided final losing only five games against fellow-countryman Marty Mulligan. By qualifying to play Laver, Mulligan became the fourth unseeded player to reach a men's singles final. He had, however, been fortunate to get past the fourth round: his opponent, Roy Emerson, the number two seed, had had to retire because of an ankle injury at one set all.

Laver, the genius, whose left forearm seemed to be twice as big as his right, achieved the Grand Slam in 1962 by winning the other three major championships (American, French and Australian). Don Budge in 1938 was the only other player to have reached this peak of sporting excellence.

Like past champions Sedgman, Hoad, Cooper and Fraser, Laver benefited enormously from the guidance of Harry Hopman. He, Rosewall and the others were described as Hopman's 'Wonder Boys'. As a player Hopman was a shrewd tactician on court but he became better known as coach and administrator of the Australian team that won fifteen Davis Cup finals in eighteen years. He was responsible for giving Laver the nickname 'The Rockhampton Rocket'; it was derived from the town in Queensland where the tennis maestro was born.

There was nothing more to gain on the amateur circuit so Laver turned professional.

In the 1961 Championship *(cont.)*

Laver kills off McKinley in 53 minutes

POKER-FACED Rod Laver committed tennis murder on the Centre Court yesterday—the cold, ruthless slaying of 20-year-old Chuck McKinley, the St. Louis college boy.

This was one of the speediest executions seen in a Wimbledon men's final since the war. It was all over in 53 minutes, with Queenslander Laver, beaten finalist for the past two years, making no mistakes in his third attempt, winning 6-3, 6-1, 6-4.

Chuck, the muscular, crew-cut, typical all-American boy, had emerged as one of the colourful personalities of these 1961 championships with his dynamic bounding all-action style.

Yesterday he had all the bounce, and almost all the heart, knocked out of him.

Off court, Laver, with his red hair, freckles, and modest manner, is just a simple schoolboyish lad from the Bush.

On court he is transformed into a merciless killer.

The ruthless streak that runs through left-hander Laver was revealed by just one sentence he spoke in his Press conference afterwards.

Sitting relaxed with his powerful arms crossed, he was asked if he had any special victory plans. He replied: " Yes, to make every shot a winner."

And he so very nearly did this. From the first set on there was only one way this no contest could end—victory for Laver.

Chuck, good sportsman that he is, said afterwards: " I don't reckon I played too badly. It was just that Rod did everything so much better.

" If I had the chance to play it all again I would not try to change anything. I don't think I could have done better."

Before he showed this venomous mood Laver had been hailed as a champion runner-up.

Apart from his two losing Wimbledon finals, he had also finished second best in the Australian, American, Italian, and British hard court championships this year.

BEWILDERED

Yesterday there was never any fear that he would emulate the dismal pre-war feat of Baron Von

By PETER LORENZO

Cramm, who appeared in three successive finals . . each time as a loser.

Chuck's American team-mates sitting just in front of me shook their heads in sympathy and bewilderment as the embarrassing slaughter went on.

Said one: " This guy Laver is fantastic. He's never played better in his life. On this form he'd give Pancho Gonzales (the world professional champion) the fight of his life."

Only for the opening six games did it seem that Chuck the Missile had any remote chance of holding Rod the Rocket.

In the seventh the Rocket decided it was time to leave the launching pad — and break through the Missile's service.

BREAK-THROUGH

A tremendous forehand winner down the line gave him the break. Laver took his own service game to love to lead 5-3 . . and everyone knew it was all over.

The first set took just 18 minutes. The second 13, with the outclassed American managing just 10 points.

In the third, Laver was content to let games go with service until the ninth, then three magnificent backhand returns of service, followed up with a cunning forehand to the baseline gave the Australian the break.

1961   Daily Herald

Rod Laver. 'The Rockhampton Rocket' had a spell as a professional which meant there was a six-year gap between his first two and last two Wimbledon victories

four Britons reached the last sixteen in the singles. At this stage the left-handers Billy Knight and Roger Taylor were beaten but Bobby Wilson, defeating the champion Neale Fraser in four sets, reached the quarter-final before going out to McKinley. The big serve of Mike Sangster took him to the semi-final but he, too, was beaten by McKinley.

Laver only took 52 minutes to beat Mulligan

LONDON, July 6 (A.A.P.). — Queensland's Rod Laver won his second successive Wimbledon singles title today when he eliminated fellow-Australian Martin Mulligan 6-2, 6-2, 6-1 in 52 minutes.

It was one of the quickest-ever Wimbledon victories, and although Mulligan fought courageously, he could not match Laver's speed and power.

Laver was brilliant, giving the best display by any one player in the tournament.

Besides having no answer to Laver's power and accuracy, Mulligan's service failed him and he spent most of the match retrieving.

The crowd was slightly stunned at the speed of it all and amazed at the severity of Laver's win.

It was a one-sided match, but this did not dim Laver's brilliance. He had taken about the same time in beating the American "Chuck" McKinley last year.

Mulligan appeared a little nervous and he made several mistakes early, some of them forced errors against Laver's accurate ground strokes.

Broke service early

Laver was quickly into form and he broke Mulligan's first two services to lead 3-0.

Mulligan, however, was not serving well. His first ball was rarely going in and he dropped service again to give Laver 4-1.

Laver at this stage looked vastly superior and he effortlessly held his own service.

Then Mulligan held his for the first time and it was 5-2.

Laver held his own service to love in the eighth game to take the set 6-2 in 17 minutes.

Mulligan was still trailing in the second set. He dropped his service in the third game, after Laver had twice outvolleyed him at the net to give Laver 2-1.

Mulligan had a point to break back in the next, but he made two errors on drives and it was 3-1 to Laver.

The crowd was right behind the Sydney boy and they gave him a tremendous ovation in the sixth game when he saved four huge smashes from Laver and ended the best volley of the match by hitting a fine winner straight down the forehand line.

This encouraged him to hold service, but Laver effortlessly held his in the next to take the second set 6-2, in the same time as the first.

Laver's display to this point was superb. He rarely made a mistake.

His volleying was brilliant and technically it was the finest display of tennis given by any one player in the tournament.

Laver dominated the game from the net, where he was cutting off Mulligan's returns or forcing him into errors trying to pass. He ran to 3-0.

Then Mulligan broke Laver's service in a long fourth game, which went to three deuces.

But his success was short-lived as Laver broke back immediately.

Laver went to 5-1 and held a match point on Mulligan's service, but outed a service return.

But the end was only delayed. Laver quickly went to match point again and won his second Wimbledon title when Mulligan put a smash into the bottom of the net.

Laver had taken the set 6-1 in 18 minutes and the match in only 52 minutes, which is one of the quickest-ever Wimbledon victories.

SHOCK WIN TO FLOYD

QUEENSLAND lightweight champion David Floyd (9.9½) scored a shock points win over world-rated U.S. junior lightweight Tommy Tibbs (9.6) at Festival Hall last night.

Tibbs appeared to take southpaw Floyd too cheaply and let him build up a good lead on points in the middle of the fight.

The American went all out for a k.o. in the last few rounds, but Floyd stood up to him, and although Floyd went down in the last round he never looked like being beaten.

Tibbs started brightly. he took the points in the first round.

The American started the second round with another burst of swinging blows, but Floyd was not rattled and fought back strongly.

Eased up

Tibbs then eased up and spent too much time posing, while waiting for a telling punch.

1963   Chuck McKinley
beat Fred Stolle
9–7 6–1 6–4

1964   Roy Emerson
beat Fred Stolle
6–4 12–10 4–6 6–3

1965   Roy Emerson
beat Fred Stolle
6–2 6–4 6–4

With no Rod Laver the 1963 Wimbledon men's singles Championship was wide open and only three seeds remained as the tournament entered the quarter-finals. One of these, **Chuck McKinley** (4) – the beaten finalist in 1961 – became the third man since the Challenge Round was abolished in 1922 to win the title without losing a set.

McKinley's final opponent was the Australian, Fred Stolle, who himself entered the record books as being the fifth unseeded player to reach this stage of the competition. The following year Stolle was seeded sixth and he had revenge over McKinley (2) in the semi-finals. He met the number one seed **Roy Emerson** and, in a rain-interrupted final, lost in four sets after narrowly failing in the second 12–10.

Emerson and Stolle were both under Harry Hopman's wing. Since Perry and von Cramm's pairing in consecutive finals in 1934 and 1935, these two 'Wonder Boys' were the first pair to contest two consecutive men's singles finals. Although it was Stolle's third final it was also his least successful and he won only ten games against Emerson. Stolle, like von Cramm and Rosewall, was therefore labelled one of the Wimbledon singles 'runner-ups'. He twice won the men's doubles title and had singles success in the French and Australian championships.

Emerson was also a brilliant doubles player. An outstanding schoolboy athlete, he could run 100 yards in ten seconds and this pace helped him cover the tennis court with breathtaking speed.

Down 9-7   Down 6-1   Down 6-4   …Out

Chuck bounds to the title

By FRANK ROSTRON

CHARLES ROBERT (CHUCK) McKINLEY, America's No. 1 lawn tennis player, became the world's top amateur in just 80 minutes yesterday when he beat Australia's Fred Stolle 9—7, 6—1, 6—4, with a muscular display of fast-serving agility, and an acrobatic speed that, at times, turned Wimbledon's Centre Court into a circus-tumbler's ring.

Chuck, watched by his pretty wife Wylita, who saw him surprisingly beaten in the second round last year when they were on honeymoon, took the men's singles title without losing a set. The last man to equal the feat—1955 champion Tony Trabert—was also a spectator yesterday.

Popular Chuck is a worthy and genial champion, a highly trained athlete with a breezy personality that enriches the game in an age of drab serve-and-volley robots.

This likeable, bounding ball of muscular energy has not the greatness of some of the classic champions of the past. But with his prodigious energy and sheer will to win, he might beat anybody.

Gripping

Stolle, the languid 6ft. 3in. thin man of world tennis, countered McKinley's madcap rushes about the court for 12 exciting games. He did so with the same slashing high-trajectory serves and chalk-raising volleys that had carried this unseeded doubles specialist so surprisingly to the final.

It was a gripping spectacle while it lasted, with Stolle still hopeful of repeating his two previous victories over McKinley, the last in the West of England championships at Bristol only three weeks ago.

But the difference in match-winning quality on the really big occasion was typified by their attitudes.

The good-natured breeziness of the mathematics student from Trinity College, San Antonio, Texas, who yelled comic remarks, contrasted with the tenseness of the Sydney bank clerk who gazed in anguish to the heavens at his failures.

The strain told on Stolle's only match-winning weapon — his service. He served seven vital double faults, compared with Chuck's three.

Somersaulting

So the end was inevitable when tumbling, somersaulting Chuck, never admitting himself beaten by any shot, broke through Fred's service in the 15th game and went on to take the first set 9—7.

McKinley had said beforehand that all he feared was Stolle's serving, and both knew it. Stolle struggled stoically to the end, but the rest was all McKinley.

As United States team manager Bob Kelleher aptly summarised: "This was a natural triumph for a 100 per cent tough games player with a great heart and an inflexible will. And it couldn't have happened to a nicer guy."

Triumphant Chuck kisses the Cup

WEETMAN ZIP LANDS GOLD

GOLF   By RONALD HEAGER

MUSCULAR Harry Weetman was the star of the command performance golf show with a scorching round of 66 which gave him the £525 Prince Philip Trophy, at Blackpool North Shore yesterday.

FAULKNER MAKES IT —JUST!

MAX FAULKNER scrambled into next week's Open golf championship after a "sudden death" play-off involving six players.

Max, Open champion in 1951, had a second round 73 at Fairhaven to total 148. Then six men went out to play for the last five places. Leading qualifiers :—

ST. ANNES
146—W Large 71, 69.
146—S Sewgolum (S Africa) 69, 71 ;
A King 74, 64.
147—N Lynch 71, 70 ; G Cayril 66, 73 ;
H Henning (S Africa) 68, 70.
142—R Sota (Spain) 70 72 ; N Drew
72, 70 ; A Grubb 70, 72.
143—H Boyle 71, 72 ; A Gillies 72, 71.

FAIRHAVEN
137—B Devlin (Aust) 67, 70
139—H Lewis 67, 72
141—C Bowman 73, 68 ; A Fisher 73.
139 ; G Mac ey 69, 73.
143—F Wilkes (S Africa) 71, 71 ; E
Lester 70 72 ; S Davies (S Africa) 72

Prince Philip dropped in by helicopter to watch big golf for the first time and stayed long enough to see Weetman start with a tremendous eagle 3 at the first where he holed a five-yard putt.

Weetman collected the handsome gold-and-silver trophy from Sir John Hunt, of Everest fame, and then said :—

"It's nice to know this trophy is mine for keeps. The others I've won I've always had to hand back. I seem to have found a bit of form.

"Not a bad effort for a 33 –1 shot for the Open, eh ?" he asked pointedly. "I think I'll back myself if I can keep this putting stroke."

Harry, of Selsdon Park, won the tournament with huge putts of five and six yards at the 15th and 16th for a birdie 2 and an eagle 3.

EDGED OUT

This edged out Parkstone's power man Peter Alliss by one shot after Peter had set up a 67 target that did not look like being beaten.

Dave Thomas shared third place and the three home men in the first five gave Britain a tremendous boost in this preview of the Open championship, starting next Wednesday at Royal St. Lytham.

EMERSON, the robot champion

ROY EMERSON, 27-year-old Queenslander, will be known as Wimbledon's robot champion. He plays the game dead-pan and at one pace, almost as if speed and direction had been pre-determined by computers.

After his 6—4, 12—10, 4—6, 6—3 win in 2hr. 43min. over fellow-Australian Fred Stolle in yesterday's final, even Emerson admitted:

"I don't think this sort of tennis was terribly attractive to watch.

"But there's nothing else you can do against players like Fred. He hits the ball so hard and I hit the ball hard, too."

Was it boring? Yes, if you look for subtleties of spin and deft-touch volleys from a Wimbledon final or for colourful, fiery heroes.

Boldness

But there were no disappointments for those with a taste for the deadly efficiency of grass-court service and volley at something approaching its best.

Proof of their efficiency is the fact that the longest rally of the match was nine strokes.

There was still much to admire, however. Supreme fitness, ruthless concentration, amazing reflexes, complete unflappability, burning determination and boldness.

Emerson won because of his electrifying speed, his greater flexibility and the sheer bravado of his service returns which Stolle could never match.

Eleven Stolle double-faults also helped Emerson to force five of the seven service breaks. Stolle is now becoming the game's best loser. It was his second successive losing Wimbledon final. This year he has also lost in the finals of the Australian and Italian championships.

Poor Stolle had his chances. A point for a service break in only the second game, a point for the second set at 5—4 with Emerson serving.

He lost them because, in vital moments like these, Emerson was relaxed and adventurous,

Stolle taut and diffident.

It took Emerson just 22 minutes to pocket the first set and another double fault and a backhand passing shot helped him burst clear for 4—3 in the second set.

But in the next game his own volleys were twice indecisive enough to give Stolle the chance to flash the ball past him. So they were level again at four all.

Vital break

It was not until the 21st game, after rain had caused a third brief interruption which meant that each time Stolle was the unfortunate one to serve cold, that Emerson made the vital break.

He missed his chance to win in straight sets when Stolle bravely recovered from love-40 in the very first game of the third set. Stolle took the set nine games later when Emerson, on his own service, missed a smash at set point.

In the fourth set Stolle was at such pains to return service that Emerson dropped only three points in his four service games.

The championship was finally decided in the ninth game when Emerson's enterprise made Stolle volley weakly, and the new champion was home and dry.

● Today Margaret Smith attempts to make it an Australian double when she takes on the Brazilian Maria Bueno in the women's final. Miss Bueno beat Miss Smith in the American final last summer: Miss Smith beat Miss Bueno in the final of the French championships more recently.

If Miss Smith can keep her nerve today I think she will win again.

Stolle's follies!
EMERSON WINS—IN MOCKERY OF FINAL

IN just five minutes yesterday it became clear that 28-year-old Roy Emerson from Brisbane was going to become the third player since the war to win the men's singles at Wimbledon two years running.

In the first game, his opponent, 26-year-old Fred Stolle, from Sydney, led 40—15.

Emerson produced some great service returns and passing shots and Stolle served the first of six double faults he was to produce in the match, to lose the game.

Emerson was 15—40 down in the second, in which HE served a double —one of only four in the match.

But he soon rallied to take the game as Stolle's returns of service began to break down.

And there you have the whole lack-lustre affair in a nutshell.

Cruel

For a great majority of the time Emerson could return Stolle's service—the challenger achieved a very low percentage of first deliveries—and Stolle could never cope with Emerson's service.

The cold statistics bring this out cruelly. In fourteen service games Emerson lost only 16 points—and don't forget four of those were "gifts" in the form of double faults.

After that second game, Stolle only four times got to 30 when Emerson was serving.

Once more the return of service proved the most important of all ground shots, and the governing factor of what only charity can describe as a match.

As though that were not enough, Stolle seemed not only incapable of putting any of his volleys away but for long stretches of even getting them over the net and into court.

Fred Stolle groans as he sees another bad shot cost him a point in yesterday's final.

Uncertain

Half-way through the second set, as Stolle became more and more uncertain with his volleying touch. I found myself irreverently scribbling "Golly, the folly of Stolle's dolly volleys"!

I know this is harsh criticism but I cannot remember a final in which the loser played worse.

The whole thing lasted 67 minutes.

There have been quicker finals—Jack Kramer's 47-minute slaughter of Tom Brown in 1947, Lew Hoad's crushing of Ashley Cooper 10 years later. And, as recently as 1962, Rod Laver's rout of Martin Mulligan.

In none of these matches did the winner concede more than six games, whereas Emerson dropped 10 yesterday.

But in all those earlier matches it was the superlative play of the winner which remains in the mind.

Yesterday, alas, it was the utter fumbling incompetence of the loser which was paramount. A desperate shame, for you couldn't

hope to meet a nicer chap than Fred.

The law of diminishing returns seems to be working with a wicked vengeance on Stolle.

Flattered

This was his third successive losing final—he's the first man to have such ill-luck since Baron Gottfried von Cramm experienced it in 1935-6-7—and his scores are declining.

In 1963 he was beaten 9—7, 6—1, 6—4 by Chuck McKinley. Last year Emerson beat him 6—4, 12—10, 4—6, 6—3. And yesterday's 6—2, 6—4, 6—4 really flattered him.

For although there was only one service break in each of the second and third sets, there never seemed the remotest likelihood of him staging a come-back.

Emerson was always as sharp as a whip—once towards the end of the second set literally toying with his opponent.

While it was impossible to assess just how good he could have been—for you can't score a knock-out when you're shadow-boxing —it was a tribute to his concentration that he never allowed his own

game to be dragged down to the level of his opponent's.

Emerson summed it all up when he said afterwards: "I played quite well possibly as well as last year but Fred never got started."

Emerson confirmed he had been made an offer of 85,000 dollars—slightly over £30,000—by the professionals, but that he had turned them down.

As he said, he has been playing top-class amateur lawn tennis for some ten years, and he wasn't sure whether he could work as hard for two or three more years as a pro.

Stolle, as anyone who knows him could have predicted, made no excuses.

He said: "Emmo played too well, he had too many winners.

"I didn't serve well. The more I tried the worse I got. But after a few days I'll forget it.

"I'll be back next year so got. But after a few times lucky.

"It's a great thrill to get to the final at Wimbledon —but it would be a damn sight bigger one to win it."

I hope he achieves his ambition; he deserves it.

1966   Manuel Santana
beat Dennis Ralston
6–4 11–9 6–4

1967   John Newcombe
beat Wilhelm Bungert
6–3 6–1 6–1

Roy Emerson tried to equal Fred Perry's hat-trick of men's singles victories but a fall in his quarter-final match was almost certainly responsible for his exit from the Wimbledon Championship. As he had done throughout his career, Emerson chased a wide ball at great speed but the damp turf caused him to crash into the umpire's chair. He managed to complete the match but was beaten by the left-handed Australian Owen Davidson.

With Emerson out, the number four seed **Manuel Santana** accounted for Davidson, thus reaching his first Wimbledon final. The Santana–Davidson match was described as one of the most sporting ever played in the Championships – quite a tribute to both players considering it was a semi-final.

Joining Santana from the other half of the draw was Dennis Ralston. Six years previously he had set a record by becoming the youngest Wimbledon men's title holder at the age of 17 years 341 days when he won the doubles with Rafael Osuna.

Ralston, the number six seed, was a strong server and volleyer but his game was blunted by the superb artistry of Santana. The Spaniard produced his full repertoire of top spin and lob shots to win in three straight sets. Santana was fêted on his return to his country and he received the Gold Medal of Madrid, which was the city of his birth.

In 1967, the Championship started dramatically with Santana becoming the first holder of the men's singles title to be beaten in the first round. His conqueror was Charlie Pasarell, a Puerto Rican who was studying at the University of California. Pasarell, who took part in another record-breaking match in 1969, won 10–8 6–3 *(cont.)*

MANUEL THE MAGICAL MATADOR!

■ Santana, the championship trophy—and a great big smile.

Ann ends in tears and pain

By HARRISON EDWARDS

WIMBLEDON finished with tears for that great fighter, Ann Jones yesterday. But not tears of disappointment at losing yet another semi-final, but of pain.

She was hit on the side of the face by a full-blooded smash from Margaret Smith during a doubles semi-final which had to be held up several minutes while she received courtside attention.

The tears were not surprising for big Margaret has one of the heaviest wallops among women players.

Ann was partnering Virginia Wade against Miss Smith and Judy Tegart, but despite a 3-0 lead in the second set they were beaten 10-8 6-4.

The doubles semi-finals were also the end of the road for Alan Mills and Mark Cox. They were out-gunned by Australians Owen Davidson and Bill Bowrey and beaten 6-2, 6-4, 9-7.

MEN'S SINGLES—Final.
M. SANTANA (Spain) bt R RALSTON (U S) 6-4, 11-9, 6-4.

MEN'S DOUBLES—Semi-finals.
K. FLETCHER, J NEWCOMBE (Australia) bt C GRAEBNER, M RIESSEN (US) 6-3, 7-5, 5-1. W. BOWREY, O. DAVIDSON (Australia) bt M. COX, A MILLS (GB) 6-2, 6-4, 9-7.

WOMEN'S DOUBLES — Semi-finals.
M. Bueno (Brazil), N. Richey (US) bt K. Krantzcke, K. Melville (Australia), 6-2, 4-1. M. SMITH, J. TEGART (Australia) bt Mrs P E Jones, S Wade (GB) 11-9, 6-4.

MIXED DOUBLES — Semi-finals.
K. FLETCHER, M. SMITH (Australia) beat P. SIEGLE (Australia), A DERIE (France) 6-3, 2-5, R RALSTON, MRS L. KING (US) beat R McMILLAN, A VAN ZYL (SA) 6-3, 6-4.

By STEVE RICHARDS

THEY HAVE never seen anything quite like it before on the so formal Centre Court at Wimbledon.

When Spaniard Manuel Santana, the people's choice, had beaten American Dennis Ralston in straight sets in the men's singles final yesterday, he bowed and kissed the hand of Princess Marina as he received the trophy that makes him world champion in the amateur game.

It was the gesture of a successful matador.

And this indeed had been a final of a tennis artist resisting the power and rushes of a young "bull" before emerging as the master and the most popular men's winner for years at the All-England championships.

Santana is only the third champion from Europe since the war and the first since Drobny took the title against Rosewall 11 years ago.

Ralston, rightly angry with himself at the end, produced a fair share of the scintillating tennis that at times lifted the final way above many of its predecessors.

BRANDS OF FAILURE

But he knew that although his service had often been frighteningly powerful and accurate, he had also served on too many other occasions like a man with a strapped-up arm.

Nine double faults in 20 service games were the brands of failure that Ralston carried on the three rackets he used in a vain fight against wily Santana and his own rumbling temperament.

That temperament, I felt, was his final undoing. He had lost the first set of skilful and exciting tennis after Santana had broken through in the ninth game with a typical forehand passing shot.

The American No. 1 knew he just had to win the second set. With considerable control and some delightful shots, he deservedly took a 4-1 lead.

He was threatening to break through again to 5-3. Santana had just hurt his back over-stretching in failing to reach a Ralston lob

Ralston hit two powerful service returns — a shot that often surprised the Spaniard in this match—and both were inches the wrong side of the line .. inches that enabled Santana to level at 4-4 and get back into the set

DOUBLE FAULTS

Ralston was never to get another chance. In the 19th, at 9-9, game the American served his fifth and sixth double faults and, as Santana broke through to 10-9, angrily threw down his racket and changed it for a new one.

Santana took this 51-minute second set with a service game to love, finishing with an ace. And Ralston changed his racket once more.

Santana shrewdly dictated the final set, broke service in the third game, continued that stream of passing shots that only added to Ralston's troubles and won the title with a forehand volley.

MRS RAND WILL HAVE BUSY DAY

By PETER CORRIGAN

ANN SMITH set herself up for a sizzling half-mile in today's Women's AAA's championships at the White City by winning her heat last night in a championship-best time of 2min. 6.6sec.

The Mitcham red-head powered home nearly 3.2sec. ahead of the field to clip almost a second off her winning time of last year.

Then she pulled out of the mile heats to save her strength for today's 880 final.

Mrs. Rand won the first title of the meeting by beating Pat Pryce in the 100-metres hurdles. Then Mary went to the long jump pit to register a qualifying leap of 19ft. 5in.

Today she bids to win the long jump, high jump and 80-metres hurdles.

Last night's proceedings were watched by 73 spectators. This is not an official figure: someone might have moved while I was counting.

SEXTON 'YES' TO ARSENAL

ARSENAL appointed Dave Sexton as chief coach yesterday after he had rejected a Fulham bid to keep him at Craven Cottage, *writes* PETER CORRIGAN.

Sexton, coach to Fulham since last February, joins Arsenal's new manager Bertie Mee on July 20.

He said last night: "Fulham made me an excellent offer to stay but my move has nothing to do with money.

"I am sick at leaving Fulham, where I have been very happy, but the challenge of helping Arsenal regain their former glory is too much to resist."

Spurs, Arsenal, Sheffield Wednesday and Wolves will play in the Football League Cup for the first time next season. Only clubs not in the competition now are Liverpool and Everton.

Cardiff have turned down the transfer request of skipper and wing-half Gareth Williams.

NEWCOMBE SPRINTS TO TITLE IN 71 MINUTES

John Newcombe shows his volleying power precision against Germany's Wilhelm Bungert, qualities which helped him bring off Australia's ninth men's singles triumph in 12 years.
(Pictures by Srdja Djukanovic.)

Wilhelm Bungert waging his unsuccessful battle against John Newcomt.

THE Lawn Tennis Championships maintained its refusal to permit a non-seeded singles champion. The Australian John Newcombe, took the major men's title this afternoon when he beat the German, Wilhelm Bungert 6-3, 6-1, 6-1.

Australian dominance was accordingly maintained. Newcombe, 23, and a good, solid player by any standard 2-6 8-6.

It was a year of upsets in the men's tournament and, at the semi-finals, only one seed was left. **John Newcombe** (3) was joined by three Europeans – Wilhelm Bungert (West Germany), Nikki Pilic (Yugoslavia) and Britain's Roger Taylor. Bungert, who had earlier beaten Bobby Wilson, ended the Wimbledon crowd's hopes of a home finalist in a two-hour struggle with Taylor. The Yorkshireman led by two sets to one but eventually lost 6-4 6-8 2-6 6-4 6-4.

The West German became the fifth unseeded player to reach a Wimbledon men's singles final but he was no match for Newcombe. In his semi-final the Australian had tamed the big serve of Pilic and in the final he was able to dominate Bungert and lost only five games.

Newcombe's victory meant that in the twelve years up to 1967 the Wimbledon men's singles title had gone to Australians nine times.

There was to be a tenth win, in 1968, but before the Championship began a very important decision was made.

became the ninth Australian singles champion in 12 years.

Beginning with Norman Brookes, who was the first overseas man to win in 1907, Newcombe is 10th in the line of distinguished Australian victors. Whether he will be a distinguished champion depends on what he does in the future for there was little, alas, that was memorable about his victory this afternoon.

This was hardly Newcombe's fault. He put forward a game of rugged excellence. His sterling qualities merited stronger opposition but, as it was, those enthusiasts who queued overnight had scant reward for their weary vigil.

TENSE FINAL
Shackling influence

By and large Wimbledon finals do not produce great lawn tennis. The occasion is too big and the atmosphere of the occasion too rich for most players to unwind from the shackling influence of nervous tension.

On Bungert's part, today was no exception. The fine genius of this German was blunted and he gave but poor indication of what he can do. While Newcombe's virtues shone brightly Bungert's negative ones were more apparent.

When it was all over, Bungert having stayed on court for only 71 minutes and won but five games in all, one could think only in terms of negation. Was there ever a briefer final than this, was there one of such poor combat value or one where the vanquished got fewer games?

In 1962, when Rod Laver swiftly dispatched the unseeded Martin Mulligan, the loser then got five games only. Five games was the tally achieved by Ashley Cooper in 1957, though the main cause of that debacle was Hoad's tremendous skill rather than the poverty of the loser.

BRIEFEST MATCH
Injured loser

Actually, the briefest final of all time so far as the number of games assesses brevity, was Fred Perry's 1936 win against the last German to be in the final. Gottfried von Cramm. Von Cramm was then an injured man.

It is an odd quirk of fate for Newcombe that the actual match by which he won his first major singles title should have been his easiest in the tournament. Even the Frenchman, Francois Jauffret, who is essentially a hard-court man, gave him more trouble in the opening round last week than Bungert contrived today.

Bungert initially promised to give Newcombe a contest worthy of Wimbledon's august tradition. Despite two double faults in his opening service game, Bungert, after three deuces, was standing well at one game-all and in the ascendancy when in the next game he broke the Australian's delivery to love.

That was 2-1 to Bungert with his own service to come. There was a stir of expectation for the promise of his delicate rapier finding chinks in the weightier Australian armour.

In fact, Bungert came three times within a point of leading 3-1. It was, though, a game of German muddle, of shots that went awry, of ambitions unfulfilled and included three double faults.

It turned out to be a symbol of all the German frustration that marked the rest of the match. Occasionally Bungert revealed his virtuosity, a forehand hit flat that searingly found its target at tremendous speed.

But how occasionally it was! The net or the area beyond the lines increasingly became the destination of a German-struck ball and the fact of Bungert leading 40-15 on his own delivery was the hallmark of a game he was bound to lose.

CHANCES MISSED
Sorry record

Bungert had two points for the eighth game of the first set and lost it. He had two points for the third game of the second set and lost it. He had three points to break Newcombe's service in the fourth and did not do it.

The German had one point for the fifth game of the second set and did not clinch it. He had . . . there is really no object in recording this sorry catalogue of German hopes that were unfulfilled. Poor Bungert, his talents deserved a better fate. As for Newcombe he deserved a chance to show his strong game under pressure.

Bungert, of course, had had a hard championship. He had a five-setter against Frank Froehling, five sets against Bobby Wilson, five sets against Thomas Koch and five also against Roger Taylor, all of which were poor preparation for a final by one who stands well short of the most robust of players.

1967 **The Daily Telegraph**

10 | 'Open' Wimbledon

1968–75

The Lawn Tennis Association took a bold step and made all tournaments 'open'; this included the Wimbledon Championships from 1968. However, this did not stop off-court squabbles and, with several top players banned in 1972, the following year saw a massive boycott by members of the Association of Tennis Professionals.

OPEN TENNIS QUOTE by MAURICE SINCLAIR, secretary of the West of England event: For a long time the expense of getting amateurs has been too high. Now we will be able to pay players on merit. We're delighted.

All the way with the LTA

Brave show of hands—and it's all but unanimous

1968   Daily Mail

In December 1967 the Lawn Tennis Association decided at their annual meeting to abolish the distinction between amateur and professional players. For six years the LTA had pressed the International Lawn Tennis Federation to accept this important change in the rules, without any success. Now, by taking this decision, they were in defiance of the world's governing body. The ILTF could have expelled the LTA but, at a meeting in Paris some three months later, the international federation accepted that each member nation could make its own rules about amateurs.

So, on 22 April 1968, the British Hard Court Championships at Bournemouth became the first 'open' tennis tournament, and two months later the great professional players returned to Wimbledon.

The LTA had witnessed the response from the public when Jack Kramer had arranged for an eight-man professional tournament at Wimbledon a month after the 1967 Championship. It was staged to coincide with the introduction of BBC-TV colour transmissions, and the final between Rod Laver and Ken Rosewall was watched by a capacity crowd.

1968 Rod Laver
beat Tony Roche
6–3 6–4 6–2

1969 Rod Laver
beat John Newcombe
6–4 5–7 6–4 6–4

Rod Laver returned to the Wimbledon lawn tennis Championship and showed that he had lost none of his brilliant strokeplay or competitive edge during his five-year absence. He had turned professional after winning the men's singles title in 1961 and 1962 and his victories in the first two open tournaments meant that he did not suffer a singles defeat in four Wimbledons. Many tennis followers were left wondering whether it would have been possible for Laver to have won nine consecutive Championships between 1961 and 1969 if he had stayed amateur.

The professionals' return to Wimbledon was greeted by appalling weather and several big names were knocked out in early rounds. Double champion Lew Hoad – whose professional career had been brief because of persistent back trouble – and Pancho Gonzales were beaten in the third round. Ken Rosewall, seeded to reach the final, was surprisingly eliminated in the fourth round by fellow-countryman Tony Roche.

Roche, the number fifteen seed, went on to meet Laver in the second left-handers final (the Neale Fraser–Rod Laver having been the first in 1960) but was beaten in just over an hour. There was some consolation in his victory in the men's doubles with John Newcombe – the second of five Wimbledon doubles titles the popular Australian duo shared between 1965 and 1974.

In the second round of the 1969 men's singles Championship it looked as though Laver would be beaten when he trailed by two sets to the Indian, Permjit Lall. However, he quickly regained his concentration and won the next three sets, only losing three games.

Laver's semi-final with Arthur

LONDON, Friday. — Australian Rod Laver was in relentless form to win the first Wimbledon Open men's singles championship here today.

The red-headed left-hander proved himself the world's top tennis player by defeating fellow Australian professional Tony Roche 6-3, 6-4, 6-2 in 60 minutes.

It was Laver's third Wimbledon singles title.

He won the first of two as an amateur in 1961 and 1962, and was runner-up in 1959 and 1960.

Roche played great tennis, but Laver was in such dominant form that no player in the world could have troubled him today.

Laver took just an hour's playing time to score one of the most decisive wins in Wimbledon history.

He took his time in settling down and did not win a point on Roche's service until the eighth game of the first set.

From then on the result was never in doubt.

Laver's serving, volleying and general courtcraft grew better all the time and there was just nothing Roche could do about it.

Roche's chances at the start of this historic first open Wimbledon were rated lowly by the seeding committee—he gained only 15th place among the 16 elite.

His previous best effort here was to reach the last eight in 1966.

Laver and Roche began in the final in bright sunshine before a huge crowd.

Laver won his opening service game to 30, although the loudest burst of applause was for a fine forehand by Roche past Laver's backhand to pull him up to 30-30.

Roche, serving brilliantly, won the next game to love to make it 1-1.

At 2-2 Laver had still to win a point on Roche's service, which he was over-hitting repeatedly.

Roche was looking the more likely to break through.

He had a point to do it after blasting a winning return off a Laver volley, but

Laver won the next three points.

That made it 3-2 to Laver with Roche to serve.

Roche won his third service game again to love.

ERRORS

Laver was not serving at his top and in the seventh game committed his second double fault, but it was the only point he lost in the game.

He won his first point from Roche's serve in the eight game—and promptly broke through as Roche began to make errors.

That was at a vital stage, for Laver led 5-3 and suddenly was serving for the set.

He won the game with difficulty, Roche having three chances to break back before putting two successive returns of service out of court.

The first set took 20 minutes. Laver won 6-3.

Roche was battling all the way and was clearly the crowd's favourite.

The two left-handers were treating the crowd to a fine, sharp display of serve-volley tennis.

The first four games of the second set went with service.

Laver's serve was becoming more accurate and he scored two aces in the fourth game.

Laver levelled at 3-3 with two beautiful drop volleys that stranded Roche on the baseline.

But he still took the Queenslander to deuce.

Laver scored the vital breakthrough in the following game with two fine passing shots and a netted volley by Roche.

Laver held his serve in the eighth game to lead 5-3, Roche taking his only point on a double fault.

Laver then served out the set. He was covering the net brilliantly and appeared to be coolly marching towards his third Wimbledon crown.

Roche was serving well, but Laver's experience was blunting his rival's enthusiasm.

Like the first set, the second lasted 20 minutes.

Some of the spark appeared to have gone from Roche's play as the third set started and he dropped his opening service game. Laver passing him on the backhand as he ran to the net.

FIGHTING

Laver held service easily for 2-0.

He was beating his younger rival in every department. Try as he might, Roche could not crack Laver's service, although he again, took him to deuce and the fourth game.

Still fighting, Roche finally made the scoreboard in the fifth game when he won his service after two deuces.

He won a round of applause from the crowd that contained a measure of sympathy for having met "The Rocket" at his most fiery.

Laver, his serve seeming to gain in power as the match progressed, made it 5-1 and the end was near.

Laver broke through again in the third game of the third set and the final looked as good as over.

Roche made it 5-2, but Laver did not need to win this one.

He won the eighth and last game with three typically unplayable volleys.

Roche had been simply outclassed.

Ashe was a spectacular match: both players hit the ball with ferocious, controlled power right from the first rally. Although beaten, Ashe, the 1968 American champion, was enormously promising.

Newcombe, the last amateur champion in 1967, qualified from the other half of the draw and, although he won the second set, there was no stopping 'The Rocket' in 1969. Laver's fourth Wimbledon title helped him to his second Grand Slam (American, Australian, French and Wimbledon men's singles titles in the same year).

The year may have belonged to Laver but the match of the Championship was a first-round clash between Gonzales, the number twelve seed, and Charlie Pasarell. Pasarell had set a record two years earlier when beating Manuel Santana – the 1966 champion – in the first round. This time he was locked in a marathon duel with the 41-year-old Gonzales that lasted more than five hours over two days.

At the end of the first day Pasarell was leading 24–22 6–1 but the following afternoon the moody and magnificent Gonzales levelled the score by taking the next two sets 16–14 6–3. In the final set Pasarell failed to capitalize on seven match points and the incredible Gonzales – conceding a 15-year age advantage – broke his opponent's serve, won his own to love and the set 11–9. He progressed to the third round before losing to Ashe.

LAVER LAPS IT UP

Rod the Robot clicks another £3,000

By MAURICE SMITH

ROD LAVER, Wimbledon champion for the fourth time, called it "my hardest final ever." But it took this tennis robot only a little over two hours to pick up £3,000—and grind John Newcombe into the turf of the Centre Court.

It was Laver's second successive Wimbledon triumph, and it was as unflurried and unhurried as the experts had predicted. Yet Rod paid Newcombe the compliment of saying: "John played well. The way he started setting up lobs really had me worried. I knew then I had to pull out my best."

Yes, it was smash-and-cash Laver all right. And so with the earlier triumph of Britain's Ann Jones, Wimbledon 1969 goes down as the first double of two left-handers.

Laver's southpaw punching from the baseline finally beat Newcombe to his knees, had him gasping and grasping, looking despairingly to the heavens when his own "winners" somehow came flashing back.

Newcombe, himself champion two years ago, set out to show this packed Centre court that his own triumph was not simply because Laver wasn't there.

"After I'd beaten him at Queen's Club a fortnight ago, I thought I had a real chance now of doing so again and proving my point," he told me.

But only at one stage yesterday did Newcombe look like making that point.

He pulled Laver back by taking the second set 7-5 after Rod had run out with the first on 6-4.

At the third game in the third set it was still anyone's match. And then Laver, the man with so few flaws, suddenly developed one.

ROD LAVER

Extra flair

On his own service in the fourth game, he double-faulted to let Newcombe go 3-1 in front. The younger man kept his service for the next game to lead 4-1.

If Newcombe had Laver's flair and variety of shots, I believe he could have forged victory and the extra £1,500 victory meant. But Newcombe the plodder is essentially predictable.

He fell back on his old strategy of baseline duelling, and the opportunity was gone.

Newcombe himself double-faulted to end the seventh game and give Laver the break-back. And the champ broke service for the second successive time in the ninth.

That was that. Another 6-4 set won by Laver, but it might so easily have turned out a 6-3 win for Newcombe.

From then on it was formality. The slow, relentless execution of a gallant fighter who could never lift his own game sufficiently to suggest any other ending.

Said Laver: "It was when I broke back at 4-2 in the third set, I knew everything would be all right.

"I managed to slow the game down from then on as I wanted to."

Warmed up

Laver said his troublesome left elbow stood up to the task without trouble.

"Fred Stolle and John MacDonald put me through a hard 30-minute warm-up before the final," he grinned.

Said Newcombe: "I played as well as I ever have done. My big chance, I thought, was to out-think him, not out-match him. You know, I think a lot more than people often say I do.

"When I led 4-1 in that third set I knew Rod would be pulling out all the stops I tried for extra, but nothing came."

That, to me, is the self-imposed judgment of a runner-up.

1970   John Newcombe
beat Ken Rosewall
5–7 6–3 6–2 3–6 6–1

1971   John Newcombe
beat Stan Smith
6–3 5–7 2–6 6–4 6–4

Britain's number one, Roger Taylor, caused one of the biggest upsets in the history of the Wimbledon men's singles event when he knocked out Rod Laver in the last sixteen of the 1970 Championship. Laver was seeking his third consecutive victory and was progressing so well that Taylor was ranked a 50–1 outsider. 'The Rocket' won the first set 6–4 but, as the temperature soared towards 90 degrees, Taylor played the game of his life to win the next three sets 6–4 6–2 6–1.

Like a true champion Laver acknowledged the Yorkshireman's performance and said after the match: 'Roger well deserved his victory. He hit the ball so well and I just couldn't put away my volleys.' Laver had reached the summit of his achievement in 1969 and the following year did not win a major tournament.

Taylor, seeded sixteen, beat Clark Graebner – a hard-serving American – in the quarter-finals but his run was brought to an end in the semi-finals by the ageless Ken Rosewall 6–3 4–6 6–3 6–3.

In the final Rosewall met **John Newcombe**, the number two seed. At two sets each and one game all it looked likely that Rosewall could at last win a Wimbledon singles final but Newcombe had other ideas. He took the next five games, and the Championship for a second time.

Laver was again the top seed in 1971 with the champion Newcombe at number two. Newcombe reached his place in the final while Laver lost in the quarter-finals to the American Tom Gorman.

Newcombe went on to his third singles title by beating the number four seed Stan Smith. It was a tough five-set match and the 6 ft 4 in. Smith, a serving officer in the American army, looked a likely winner when leading by two sets to one.

NEWCOMBE TOO STRONG

ROSEWALL GREAT IN WIMBLEDON THRILLER

THE Wimbledon champion's crown sits once more on the handsome head of 26-year-old Australian John Newcombe, writes **KEN MONTGOMERY.**

But the sympathy of everyone must go out to 35-year-old Ken Rosewall, who trudged off the Centre Court beaten 5—7, 6—3, 6—2, 3—6, 6—1.

"Muscles," as that little master is nicknamed, can now order the engraving on his tombstone . . . "The greatest player never to win Wimbledon."

LEG-WEARY

Now it seems certain that he never will.

The fifth seed lost more than just his third Wimbledon final. He lost his life's ambition.

Yet Rosewall lost no face in a magnificent match of fluctuating fortunes.

A memorable two hours and forty-three minutes, the first five-set final since Ted Schroeder beat Jaroslav Drobny in 1949.

Through it all we saw what we suspected — the Rosewall spirit and skills are still superbly strong, but the legs, alas, are weakening.

Rosewall, beaten in 1954 by Drobny, and in 1956 by Lew Hoad, received an ova-tion normally reserved for victors as he stepped up to receive the runner-up award from Princess Margaret.

An emotional crowd seemed determined to console the little man they had been willing on to the win that would have put the final touch to a remarkable career.

But the taller, stronger and more athletic No. 2 seed lasted the pace just that bit better.

GALLOP

Rosewall got off to a start everyone hoped for.

He took the first set after forty-five minutes when he came from 40-love down on Newcombe's service in the eleventh game to break, then hold his service after three deuces.

The second set was settled by one service break. Newcombe getting it in the sixth game when Rosewall served his fifth double fault of the match.

Newcombe took the second set 6—3 in thirty-six minutes and galloped through the third in twenty-seven minutes.

As the scoreboard flashed out Newcombe ahead two sets to one, 14,000 fanatically pro-Rosewall fans were resigned to seeing their little hero demolished.

NERVOUS

But no. Although he dropped service in the opening game of the fourth set, the little man was not yet mastered.

Newcombe held his service game to lead 2—0, then it went 2—1, 3—1 and at that point the championship almost turned.

"Muscles" hit a monumental purple patch, winning twelve consecutive points to go 4—3 up.

When he broke service in the eighth game, the match was alive with a vengeance.

Rosewall served out to take the fourth set 6—3 in twenty-six minutes and Newcombe showed signs of nervousness when he strode off court in the middle of the ninth game to change his racket.

It seemed to have the desired effect, for the final set took only twenty-five minutes.

Rosewall's service was broken in the fourth game and in the sixth, but he fought on and Newcombe had to battle from 30-40 to take the title on his second championship point.

The result was just about right. Newcombe deserved his second Wimbledon win in four years.

When asked afterwards if he felt sorry for the three times loser the reply was old fashioned Aussie: "A little sorry, but not overly sympathetic. Hell, I wanted to win it myself."

Rosewall announced it was too early to say whether he would play Wimbledon again but said the chances were likely.

"Of the three finals I have played in I think Lew Hoad was the most fluent," he added. "He was a dangerous player."

RESULTS

WOMEN'S DOUBLES FINAL.—R. CASALS and Mrs. L. W. KING (U S) bt F. Durr (Fr) and S. V. Wade (G B) 6—1, 6—3.

Mixed doubles semi-final.— NASTASE (Ru) and Miss R. CASALS (U S) bt F. D. McMillan (S A) and Mrs. D. E. Dalton (A) 6—7, 6—1, 6—4. FINAL.— NASTASE (Ru) and MISS R. CASALS (U S) bt A. Metreveli and Miss O. Morozova (U S S R) 6—3, 4—6, 5—7.

VETERANS' DOUBLES FINAL.— J. Drobny (G B) and R. L. Riggs (U S) bt G. R. MacCall (U S) and D. P. Segura (Ec) 6—1, 6—1. .

MEN'S PLATE FINAL.—R. R. MAUD (S A) bt R. R. Barth (U S) 6—4, 6—3.

WOMEN'S PLATE FINAL.—E. F. Goolagong (A) bt L. Liem (Inds) 6—1, 6—1.

JUNIOR BOYS' SINGLES. — B. Bertram (S A) bt F. Carbert (G).

JUNIOR GIRLS' SINGLES FINAL.—S. Walsh (U S) bt M. Kroshina (U S S R) 6—4, 6—4.

End of memorable era in history of Wimbledon

By Rex Bellamy
Tennis Correspondent

The lively strains of "Waltzing Matilda" rang through the plush sobriety of Grosvenor House as Evonne Goolagong and John Newcombe, the Wimbledon champions, opened the Lawn Tennis Association ball on Saturday evening. That was a good moment for Australia after all the heat and dust of battle. Newcombe precariously defied the challenge of young America; in the women's event, Australia had the final to themselves for the first time.

As Newcombe and Miss Goolagong circled the floor, we reflected that here was the end of a memorable era. Rod Laver, Ken Rosewall, Margaret Court and Billie Jean King—who between them graced a Wimbledon singles final 20 times—were all beaten in straight sets. Three Americans, Stan Smith, Cliff Richey and Tom Gorman, pushed their names forwards for future reference. Richey and Rosewall gave us the finest match of the championships Smith and Miss Goolagong took the lead in the Pepsi Grand Prix series.

The tournament was lucky with the weather, ended with two days of smouldering heat and humidity, provided a consistently appetizing diet of matches richly flavoured with skill and character, and attracted almost 300,000 people—an advance of more than 15,000 on 1970. The courts were soft and worn, so that the players most in need of a true bounce were most in difficulty. The experiment with the tie-break was almost irrelevant. In the singles, it applied in roughly 6.4 per cent of the men's sets and 2.3 of the women's. But it abbreviated the monotony of some service-and-volley exchanges and it added a little dramatic garnish to the dish. The only improvement suggested is that, in the variable conditions of the outdoor game, players should change ends fter four points rather than six.

Three times in five years Newcombe has been champion. He has never been top seed ("I think it might be bad luck") and he has never been champion of France or his native Australia. He still has new peaks to climb: if the game's administrators allow him the chance. But he reigns supreme—the strongest card in a temporarily weak hand held by World Championship Tennis.

Newcombe needed all his strength, skill and competitive experience to beat Smith 6—3, 5—7, 2—6, 6—4, 6—4, in a final that lasted two hours and 50 minutes. At first Newcombe was firmly if marginally in charge ("Stan was nervous and a little tentative"). One service break gave Newcombe the first set. Conceding only nine points in his first nine service games, he had four break points in the second set before Smith broke through for the set.

In the third set Newcombe led 2—0 but then lost seven successive games. "At the beginning of the fourth I had a small feeling of being a loser", said Newcombe. "I was a bit shaken up. I felt I had gone, mentally. Stan had picked up his game extremely well and I started to drop my shots shorter. One gets a little tentative. You've got to keep the ball deep against Stan."

In the fourth set Newcombe soon regained his composure. He did not lose a point in his five service games until he led 5—4 and 40-love. "It was Stan's first final", said Newcombe later. "Maybe he was wondering about dancing with Evonne tonight—he's almost two feet taller—and what he was going to say in his speech." In the fifth set Newcombe achieved a break to 3—2 when Smith played a loose game that included two successive double-faults. In the next game Newcombe was 30—40 down but saved himself with a service and a forehand volley After that, the last few pieces of this vivid jigsaw were quickly put together.

Newcombe: retained the men's singles trophy at Wimbledon.

The final was an exemplary display of grass court tennis stripped to its essentials. It would be unreasonable to expect charm and the subtlety of the chessboard from a men's final at Wimbledon. The prerequisites are strength and speed, fitness and reflexes, a thrilling violence, and sufficient imagination and touch to break up the pattern of lightning shots. Newcombe and Smith supplied all this with admirable skill and concentration. Yet at times it was so quiet that you could hear a bird singing. The power of it all was sometimes insufficiently spiced by variety.

At first we admired Newcombe's wonderful forehand volley, his delicate touch on the short angles ("I tried to vary it all the time") and reflected that this fine player is still improving. The more stereotyped Smith kept getting caught by dipping cross-court shots that buzzed past his ankles. Newcombe's service returns were better, especially on the backhand. He was the more flexible. Smith could never be sure what would happen next, except that it would be quick and awkward. But giving Smith lobs was like feeding buns to an elephant.

As the second set progressed, Smith showed that he was learning all the time—and learning fast. Suddenly, he knew what to do. He was no longer tentative. He was moving better and bending more freely. His whole game moved up a gear. By contrast, Newcombe's forehand began to look vulnerable and his touch on the short game lost its splendid certainty.

During that masterful run of seven games, Smith looked as if he had been winning finals on the centre court all his life. Every aspect of his game matured as he took a lead of two sets to one. Newcombe blinked, felt the chill of adversity upon him—and doggedly, sensibly, skilfully worked his way out of trouble and back to his best form like the great competitor he is. Even so, he had to concentrate 100 per cent. Smith ruthlessly punished anything loose. Smith's own precision was threatened by similar apprehensions.

The crux came when Smith served those two double-faults in the fifth set. He stands 6ft 4in and stretches upwards to the fullest extent, plus the length of arm and racket: yet he can still double-fault. It is like trying to kill an ant with a sledgehammer—and missing. But Smith, of course, had to gamble with his second service. He gambled and he lost. But he had shown us that he is a champion of the future.

1971   The Times

There were several nicknames to describe Rosewall (including 'Muscles', 'Iron Man', 'Little Master') and once again he featured in the 1971 Championship. His quarter-final with Cliff Richey was 'the match of the year' although, at one stage, it looked like being a straightforward win for the American. Richey led 8–6 7–5 4–2 but, using a variety of drop shots and lobs, Rosewall wore down his opponent and won the last three sets 6–4 9–7 7–5. The game had, however, taken a lot out of him and he lost easily to Newcombe in the semi-finals.

The tie-break system was introduced in 1971. At first, the Championship committee decided that the tie-break should commence at eight games each. The set would be won by the first player to score seven points. At six points all a two-point gap would be needed.

1972 Stan Smith
beat Ilie Nastase
4–6 6–3 6–3 4–6 7–5

The 1971 Championship ended on a sour note with Lamar Hunt, son of a Texan oil millionaire, stating that many of the world's top players would not take part in future tournaments unless appearance money was paid. Thirty-two of the players were contracted to Hunt's World Championship Tennis group and were to be allowed to keep all the prize money from tournaments. Hunt suggested that Wimbledon should pay £20,000 to the WCT for the services of their men.

Disputes about fees and the role in which the WCT should serve tournaments led to the International Lawn Tennis Federation placing a ban on all WCT players from 1 January 1972. A compromise was reached in time for the players to take part in the American championships in September but, unfortunately, not soon enough to allow Rod Laver, John Newcombe, Arthur Ashe and Ken Rosewall to enter for Wimbledon. It was unfortunate for Newcombe who was chasing a third consecutive men's singles title and, although he made a private application, the committee had to refuse it and abide by the ILTF ruling.

In the absence of the 'Big Four', **Stan Smith** and the Roumanian Ilie Nastase were seeded one and two respectively. The players reached their nominated places; it is unlikely that there will ever be a more contrasting couple of contenders. Smith, the blond, well-mannered, clean-cut American contrasted with Nastase, the dark, unpredictable genius of tennis whose temperament could explode at any time.

Rain forced a twenty-four-hour postponement of the eagerly awaited final and it became the first ever to be staged on a Sunday. The delay had no effect on the players and they proceeded to enthral the centre court crowd with one of the best finals in Wimbledon's illustrious history.

Stan's armoury wins it

WIMBLEDON opened its gates on a Sunday, and our eyes to a new tennis world, when Corporal Stanley Roger Smith of the United States Army defeated Ilie Nastase, of Rumania, 4–6, 6-3, 6-3, 4-6, 7-5 in a match which can be argued by old men as the greatest final ever played.

For two hours 43 minutes, these two, who differ in almost everything but the colour of their skin, shared the same torments of ambition and the same fears.

They suffered . . . how they must have suffered, as classic shots, worthy of winners, came back again and yet again, making almost impossible demands on mind and muscle. You couldn't tell where genius ended and instinct took over.

Until this match, Smith, a blond giant of 6ft. 4in., was grossly under-rated. Although he won Forest Hills, the Grand Prix, and the Davis Cup for his country (against Nastase) a year ago, he has been wrongly classified as a serve-and-volleyer.

Most of these championships he has done little to discourage this view, but yesterday, against a world master of stroke play, Smith proved he can produce every shot in the book.

Hundred-mile-an-hour screamers, which brought up dust from the crumbling court, were broken up with gentle stop-volleys when the ball seemed to float over the net like a giant snowflake. Early on these were morale-destroying; later Nastase stared at them as if they were knives ripping out the heart of his game.

Little bit of luck

Describing the climax, Smith later told me: 'In the end it was 80 per cent guts and the rest just a little bit of luck.'

By LAURIE PIGNON

● The mark of a champion as Stan Smith shows he has the shots with an almost impossible back-hand return.

Nastase did not lack courage either. If he had there would not have been a match which had the crowd standing and cheering as if they had just seen a Briton winning Olympic gold.

But Nastase did have troubles . . . lots of troubles.

Strange nightmares were going on in the windmills of his mind.

When he was on the rack he kept changing rackets, complaining in any one of his half-dozen languages that the stringing wasn't to his liking. At one time, he had so many rackets in use that he looked in need of a caddie.

The prologue to thrills to come was the fifth game, when Smith had his first taste of pressure, when Nastase had three break points and was only able to win the game at his fourth chance.

There were doubts that Nastase's temperament was strong enough to stand up to the demands of a Wimbledon final. These, temporarily, seemed justified when the atmosphere began biting into his nerve as early as the seventh game.

In the ninth game, in which Smith had double-faulted for a second time, Nastase, aided by some bad volleying by Smith, got the first service break at his sixth game point.

The second set had a surprise beginning when the first two games went against service. There were three other service breaks, with Nastase losing his twice more.

At set-all an hour had passed, and there was nothing in the match except a sneaking inner-feeling that somehow Smith would win.

Nastase won the first eight points of the third set, and then, winning only one more game, seemed to blow.

Seeing his chance running away from him like a car without brakes, the Rumanian pulled himself and his game together.

In the fourth set, he was superb and gained the single break in the ninth game.

The test for Smith came in the fifth game of the fifth set, which went to seven deuces before he was able to hold his service with a stop volley that seemed to melt into the ground.

The Rumanian, desperately snatching at half chances, saved two match points in the 10th game, and one in the 12th.

At the fourth, Smith, under pressure, put up a short lob which was awkwardly placed over Nastase's backhand shoulder.

He made the shot which he had done successfully a dozen times before. But now, when he needed it most, it folded on him and the ball fell into the net.

It was like a curtain falling at the end of a great opera. . . .

Stan Smith. He won a magnificent five-set final against Ilie Nastase in 1972

1973 Jan Kodes
beat Alex Metreveli
6–1 9–8 6–3

With one dispute settled another started before the 1973 Championship when the International Lawn Tennis Federation suspended Nikki Pilic for failing to play in a Yugoslavian Davis Cup match. As a result, the Association of Tennis Professionals requested that its members withdraw from the Wimbledon Championships and seventy-nine players did – including thirteen seeds. Two notable exceptions were last year's runner-up Ilie Nastase and Britain's Roger Taylor.

Nastase, the 1972 American champion, was a hot favourite at Wimbledon but was beaten in the fourth round by Alex 'Sandy' Mayer in four sets. Mayer reached the semi-finals – having accounted for a 20-year-old Jimmy Connors on the way – but was beaten by the Russian Alex Metreveli.

Taylor, the number three seed, reached his third Wimbledon semi-final but only after a tremendous five-set match against 17-year-old Bjorn Borg. The Swede already needed police escorts to protect him from the teenage girls.

Taylor's opponent in the semi-final was the number two seed **Jan Kodes**. It was a see-saw struggle and, with the score at 9–8 7–9 7–5 4–6 5–4 in Taylor's favour

the match was halted because of rain. As it was just after twenty past seven in the evening Princess Alexandra and some of the 14,000-strong crowd had left the centre court thinking there would be no more play. However, the two players came back on court just before eight o'clock and the stoppage seemed to affect Taylor more than the Czechoslovakian who won the next three games and the match.

In the final Kodes beat Metreveli in straight sets. Nastase was rewarded for defying the ATP's request by winning the men's doubles with the up-and-coming Connors.

3am news: Stars say final 'no' to Wimbledon

By LAURIE PIGNON

THE world's top tennis stars said a final 'no' to Wimbledon at 3 a.m. this morning after a 4½ hour meeting in an hotel bedroom.

Cliff Drysdale, president of the Association of Tennis Professionals, told reporters the players' board had decided by six votes to two to boycott the tournament.

Friday June 22, 1973 Daily Mail

Jan Kodes and Alex Metreveli. Still friends – winner Kodes (on the left) and Metreveli were pictured in the Sunday People *after the 1973 Wimbledon men's singles final*

Curtains, comrade

PETER CORRIGAN

IT WAS Wimbledon's longest day, the highest hurdle to clear in her determination to carry on regardless of deprivation and she welcomed Jan Kodes, Czechoslovakian, intense and efficient, to an embrace no less outwardly rapturous than that which has enfolded a long list of colourful and brilliant men's champions.

The sincerity of the Kodes reception must not be doubted but in the match leading up to it one could be forgiven a feeling that we were there to await a victor, not accompany him through the trial.

There was always a chance that Kodes and his final opponent Alex Metreveli, of the USSR, would have produced a contest to match the occasion or that one or the other would have gathered enough sympathy to provide the crowd with a favourite.

But no, it was an average game of tennis, played honestly without emotion, which drew nothing from its presence in the sport's greatest arena and which gave nothing to an audience resigned to endurance rather than enjoyment.

It was a mystery trip on an Eastern Europe express and points of interest on the way were politely applauded.

The peak of Metreveli's performance was to reach set-point on Kodes's service at 5—4 in the second set. He returned the service, backhanded, low into the net and dropped to put his face to the grass, giving us a fleeting moment of emotion and a realisation that their hearts were beating if ours weren't.

Metreveli had said before the match : ' I would have preferred to play Taylor in the final for Roger sometimes makes mistakes. Kodes is fairly steady.'

And fairly steady he remained, far steadier than Metreveli, who produced the occasional touch of flair but was always staring down the barrel of a superior marksman.

Kodes whipped through the first set in 18 minutes, settling immediately into a rhythm of concentrated and forceful efficiency. Metreveli's serve failed at the first time of asking and then again when the set stood at 4—1 against him. It went to Kodes 6—1.

There was some drama in the confrontation, especially on Metreveli's serve. Both have an individual rite to perform. On serving, Metreveli bends over, bounces the ball, waggles his racket behind him and glances at the target. He repeats this operation in strict order depending on the concentration he requires.

While this is going on Kodes crouches at his receiving station and clenches his whole body into a motionless statue. It is rather like one of those dynamic tension exercises Mr Charles Atlas would send you through the post. Then Kodes would relax and be bouncing on his toes as the ball came over.

It was a private ritual that seemed to emphasise the privacy of this test of strength that had little room for the spectacular. The second set wavered on for an hour. Kodes's powerfully accurate return of serve, dominating in the first and third sets, was matched by Metreveli's greater adventure in the second. The Georgian took the initiative at first, breaking Kodes's serve with a cross-court winner to lead 2—0. The Czech broke back to 2—3 but Metreveli once more broke Kodes's service forcing him twice to volley into the net and stand there scowling at it.

The first, and only, real rally of the match took place in the tenth game of the second set and Metreveli's surer touch gave him set point, but he was unable to take advantage of it. Then the set moved on with service, and boringly so, to the tie breaker by which times Kodes was once more matching his strength with his former accuracy.

The Czech whipped through to lead 5—2 in a matter-of-fact way. Metreveli produced two aces from his almost depleted armoury to make it 5—3, then Kodes, serving for the match, saw the second of two match points become his when Metreveli netted a forehand.

Kodes jumped the net in traditional style, smiling for the first time and Wimbledon was ready to grant him her acclaim.

The comparative silence which attended the efforts of Kodes and Metreveli was frequently interrupted by the noise from next door where Ilie Nastase and Jimmy Connors, the No. 1 seeds, were winning their men's doubles final against the Australian veteran Neale Fraser and John Cooper.

The match went to the fifth set which Nastase and Connors won comfortably after the fierce struggle that had gone on before. The Australian pair fought back to level sets at 2—2 after being 2—1 down, Fraser standing up extremely well to the pressure not only of the match but of the traditional clowning of their opponents.

In the second game of the third set Nastase exchanged his racket for the camera of a Press photographer and urged him to take his place in the game. The cameraman bravely tried a service and although the crowd enjoyed the break Fraser seemed annoyed and was ruffled still when he lost his service in the next game.

1974   Jimmy Connors
beat Ken Rosewall
6–1 6–1 6–4

1975   Arthur Ashe
beat Jimmy Connors
6–1 6–1 5–7 6–4

Following a two-year absence Ken Rosewall and John Newcombe returned to the Wimbledon Championship and qualified to meet one another in the 1974 men's singles quarter-finals. Rosewall, now thirty-nine, beat the triple champion, Newcombe, to set up a semi-final clash with Stan Smith. The veteran Australian looked finished as Smith served for the

match at 8–6 6–4 5–4. However, back came the evergreen Rosewall and, after taking the third set in a tie-break, he won the match to reach his fourth singles final.

By comparison, his final opponent, **Jimmy Connors**, a 21-year-old from St Louis, was playing in his first centre court singles final. The Wimbledon crowd who had beckoned Drobny to victory against Rosewall in 1954 were now, twenty years later, hoping that 'The Little Master' could at last become champion. They were silenced from the start as Connors played exhilarating tennis to crush the unfortunate Rosewall for the loss of only six games.

The following year Connors himself was on the receiving end of

a final beating by a player at the height of his game. **Arthur Ashe**, the number six seed, backed up his solid game with a special plan to blunt the buoyant approach of Connors. After watching some of his opponent's matches, Ashe decided to slow-ball the champion and upset his game by chipping and slicing his returns. It worked wonders for Ashe and he won nine games in a row to lead by two sets to love (6–1 6–1).

In the third set Connors overcame his problems and raced into a 3–0 lead in the fourth. It looked as if Ashe was finished but, incredibly, he re-asserted his authority to win six of the next seven games, and became the first black men's singles champion.

It's His-and-Hers Titles for Connors and Evert
ROSEWALL ROUTED IN MEN'S FINAL, 6-1, 6-1, 6-4

WIMBLEDON UP—"I played unbelievable tennis," 21-year-old Jimmy Connors said Saturday after a 6-1, 6-1, 6-4 victory over Ken Rosewall for the men's singles title at Wimbledon. "I've never played that well before."

Connors spoke to newsmen while holding hands with his fiancee, Chris Evert. She won the women's singles title Friday, beating Olga Morozova of the Soviet Union, 6-0, 6-4.

Connors, of Belleville, Ill., and Evert, 19, of Ft. Lauderdale, Fla., will be married in November.

The victory was worth $24,000 and Connors dutifully turned the check over to his bride-to-be, who had collected $16,800 for her title.

They took the traditional first dance at the Wimbledon ball Saturday night, a dance reserved for the men's and women's singles champions. Asked after his match if they were looking forward to that dance, Connors said, "Yes and no. Yes, because we both won the championship. No, because I don't think we dance so well."

Connors paid tribute to his coach, Pancho Segura, for tips that helped him beat Rosewall. "Pancho played

Ken for about 30 years," Connors said with slight exaggeration. (Rosewall will be 40 in November and has played Segura for some 20 years, anyway.)

"'When I played Rosewall I did this,'" Jimmy quoted Segura as telling him. "'You play the same way, so you do one the same thing.'"

One bit of advice, Connors said, was to stand back at the baseline after serving and rush the net only after the third or fourth stroke. That took away one of Rosewall's best weapons, the passing shot on return of serve.

Connors brought back memories of the game's immortals—big Bill Tilden, Don Budge, Pancho Gonzales and Rod Laver—as he destroyed the rhythm of one of the sport's great shotmakers and turned the match into a rout.

"He hit every line on the court," the 5-foot-7, 142-pound Rosewall said. "He scrambled for every ball.

He made all the right moves. He never hit a soft shot.

"I am disappointed at the score. I am disappointed that I did not play better but you can't take anything away from Jimmy. His confidence kept getting stronger as the match went along. I never felt I might pull it out, as I did against John Newcombe and Stan Smith."

Connors swept through the first two sets in less than an hour, never

> 'He's a killer. The tougher the situation is, the tougher he gets. That's ... a champion'
> PANCHO SEGURA

permitting Rosewall to win a service after the deuced first game.

Connors hardly made an error as he engaged Rosewall, the master backcourt tactician, in long rallies, always hitting deeper, always producing the sharper angle and always keeping him on the defensive.

"I never was able to put good points close together," Rosewall said. "I was never able to put pressure on Jimmy because he kept pressure on me."

Dick Stockton, who lost to Con-

nors in the semifinals, said, "Playing Connors is like fighting Joe Frazier—he keeps coming at you."

Segura said Connors is the best tennis player in the world.

"He is another Rod Laver," Segura said. "He has the right mental approach and pride. He keeps steamed up all the time. He's a killer. The tougher the situation is, the tougher he gets. That's what makes a champion."

Segura said he has been coaching Connors since the youngster was 15.

"He is great at returning serve," Segura said. "He is quick at the net and his volleying today was the best I've ever seen him do.

"He has a fantastic mentality. I asked him if he wouldn't have preferred to play Stan Smith and he said, 'No, I want to play Rosewall. He beat me once.'"

Connors said his strategy was "to keep the ball in play, stay back and rally with Ken until he tired. I made the first returns to the center of the court and then began shooting for angles. I didn't care if I broke my back doing it—I was determined to go for every point."

1974   The New York Times

Arthur Ashe. The 1975 Wimbledon men's singles champion was the first black player to succeed at the highest level of the game

Before Arthur Ashe met Jimmy Connors in the South African final at Johannesburg in 1973, that match which meant so much to him, he wrote in his journal : " I have a fair right to be confident. My best strokes go to his weaknesses. My backhand is better than his forehand, so I'll play him down the line a lot, or right down the middle and refuse to give him the angles he likes. Also, because he likes to work with speed, I'll try to vary the pace on my shots. I expect to attack his second serve and lob him because his overhead is lacking. I'll hit over the ball, too."

Connors won that match 6-4, 7-6, 6-3 after Ashe had held a point for the second serve. Never anything but tidy, studious and methodical, he afterwards noted the force and accuracy of Connors' ground-strokes (" I was more impressed than I expected to be "). But he found Connors' serve "nothing special," and when at last he worked in a few lobs, he felt he could hit with him off the ground.

At Wimbledon, where Ashe at last beat him by 6-1, 6-1, 5-7, 6-4, Connors had left behind a trail of destruction on the way to the final. There had been explosions everywhere. His aggression had been like Hemingway's description of artillery : " You see the flash, then you hear the crack and at last the shell comes." Ashe, who had decided earlier in the year that he would meet him in the final, watched Connors against Raul Ramirez (" Ramirez had the right idea, but he changed his game ") and in his devastating semi-final against Roscoe Tanner (" Watching Roscoe told me how not to play him. I knew that I had to be restrained in my game "). For Ashe with the experience of South Africa and a week of close observation to draw upon, the final was an exercise in the art of taming a champion.

He approached it almost as though he was going to play Connors at chess with a strategy deeply considered and carefully rehearsed. Connors's idea of preparation for the final was to go out to one of Wimbledon's distant courts, watched by a large crowd, and practise hilariously with Nastase, who entertained himself by parodying Ashe's style. Funny, certainly, but would the business-like Mrs King have allowed Martina Navratilova and Julie Anthony, her sparring partners in the last hour before the women's final, the amusement of imitating Mrs Cawley ? " Connors didn't train for this Wimbledon like he did for his challenge matches at Las Vegas against Laver and Newcombe," said Ashe.

The beginning was important on Saturday. Connors might have exploded at the start, kicking over the chess board and breaking the pieces before Ashe could lay down the tactical lines. But he seemed to take the match too lightly. It is hard to be an odds-on favourite in an individual sport like boxing or tennis and maybe he had been too dominating in the early rounds. Or perhaps he was over confident because he had beaten Ashe in three previous matches.

He won his first service game— 40-love, slipped to 40-30 before Ashe returned a backhand into the net—but then he did not win another game until he held service for 1-3 in the first game. Ashe took charge immediately, winning his first service game comfortably.

The first break was dramatic. Connors' lash of a smash was well out, but the linesman did not call and the crowd, who had become so critical of umpiring standards in this country since that disastrous day at Bournemouth, roared and bellowed at him until he told the umpire that he had been unsighted and the point was rightly given to Ashe.

There had been a great deal of emotion before the match. The lawsuit and all the other rivalries had added to the tension and that incident enabled the partisans on both sides to show their allegiance. " Is this Wimbledon ? I have been coming here for 20 years and never heard the crowd like that before," said a Turkish journalist.

Connors played the next two points as though he was determined to be revenged on the whole pack of them, but then Ashe took command again, making everything as difficult as possible for him. The South African strategy was plain. Nothing to hit ; variations of speed ; a great deal of awkward slice, doubly effective on the dry court ; lobs in plenty (which must have been a surprise because Ashe is famous for forgetting to use the lob) ; fine bowled smashes to counter Connors's lobs ; accurate serves, particularly those kicks to the left-handers double - handed backhand, which were such a joke when Nastase counterfeited them (" Playing Roche in the semi-finals gave me the practice I needed for serving to a left hander," said Ashe) ; and—most surprising of all—brilliant volleying. He always seemed to be guessing right at the net. He was always in position to put the ball away.

This was Ashe's eleventh Wimbledon and up to now the low forehand volley has always been his glaring weakness. Laver in particular profited from it on the Centre Court, but on Saturday against another left-hander he took total command of the net. " It wasn't difficult to volley well against a guy who just hit the ball at 100 mph. If I put my racket there, it went screaming back," he said. Everything else went according to plan. The lawn tennis thinker was in total intellectual control. Hamlet had spotted Laertes, was thrusting the poisoned cup down the King's throat and winning envenomed points everywhere. Against Roche he had hesitated, but the last act was crammed with dynamic action.

As Connors struggled and Ashe ruled, the crowd became totally involved. Double faults were applauded passionately and there were so many cries from the galleries that the umpire angrily demanded silence. " Come on, Connors," shouted one man at 0-3 in the second set. " I'm trying, for Christ's sake," said the American. One romantic foreign journalist, who clearly had not been reading the gossip columns, thought he said : " I'm trying for Chrissie's sake." " He likes all that stuff with the crowd," said Ashe afterwards.

He meditated between points, shutting his eyes and sitting totally relaxed. Neither his friends nor his opponents were able to do that. Bill Riordan, Connors' manager, kept bouncing up and down in the courtside box. Donald Dell, ATP's lawyer and Ashe's agent, was in front of him, almost biting off his own right hand with anxiety, with Marty Riessen. Next to Riordan was an unidentified man, loudly applauding everything that Ashe did. Exasperated, Connors' manager asked him who he was. " I'm Arthur's personal physician," said the stranger. Mrs Connors made gestures of encouragement to the falling champion, but the second set had gone before she showed signs of coming to terms with Ashe's shrewd attack. All those coaches who criticised the double-handed backhand must have been delighted to see how Ashe exploited the vulnerabilities of the best double-handed backhand in the world on Saturday.

He could have won in straight sets. He broke Connors for 3-2 in the third then lost his service but had half a dozen points to break in other games. Connors had looked at the message of advice that he keeps in his sock, but it had not done much good. Then when Ashe was serving at 5-6 and 30-all, a pigeon flew low over the court. Was it carrying another message for Connors ? Certainly, he responded by hitting two fierce forehands to take the set. He led 3-0 in the fourth but Ashe counter-attacked immediately. " I expected him to break my serve a lot, maybe more than he did. At 0-3 in the fourth, I didn't worry too much. It was only one break against me," said Ashe.

After that the rest was comparatively silent. The odds - on favourite was lobbed, dinked, teased, passed, out-rallied and frustrated. " Today I just lost. Everyone must realise that every time I go on to court I can lose. You guys in the press have to realise that as much as anyone. He played well and did everything well today. I don't reckon I had an off day. It was just that I was playing a better Arthur Ashe. I can't pinpoint any one thing he did that put me off. His forehand was good. His forehand volley is usually his weaker side, but that was good. He returned well. He served and volleyed well. That sort of thing is pretty hard to play against. I played hard, but it was all in vain. If I could have won that fourth set I felt that I would have been in with a chance. I had a point for 4-1 and I saw the ball well but it came blistering by me. But I walked into this tournament with head high and I go out with my head high."

The last shot was a smash as Ashe hammered the ball into an empty space with Connors yards away beyond the far sideline, the first cheers coming from William Hill, the official bookmakers.

1975   The Guardian

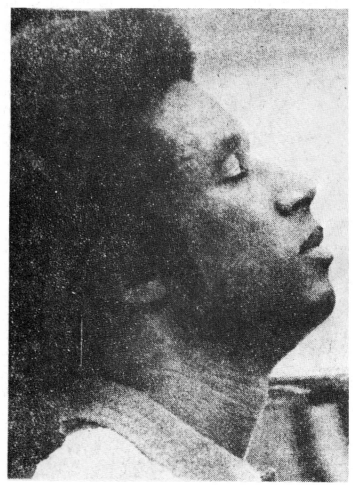

11 | Bjorn Borg – the Ice-cool Champion

1976–80

Bjorn Borg achieved a remarkable run of five successive Wimbledon men's singles title victories and a record sequence of forty-one unbeaten matches.

Bjorn Borg. The revered champion launches himself into another exciting double-backhanded shot

1976   Bjorn Borg
beat Ilie Nastase
6–4 6–2 9–7

1977   Bjorn Borg
beat Jimmy Connors
3–6 6–2 6–1 5–7 6–4

1978   Bjorn Borg
beat Jimmy Connors
6–2 6–2 6–3

1979   Bjorn Borg
beat Roscoe Tanner
6–7 6–1 3–6 6–3 6–4

1980   Bjorn Borg
beat John McEnroe
1–6 7–5 6–3 6–7 8–6

Bjorn Borg started his phenomenal run of five consecutive Wimbledon men's singles wins in 1976. From then until his defeat by John McEnroe in the 1981 final he won a record forty-one consecutive singles matches at the Championships.

Since the Challenge Round was abolished in 1922, Fred Perry had been the only player to hold the title three years running (from 1934 to 1936). Rod Laver achieved four undefeated Wimbledons but there had been a six-year gap between his second and third victories.

Borg was just 20 years and 27 days old when he lifted the Challenge cup for the first time. He was to prove to be indisputably the world's best tennis player of the time as, during his reign, all the top players were competing, there being no amateur-professional distinction. His dominance of the Championship was, therefore, remarkable. Coached by Lennart Berglin, one of Europe's leading players in the 1950s, Borg's ability and temperament were such that he

was able to stay at the top until he decided to retire.

In 1976 – three years after he had reached the quarter-finals of the boycotted Championship – he had already matured into an outstanding player and was seeded number four. His path to the final was opened up by the surprise defeats of the 1975 finalists Arthur Ashe and Jimmy Connors.

Roscoe Tanner, who had served nineteen aces against Connors, faced Borg in the semi-final but was beaten 6–4 9–8 6–4. In the other semi-final Ilie Nastase reached his second final with a straight sets win over the Mexican Raul Ramirez.

The young Swede, faced by the temperamental Nastase, displayed a coolness beyond his years. He had been troubled during the tournament by a pulled stomach muscle and Berglin had suggested that he scratched even before his match with Tanner. However, a Harley Street specialist gave him pain-killing cortisone injections which helped him through the final. He became a Wimbledon champion for the first time in true style: he had not dropped a set throughout the tournament.

In the Championships Centenary Year of 1977 one of the great Wimbledon matches of all time took place when Borg met Vitas Gerulaitis, a 22-year-old from Brooklyn, in the semi-finals. For over three hours the centre court crowd was spellbound by the magnificent tennis from the two young stars. Borg won 6–4 3–6 6–3 3–6 8–6 and afterwards his opponent said: 'I was surprised we could play to such a high standard, although I am choked that I lost.'

By comparison the other semi-final was disappointing. John Patrick McEnroe, an 18-year-old, had originally come to Wimbledon as the number one seed in the junior

tournament, held in the second week of the Championships fortnight. Meanwhile, he had qualified for the senior event and had now reached a place in the last four. It was McEnroe's first appearance on the centre court and the more experienced Connors won 6–3 6–3 4–6 6–4.

By beating Connors in the 1977 final in five sets, Borg fittingly became the men's Centenary Champion. A year later, the two players were to meet in the final again. Borg equalled Perry's hat-trick of victories with a straight-sets win against a disgruntled Connors.

For the 1979 Championships it was decided to bring Wimbledon into line with the rest of the major tournaments by introducing the tie-break at six-all and not eight-all.

For the third year in succession Borg and Connors clashed in 1979, this time in a semi-final. The result was the same and Borg proved his continued superiority over the American by losing only seven games – the same amount as in the final twelve months earlier.

Borg's surprise opponent in the final in 1979 was the 27-year-old American, Tanner. A beaten semi-finalist in 1976, Tanner had a new-look curly hairstyle which earned him the nickname from his fellow professionals of 'Bubbles'. Against Borg he played the match of his life, losing finally in the fifth set.

In an earlier round that year McEnroe, whose career had progressed with such speed as to make him the number two seed, was knocked out in the fourth round by Tim Gullikson. Ironically, McEnroe had beaten Tim's twin brother Tom on his way to their meeting, but the number two outside court – often the graveyard of top players – claimed him 6–4 6–2 6–4.

BJORN IS THE KING!

Pain-killer Borg turns on magic and kills Nasty's 'last' title dream

Kiss and be friends

AFTER the game is over. . . . All pals together when the heat's off as Borg and Nastase seal the big tennis triumph

BJORN BORG is the first Viking to conquer Wimbledon.

The 20-year-old bearded Swede, with the bright headband round his blond hair, brought off one of the Centre Court's biggest upsets by thrashing temperamental Ilie Nastase in straight sets, 6–4, 6–2, 9–7.

Borg, who had three pain-killing injections for a pulled abdominal muscle and sprayed himself with an aerosol pain-killer between games, didn't give the inconsistent Rumanian a look in.

The Swede outserved, outvolleyed and outdrove Nastase with forehand and double-gripped backhand.

POWER

And what was even more demoralising for the Rumanian was that when he desperately changed tactics and slowed down the game, hoping to break-up the power and consistency of Borg, but the Swede beat him at his own game of cuts, top-spin and half-volleys.

Nastase's tactics were disastrous. He slowed the game so much and with badly-judged volleys which often went either to the bottom of the net or over the base-line. This pat-ball style by the Rumanian made Borg look even

FRANK BUTLER on the Centre Court

better, and the Scandinavian gained more and more confidence as he swept Nastase off the court with brilliant serving, volleying and forehand drives put away to the corners.

Nastase couldn't make up his mind what to do next. He stayed back and failed. And when he went halfway to the net he ended in no-man's land.

Nastase looked a sad dejected figure. Though ten years older than Borg, he played like the boy and Borg like the man. He's 30 next month and admits that his last chance of winning Wimbledon has probably gone.

Some of the Rumanian's strokes became incredibly bad. He had produced all his old magic in the first three games. Then suddenly the magician produced rabbits from nowhere with strokes more expected from a park player.

When he led majestically at 3–0 it seemed that Nastase was about to become the only Communist citizen

this weekend to become a monarch of all he surveyed. A tennis king with a £12,500 first prize to add to estimated earnings from tournaments and contracts close to £500,000 this past year.

Winning Wimbledon would have been worth £1 million to him in the next 12 months.

He revealed his first lack of concentration when he double-faulted—his first of three—in the fourth game.

COOL

All this suited the ice-cool Viking. As Nastase tortured himself, Borg became more confident. He showed no sign of distress or pain and served aces, leaving Nastase flat-footed.

Either Borg had been given a miraculous drug or he had made a miraculous recovery. Perhaps it was all psychological. I'm sure Nastase felt he had been slightly conned.

Nastase was never in the match after Borg broke his

service and then pulled up to 3–3. The Swede broke again to lead 5–4 and, serving superbly, took the first set 6–4 in 38 minutes.

The Rumanian won the first game of the second set, but was never in front again and was subdued 6–2 in 26 minutes. Nastase now lost more concentration and seemed to have no stomach for a fight-back until Borg led 5–3.

At last he managed to break the Swede's service to make it 5–3, saving a match point, and went on to lead 6–5. But too many poor shots followed and Borg, serving brilliantly, crashed through to take the set and match 9–7 in one hour 50 minutes.

For the first time, the ice-cold Scandinavian melted and showed emotion, tossing his racket and a ball high into the air. A sad Nastase quietly jumped the net and embraced his conqueror.

Borg is the first Swede to win Wimbledon, but he is not the youngest champion. Wilfred Baddeley (1892) and Sidney Wood (1932 by default) were both 19, but I have a feeling that the Swede will come back and win again — especially as he never dropped a set in two weeks.

CALLS

Though Nastase was his temperamental self, he showed sportsmanship on several calls and was a splendid loser.

It was a good day for Sweden. Borg's manager, Lennart Bergelin won the veterans' doubles with Budge Patty.

Total Wimbledon crowd was down from 338,591 last year to 313,557—because of the heat wave.

NO HIDING PLACE — Nastase takes a breather after being crushed by Borg and the heat

MY BIG ERROR —ILIE

■ BJORN BORG said after his victory: "I knew that Nastase was very nervous in the dressing room. I saw it then and I've seen him like it in the past. But I was feeling good. I slept well.

■ "I've never played better on a fast court and although I always try to win in straight sets I have to learn to be more aggressive."

■ Sad and dejected loser Nastase, who at first refused to be interviewed, said : "I guess I used the wrong tactics. I played him from the baseline and that was a mistake. I that was a mistake.

KING'S NO QUEEN

BILLIE Jean King's ambitions to win a record number of Wimbledon titles foundered yesterday.

Partnered by Betty Stove of the Netherlands in the final of the women's doubles, she was beaten 6–1, 3–6, 7—5 by new singles champ Chris Evert and Martina Navratilova, the self-exiled Czech. So Billie Jean still shares the record of 19 wins with Elizabeth Ryan, achieved between 1914–1934.

And she may sacrifice the chance of coming back next year for another attempt.

After her defeat, 33-year-old Billie Jean said she was backing the women's threat to boycott Wimbledon next year unless they got prize-money equal to the men's.

"I won't come back if the women don't come back," she said.

Speaking of her future, she said, "I would love to see British tennis come up and I would love to coach the British."

1976   News of the World

Towards the end of the seventies the Championships witnessed bad behaviour and consistent arguing with the umpires by the likes of McEnroe, Connors and Nastase. This reached a new height during the 1980 semi-final match in which McEnroe beat Connors 6–3 3–6 6–3 6–4. McEnroe received a public warning during the match and when he went on court for the final against Borg he was booed and jeered – the first time that this had happened in the history of the Championships.

Borg, as always the perfect gentleman, obviously felt the enormous pressure of trying to win the title for a fifth year and McEnroe produced brilliant tennis to win the first set. The Swede won the next two and then came a dramatic fourth set tie-break of thirty-four points that lasted twenty minutes before McEnroe took the match into a fifth set.

Borg won the deciding set and, for a fifth time, the title. At the end of a superb contest, the centre court crowd applauded McEnroe as much

as they did the champion. There had been no tantrums and the 1980 Championship – one of the coldest on record – ended on a warm note.

For the first time an electronic eye device invented by William Carton was used that year to help line judges make their decisions. This device would obviously prove an essential part of the professional game, now that the stakes and the emotions run so high, the latter often to the extreme discomfort of linesmen and umpires.

107

The last game is played . . . the last point is won . . . and Borg is still champion.

BJORN BORG rules the world. The blond Swede proved beyond doubt yesterday that he is the greatest tennis player of them all.

He took the Wimbledon title for the second successive year, and gave Jimmy Connors a lesson in tactics.

Then Borg left the Centre Court after his 3-6, 6-2, 6-1, 5-7, 6-4 triumph and went in search of a really close shave, by getting rid of his beard.

He said: " I only grew it for this tournament because I had one when I won last year. It's very lucky for me—but I don't really like it."

Connors, seeded No. 1, had lost only two of his previous 10 games with Borg, but in the one that mattered most the Swede knew all the answers.

Borg turned, arms held high in victory to couch Lennart Bergelin at the end of the 3½ hour marathon.

For between them they worked out a plan that left Connors outthought and outrun. For once the crafty fox had beaten the fleet-footed hound.

By BRIAN MADLEY

Ice-cool Borg is really the World No.1

CLINICAL

The game contained little of the breathtaking excitement of many finals in Wimbledon's 100-year history, but for its clinical professionalism it will rank with any.

Borg's refrigerator brain saw him through after Connors had made a desperate late attempt to regain the title he won in 1974, coming back from 4-0 down in the final set to level at 4-4.

Borg admitted: " I thought the match had slipped away. If he had won the next game I would have been in big trouble."

And Connors groaned: " If I had played a tighter game at 4-4 I would probably have won, but instead I played like a klutz."

But Borg refused to panic and on the hottest day of this year's Wimbledon he remained the coolest man on the Centre Court.

Connors will look back to a point earlier in this match and remember the 45-minute nightmare that undoubtedly was his undoing.

He had won the first set in 36 minutes by breaking Borg's serve to take a 5-3 lead.

By three o'clock everything seemed to be going his way. He had not put a foot wrong and there seemed nothing Borg could do to stop him.

Then Borg switched tactics. Instead of going for winners that Connors was snapping up and zipping back, the Swede slowed the game down, concentrated on keeping the ball in play and waited for Connors to make errors.

It worked, and by 3.45 the whole match had changed, with Borg storming through the next two sets.

CLAWING

Connors lost five successive serves and won only one out of 10 games. Then he decided that if it was going to be a slow final, he would add his share to it. He took an age between each serve, stayed on the baseline, and slogged it out.

Slowly his form came back. He broke serve to take a 4-2 lead in the fourth set and eventually clinched it 7-5.

The effort of clawing back had taken too much out of the American, and Borg breezed into that 4-0 lead in the final set. He was within a point of making it 5-0, but a net cord let Connors off and gave him the inspiration for his tremendous fight back to 4-4.

But champions don't give in easily, particularly Borg—he's a born winner.

He broke back immediately to make it 5-4, then put together four of his best serves of the match to clinch the title with a love game.

Borg said: " Beating Jimmy was very important to me. I think I am now the No. 1, and that makes me very happy."

His ambition now: " To win Wimbledon three times."

Connors said: " I don't necessarily think this win makes Borg No. 1. The year is only half over and there is still Forest Hills to come.

" But you can bet I'll be here next year to try to win this title back."

1977 Sunday People

KING-AGAIN BORG —I'VE NEVER PLAYED BETTER

by ALAN HOBY

SO NOW WE KNOW beyond all argument. The world's No. 1, the unchallenged king, the super-superstar of international tennis is Sweden's Bjor Borg. In a murderous display, highlighted by a massive first serve (five aces), a crucifying double-fisted backhand cross and a surprisingly subtle slice to the loser's suspect forehand, he crushed Jimmy Connors 6–2, 6½2, 6–3.

The execution took one hour 48 minutes and as the desperate Connors' final forehand volley flashed out, Borg, knelt on the Centre Court's frayed grass clutching his hands as if in prayer! It was a "nice guy's" gesture of utter delight as he became only the second men's champion in Wimbledon's history to complete a hat-trick. The last to do it (1934-35-36), Britain's Fred Perry, was the first man on the court to congratulate the 22-year-old Swede.

The cheering lasted for minutes and was redoubled when this great, young champion received the trophy from the Duke of Kent.

The 26-year-old Connors, who had vowed to win back the title he took in 1974, could only look on with an expression which said it all.

It was one of sheer self-disgust, although he did rouse himself sufficiently when Borg held up the cup to clap—just three times !

PRESSURES

Borg said: "It was probably the best I've ever played. I wanted to win so much. I felt the pressures before and during the match."

Swigging a bottle of beer Borg, a model sportsman, said that he knew it was going to be difficult. "I knew I had to play on top of my game. To beat Jimmy you have to serve well, although he did not serve very well this time."

Borg came to Wimbledon as champion of France and Italy. Now for the third time he has won the finest crown of all. "I will now try to win the U.S. Open and the Australian titles to complete the Grand Slam," he said.

And he is just 22.

Connors said : "I had a day off. I don't know what happened. I was physically into it and eager but I never got into the match mentally."

When he was told that Borg had said he would go for the Grand Slam, Connors said : "I'll follow him to the ends of the earth. If I have to, I'll follow the son of a bitch anywhere."

SECRET

The secret of Borg's overwhelming success lay in a special 10 a.m., 45-minute practice at Hampstead. In this session, his coach, Lennart Bergelin, concentrated on Bjorn's service and volleying. "Throw the ball higher," Bergelin directed. "I don't want any double faults today."

During the match Borg did not serve a single double and only dropped his service once—in the second game when Connors had a point for 3–0.

Borg, whose volleying touch surprised the American with its firmness, then had a run of six games to take the set 6—2. It was not a Connors's collapse. It was a total eclipse.

In the second 37-minute set—the same time as the first—Connors, who had said he would "die on the court," never got anywhere near that desperate state.

Under Borg's relentless barrage—he broke two rackets—and magnificent return of service, he simply faded away.

The only time Borg was in danger came in the fourth game when Connors had three break points for 2–2. The icy Swede clawed back to deuce, staved off another break point and then left the charging American stranded with another scorching backhand cross. 3—1.

Then we began to see the muscular Borg ballet. The vicious top-spin drive, cross-court or down the line with the racket face rolling right across the ball, the disguised slice, the looped, dipping passes, the incredible reactions which would leave a cat a bad second . . . they were all there.

Breaking Connors's erratic serve again in the eighth game,

Borg left the crowd gasping with two successive aces to clinch the set 6—2 with another unstoppable two-fisted cross. He was almost home.

HEART

In the third set Connors, fighting for his life—and he has a heart as big as a tennis court—staged a brief deceptive rally when he led 2–1 after Borg had lost two break points.

Suddenly "Jimbo" had raised his tempo in a match which had been brutally fast from the first ball.

In one absorbing rally he caught Borg coming in with a beautiful forehand pass and then volleyed decisively for the game.

This was the crisis. Was the towering Borg about to falter ?

His answer was instant and lethal.

Serving ferociously and producing one exquisite drop, Borg levelled at 2—2. Seldom have I seen such severity on the smash.

The score jittered to 3—3 and one wondered if Connors could come back from the grave. But in that crucial eighth game it was Connors who double-faulted at in (his fourth) and it was Connors who failed in the crunch at 30-all.

He saved one break point at 30—40 with a service that sent the chalk flying. Deuce. Then in a rally, which had the crowd humming, Connors somehow reached yet another Borg backhand only for the American's stretching forehand to hit the lip of the net and fall back.

It was almost over. Borg held his service 5—3 and then broke devastatingly again in the ninth game when Connors, under ruthless pressure and with the score at 30—40, slammed a forehand volley wildly out.

I'VE DONE IT! Jubilant Bjorn Borg sinks to his knees as he wins the men's singles . . . and waits for the umpire — and scoreboard— to make it official.

Bjorn yesterday and for ever

HALF AN HOUR after the mighty fifth set crescendo of his fourth successive Wimbledon title, an historical feat in itself, Bjorn Borg was happy to concede that if the fates consign him to win yet more crowns, "maybe one day they will say, you have been the greatest player of all time."

Borg left no one on the Centre Court in any doubt about his current status. For two hours and twelve minutes he endured the colossal serve of Roscoe Tanner, with the ball kicking and fizzing at him nastily from the turf, before he finally probed in front for the first time.

After all the torment in the capricious wind, all the scraping and struggling against an inspired Tanner, who reacted to the Wimbledon final with one of the most carefully considered and practically correct performances of his life, Borg's backhand down the line to earn a service break at the start of the final set was his first premium shot of the match.

It meant that Tanner, after the heady delights of leading by one set, then by two sets to one, had suddenly to contend with the most authoritative player modern Wimbledon has known holding the advantage in the home straight. Tanner was not quite ready for it. But he gave his all, lunging and fighting and searching for the sneak shot that could turn this final his way again.

But the abiding memory of Borg in this final was his ability to hold on to that which was so doggedly won. Even playing a degree below his best—and surely that was against Jimmy Connors in the semi-finals—Borg had so much commitment to the task that he could sense a victory.

It came in the end, by 6-7, 6-1, 3-6, 6-3, 6-4, but not until the fifth set had taken both men to their limits.

Having shared triumph and disaster in their differing ways, Borg and the left-handed Tanner, the lawyer's son from Tennessee, were at least agreed on one fact — that the crucial point of two hours and 49 minutes of tennis came when Borg, 4-3 in front, was 15-40 behind on his serve in the fifth set.

Tanner came up to play his most reliable shot, a forehand down the line, but his desire for pin-point accuracy overcame the need for the straightforward stroke and he clipped the ball into the tramlines.

"Basically that one point was the match," said Tanner. "He was dominating it, but once it was four-all in the fifth, if I could have got there, it's anybody's match."

Borg, all concentration under his headband, now believed it was his. "In the beginning I was a little bit unlucky in the important points, but in the fourth and fifth sets I won all the important points. That made all the difference."

With Tanner's major chance gone, there were only a few important points left to play. Tanner held his serve, leaving Borg at 5-4. But now Borg, with all the massive experience of three finals behind him, had to serve for the match. "I have never been so nervous in my whole life," he said. "I almost couldn't hold my racket."

But somehow Borg did, rushing to three match points, and unbelievable luxury, with a backhand down the line. It all looked over, game, set, match, neat and tidy and a call to the Wimbledon signwriter to bring the gold paint and go to the honours board and copy the name that occupies the bottom three places.

Tanner had other ideas. "I figured I should keep trying, keep working at him, because even being down a break wasn't impossible. In the last game I just had to swing away, against Borg you can't pull in and play safe."

Tanner swung away, chiselling away match points in rapid succesion — a backhand down the line, a volley and a volley error from Borg. The Swede hung his head and said to himself that if the set went to 5-5 there was no way he would win and turn his dreams into reality.

Borg crunched in another serve. A winner. And fourth match point. A brief rally, a bad bounce to Tanner's backhand, and the ball floated out of court.

Borg sank to his knees in desperate but joyous relief. It was the opposite end to where he won against Connors last year, and if he keeps this up he will have knelt on every part of the Centre Court baselines.

It was a solidly won achievement by the 23 year old Swede, whose parents saw him pull off the unique four in a row. No wonder his mother wept at the end. No wonder Borg could not quite believe it all.

And no wonder Borg paid tribute to Tanner, saying: "This was the most difficult of my four finals, even against Connors in 1977, because here I was always behind till the last set. The way Roscoe was serving . . . It was so difficult to break his serve. That puts more pressure on you."

Tanner served with so much menace that Borg would often stand three yards behind the baseline to try to read and cope with the darting ball. Tanner produced 14 clean aces, against four by Borg, and this show of defiance gave him the first set before the Swede had settled down and worked out what he should do.

After losing the first set tie break by 7-4—there was not a single break of serve to precede the tie break—Borg prevented Tanner running away with the final with a tactical change, going to the net himself to ask more of Tanner's ground strokes.

The American, relaxing after the tension of the first set, lost the second set in 20 minutes. But he hauled himself ahead 3-0 in the third and survived three break points in the seventh game, the last of them with an ace, and closed out the set with another impressive bout of serving that must have made Borg wonder whether at this Wimbledon he had come one match too far.

Borg mistimed in the wind. He hit the wood and he missed smashes, and sometimes he looked totally dissatisfied. But he never stopped thinking and trying and with his abilities as a match player in question he came rambling back with a single break of serve in the fourth game.

The fifth set said it all, the ultimate display in conviction by Borg whose persistence at the highest level of the game is so difficult to challenge.

Tanner felt that he had at least pressed Borg enough to worry him. "I know that I bothered him today and that my strategy presented him with a few problems. It comes down to one or two points. Overall I felt it was a heck of a lot better than I have done in big matches at this tournament. Being in the final ain't all that bad."

Borg, who must have raised his unusually low heart beat of 38 during this long-haul final, has now won 28 matches in a row at Wimbledon. He needs three more next year to equal Rod Laver's feat of 31 wins.

Laver won four titles, but not in successive years. He won in 1961 and 1962, was then prevented from playing for five years because of the ban which existed on professionals. and won again in 1968 and 1969. He also won three matches in 1970. "I want to go for Laver's record" said Borg.

He has met all-comers, all types of serving, varying stylists, and players with the optimism to beat him. But he has taken care of the lot.

Yesterday was Bjorn's 8,451st first day on earth. Time and Wimbledon chose that to bequeath tennis immortality.

1979   Sunday Telegraph

BJORN BORG won his fifth successive Wimbledon men's singles title in a marathon thriller that lasted seven minutes short of four hours yesterday. The 24-year-old Swede defeated John McEnroe, the American left-hander, by 1-6, 7-5, 6-3, 6-7 (18 points to 16), 8-6. He won, incredibly, on his eighth match point with a double-handed backhand pass that left McEnroe lying on the ground near the net. Borg had made more tennis history and, as is his custom, he sank to the scorched brown turf on his own baseline and several times bowed over in an attitude of prayer.

Borg later reflected: "I gained more satisfaction from winning a match like this than from an easy one. It was the best match I have played at Wimbledon so far. I kept telling myself not to get tight or nervous. Like Connors, McEnroe never gives up until the last point. It's not going to sink in until tomorrow that I have won my fifth title. It was exhausting out there, not physically but mentally. My biggest ambition is to be remembered as the greatest player of all time and I will be coming back to try to win my sixth Wimbledon. Next week I have a Davis Cup tie against Italy, and then I go on to Toronto for a tournament there before my marriage [on July 24]. I am going out to get drunk tonight, you may be sure of that."

McEnroe observed maturely, for a 21-year-old: "I am disappointed but I tried hard and it was a good match. I can't complain for I never had a break point in the fifth. I didn't get a good hand from the crowd at the beginning, but eventually I felt a change in the attitude. But they always wanted Borg to win. You'd think that maybe after four wins he would let up and forget it. But no such thing. He hits the ball harder than ever these days and has also improved his volley, which makes him difficult to beat. Already he is one of the greatest players in history. If he wins the US Open this year it will prove that he is the greatest on all surfaces. I am surprised that he has never won it and will be even more surprised if he never does."

McEnroe, who was unfairly greeted by some booing when the players came out at 2.17 following an unexpectedly long mixed doubles final, totally redeemed himself and reconstituted his 'Superbrat' image.

As Borg lifted and kissed the golden trophy to each corner of the packed stands, waves of applause and a forest of waving arms, especially from the "promenaders" in the standing areas, showed where the heart of most of the spectators lay. But McEnroe, who had demonstrated true grit and had played throughout with hardly a scowl or a pained look, was given a tremendous ovation by the 14,000

Etched in our memories for ever: five times Wimbledon champion Bjorn Borg . . .

Report by John Ballantine
Photographs by Chris Smith

spectators who knew that they had witnessed an historic final.

It was the most exciting men's final I have seen since 1949 in terms of match points saved by McEnroe and set points lost by him in the highly dramatic fourth set. It was also distinguished by the burning quality of the magnificent strokes hit by both men in the many crises.

The actual tennis itself was patchy, especially in the first two sets. But it was developing after a very slow start almost along the lines of a major concert work by a great composer, worthy of the title "Symphony of a Thousand Points."

Borg, as nervous as a frisky thoroughbred racehorse at the start, immediately served the first of many double faults and hit two backhands into the bottom of the net. McEnroe, in an eager and ruthless mood, crushed him 6-1 in 27 minutes.

The first big crisis came in the ninth game of the second set. The American held three points to break through the champion's service and the way

he was serving himself at the time made it appear sure that if he did he would quickly take a two-set lead. But Borg, holding on by his very finger-tips, served deep to the corners and rushed to the net to volley winners. After getting through the trouble Borg levelled the score by breaking through in the 12th game to take the set 7-5.

Forty-nine minutes had now passed and the match entered a very different phase. Most of the unforced errors disappeared as both became fully tuned up. Borg won an early break in the second game of the third set and went swiftly to 4-1 despite serving his fifth and sixth double fault of that game. In the seventh game McEnroe, flat out and attacking with everything he had, again put enormous pressure on the Swede's service in an attempt to break back. He held no fewer than five break points but Borg rose again to the very heights to pull through and lead 5-2. He won the set 6-3 on service.

The final had now swung

round Borg's way. It was McEnroe, who had played two matches on Friday when the Swede was resting, who began to look a little ragged and tired although later he denied that he had suffered any loss of stamina. The absorbed crowd, used by this time to crises, were taken by surprise, even more so by the splendour of the tie-break after McEnroe had saved two match points in the tenth game. Both men seemed absolutely determined not to give an inch and from 5-5, match points to Borg and set points to McEnroe followed each other with bewildering rapidity.

Some of the rallies defied belief until Borg missed a forehand stop volley on the American's seventh set point to lose the tie-breaker 16-18. It seemed impossible for the pace and the level of play to be maintained in the fifth set and indeed, Borg served two tentative double faults before holding service in the opening game. McEnroe responded and a bitter duel evolved which ended with Borg hitting a magnificent backhander for victory in the 14th game. They played the whole four hours as if both of them had spent their lives and careers preparing for this one match. And what a match it was.

1980   The Sunday Times

12 | John McEnroe to Boris Becker

1981–85

The controversial John McEnroe won three titles during these years; Jimmy Connors won his second in eight years and the ninety-ninth singles champion was the 17-year-old Boris Becker.

John McEnroe. A controversial but highly talented Wimbledon men's singles champion

1981 John McEnroe
beat Bjorn Borg
4–6 7–6 7–6 6–4

1982 Jimmy Connors
beat John McEnroe
3–6 6–3 6–7 7–6 6–4

If **John McEnroe**'s arrival on the Wimbledon scene in 1977 had been

dramatic it was nothing compared with the furore that followed his Championship victory four years later.

In a repeat of the 1980 final pairing, he became the first player to beat Bjorn Borg at Wimbledon since 1975. Within two hours of his victory, however, the Wimbledon authorities had recommended to the International Professional Tennis Council that they fine McEnroe for his conduct during the

Championship fortnight. A figure of $5,000 was agreed but, following an appeal by McEnroe, an arbitration panel squashed the verdict, to the disgust of the British media.

The surrounding controversy led to McEnroe having the dubious distinction of being the first men's singles champion not to be offered honorary membership of the All England Lawn Tennis Club.

So the 1981 Championships (*cont.*)

MIGHTY MOUTH!

6 It was superb to see him beat his own temper 9

McEnroe ends Borg era—and walks into a £5,000 fine

JOHN McENROE ended the remarkable era of Bjorn Borg on the Centre Court yesterday by destroying the dream that the remarkable Swede could go on winning Wimbledon for ever.

The left-handed New Yorker outserved Borg to win 4—6, 7—6, 7—6, 6—4 in three hours 22 minutes—half an hour shorter than last year's epic five-set final.

It was Independence Day and the 22-year-old American was delighted to call a halt to what would have been Borg's sixth successive win. An American had not won the Wimbledon singles since 1975 when Arthur Ashe, the first black champion, beat Jimmy Connors.

Since then the Swede had not been beaten in 41 matches at Wimbledon. He fought the best he could yesterday and the second and third sets went to McEnroe on tie breakers.

On the day McEnroe deserved his victory. He fought all the way, especially in the third set when Borg led 4—1, but Mac pulled him back to 4—4 and took the set 7—6.

The big difference was in service. McEnroe was aggressive and effective, even though at times he lost concentration and served ten doubles to Borg's four. Yet he has not served better at Wimbledon the past fortnight and this was the important day.

POOR

Equally, I have never seen Borg serve so poorly in an important game. He had seemed to get his service going after winning the first set, but then it went to pieces. He served all over the place and so often into the net.

The old Borg magic was missing. And no man not even Borg, can beat as strong a player as McEnroe with those service odds.

And the weakness of the Swede's service was emphasised in the tie-breaker of the second set. Borg had had an inspired spell with his volleying and passing shots and in

FRANK BUTLER reports

Wimbledon '81

the twelfth game pulled up to 6—6. Then the tie-breaker began, McEnroe served and made it 1—0.

McEnroe trailed 0—2. Then McEnroe served and led 2—1 and then all the way up to 7—1 to take the set 7—6.

Never was it more clear that McEnroe was always superior serving. And the Swede couldn't motivate himself sufficiently to get himself set and as well as he played his two-grip backhand and showed flashes of his old magic with volleys, Mac had the edge on him.

I would say even greater than McEnroe's first Wimbledon singles title was his victory over himself. Let's face it, he has had an awful Wimbledon because of his own loutish and insulting behaviour.

Yesterday his father advised him to fight against aggro and, to young Mac's credit he controlled himself, even when he felt sure there were two wrong calls against him.

Twice he gripped his head almost in despair. In the fourth game of the fourth set he looked close to tears when he felt an injustice had been done.

It was superb to see him

win the battle against his own temper, grip both fists so tightly that they drained white and decline to abuse authority.

I am sure that, now he has digested his first Wimbledon success, he must see how foolish was his nastiness early in the championship when he not just queried calls but insulted officials.

Even the so-impassive Borg queried a couple of calls against him, but the Swede as always, was polite and accepted the umpire's verdict. That is what true sportsmanship is all about.

SNUB

As winner of the title, John McEnroe normally would be invited to become a member of the All-England Club. Now the committee could be embarrassed. If he isn't invited, he'll be the first Wimbledon champion snubbed.

Two hours after winning he was censured for his behaviour against Rod Frawley in the semi-final. The recommendation has been to fine him £5,000, bringing his total for the two weeks to £7,375—a third of his £21,600 for winning.

As a millionaire, the fines won't worry the American, but he could face a suspension if the advice is accepted by the men's international professional council which

meets in New York in September.

McEnroe would not say whether he intended returning to Wimbledon next year. But despite his victory, few sportsmen want to see a repeat of his '81 behaviour.

To his credit, John McEnroe was gracious in victory and praised the vanquished Borg, who, as always, was charming and refused to make excuses, except to criticise his own service.

Looking back on the final, it wasn't as great as last year, but it revealed how evenly the pair were matched. Mixed with some of the greatest volleying, passing forehand and backhand driving by both players, there were many mistakes.

Yet, summing up, McEnroe deserved to win. He fought back as he has never done before. He served better than any time this year and forced Borg into some of those mistakes. And despite some of the Swede's passing shots that were sheer genius, this was McEnroe's day.

McEnroe couldn't have chosen a better one—July 4—to win for America. He couldn't have beaten a better champion than Borg. Now I hope he has learned a lesson and will try to behave himself in future.

Only with such insurance would most sportsmen want him back at Wimbledon.

THE three faces of Wimbledon yesterday. OUT goes five-times champion Bjorn Borg. DOWN goes Supermouth John McEnroe . . . but not for long as he ends the era of one of the all-time tennis greats

1981 News of the World

By NIGEL CLARKE

JIMMY CONNQRS, champion in 1974, yesterday blasted the Wimbledon crown from John McEnroe's head in the longest final in the history of the championships.

It was staggering, strutting performance by the man who came back for a 3-6, 6-3, 6-7, 7-6, 6-4 victory in a battle lasting 4hr 14 min.

The emotion and excitement that Connors whipped up from a 14,000 crowd

JIMBO BLASTS BACK

MARVELLOUS moment! Jimmy Connors with the trophy he last won eight years ago.

psyched him up to such an extent that at the end he was in irresistible form, and McEnroe became a doomed, despairing figure unable to dodge Jimbo's barrage.

As Connors crowded on the pressure in a final set that crackled with tension, so the determination seemed to drain away from the troubled title-holder.

Prancing the court with fists clenched in determination and striking himself to give greater effort, Connors ruthlessly closed in for the kill.

And when he finally put McEnroe away, there was a leap of delight, the arms raised to the heavens in exultation, and a guttural yell of triumph.

Yet at one time it seemed Connors had committed Centre Court suicide as he let slip a 3-1 lead in the first set, and again when he served for the third set.

Seized

Both times McEnroe broke him so comprehensively that Jimmy seemed ready to go.

At 5—4 in the third set, Connors double-faulted twice in succession as his service seized up.

But when McEnroe had him down, he couldn't put the boot in and Connors, so courageous, strong-armed his way back into the battle again.

McEnroe, muttering and cursing to himself, was in a strangely muted mood. He was caught in no-man's land, not knowing whether to protest at

line-calls that troubled him, or turn his back and ignore them.

McEnroe needs to explode to play his brilliant tennis, needs to shout and scream to create his own adrenalin.

But, like a puppy on a too short a lead, he let his play become strangled as he choked back the emotions that run riot within him. And Connors was always the stronger man.

Connors admitted afterwards: "It was a rough ride for both of us, it was a case of kill or be killed."

But even at the end Connors made us suffer. At 5-4 and 40-love he was home and dry.

He wound up that vicious flat service and promptly double-faulted— for the thirteenth time— on match-point.

Even McEnroe allowed

himself a wry smile as he looked up at the gods and nodded. But the next point was decisive.

So Connors, in supreme style, won his first major title since the U.S. Open in 1978.

"I almost double-faulted the match away," he said. "That cost me the final against Borg in 1977.

"I know I was a very unpopular champion in 1974, but I was not thinking about the crowd and who was their favourite to win.

"You have to battle for every point against McEnroe and I was ready to fight to the death.

"Since 1974 I've had three chances to win the crown and let them all slip away. I was determined the same would not happen this time."

1982 Daily Mirror

It's double trouble for feeble Mac

By JACK STEGGLES

TIRED John McEnroe also saw his doubles title slip away in the gathering gloom of Wimbledon last night.

Reigning champion McEnroe and partner Peter Fleming were wiped off the court in just 43 minutes by Peter McNamara and Paul McNamee, who won 6-3, 6-2.

And it was hardly surprising. For McEnroe—back on the Centre Court fifty minutes after his five-set marathon against

Jimmy Connors—hardly had the strength to lift his arms.

Britain lost the chance of the first men's champion since Fred Perry in 1936, when John Lloyd was beaten in the final of mixed doubles.

He and partner Wendy Turnbull, winners of the French Open, took the first set 6-2 off Kevin Curren and Anne Smith. But they dropped the next two 3-6, 5-7.

– which were to be Borg's last – ended on a sour note.

In the magnificent semi-final match with Jimmy Connors, Borg had looked beaten for two sets but had pulled back from 0–6 4–6 to win the next three sets 6–3 6–0 6–4. (Even the ice-cool Borg was excited by this victory which he described as 'probably my greatest comeback'.) Finally, McEnroe was the one to beat Borg, but his achievement was marred by his court behaviour and his decision to

ignore the annual Champions' Ball.

A year later, the Men's International Professional Council were once again in the news when they refused Borg special entry into the Wimbledon draw. They insisted that he pre-qualified as he had not played in the minimum number of tournaments on the circuit. The five-times champion decided not to do this and retired at the early age of twenty-six.

Jimmy Connors, who had lost to Borg four times in the last five

Wimbledons, must have been delighted about the Swede's absence. He won through to meet the holder McEnroe in a left-handers' final.

There had been a lot of build-up to this encounter as both players had similarly aggressive natures, and the contest lived up to expectations. The longest final on record, it was a bracing 4 hours and 14 minutes before Connors lifted the Challenge Cup for the second time in eight years.

Jimmy Connors. His two singles victories at Wimbledon spanned eight years

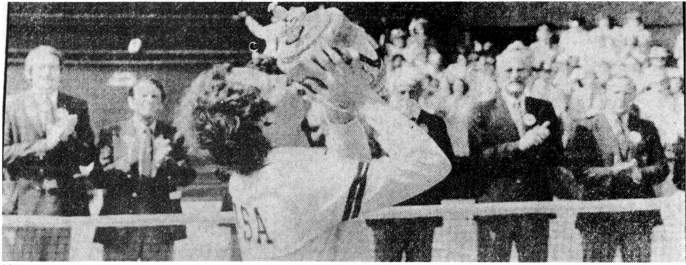

LOVING CUP . . . John McEnroe shows unrestrained, and unusual, joy at winning his second Wimbledon title.   Picture by Kenneth Saunders

David Irvine on the men's final

McEnroe's tide swamps Lewis

WIMBLEDON '83

JOHN McENROE regained the Wimbledon men's title yesterday by devastating the unseeded New Zealander Chris Lewis 6-2, 6-2, 6-2 in the most one-sided final for nine years. On a golden, sunny summer's afternoon, the last of the '83 championships, the monochrome of the tennis contrasted starkly with the technicolour of the setting.

"I lost to a player who was in another class," admitted Lewis. That summed it up precisely. The match lasted just 85 minutes, the shortest time recorded in the "open" era, and Lewis was as powerless as Canute against the incoming tide. "Even my speed around the court was useless. He made so many cold winners."

So the catalogue of non-seeded failures was increased Lewis took one more game than Wilhelm Bungert of Germany, the last to make the final in 1967, and Marty Mulligan in 1962. But he shared with his six predecessors the dubious distinction of not winning a set.

In many ways it was a predictable anti-climax to a fortnight of surprises. At the end McEnroe, who seemed more relaxed and at home than at any stage of the tournament, shed his perpetual mask of anguish to share his obvious delight with the crowd.

"I was glad I was able to win it the way people wanted me to win it," he explained later. And so say all of us. Gifts such as he possesses are rare — too rare for him to submerge them with rage.

Having already won the doubles title for the third time with Peter Fleming on Saturday — they beat the Gullikson twins 6-4, 6-3, 6-4 — McEnroe ended the championships £79,914 richer. Lewis was compensated with £33,872 but more important than the money, he said, was the confidence Wimbledon had given him. "The incentive is there now."

Lewis, certainly, had no need to feel distressed at his loss, disappointing though it was. He contributed to the best match of the championships, when he beat Kevin Curren in the semi-finals, and knew that it had taken the best player in the world to beat him. He praised McEnroe as "an artist with a racket." His efforts were worth a title too ; an artisan with the heart of a lion.

It was always evident that Lewis would have to play at least as well as he did against Curren to have any chance at all. Knowing that, McEnroe was determined to impose himself from the start. "Chris is the sort of player who, if you let him into a match, will make you work for it. I was determined to keep all over him and make him work for every point."

Whenever a rally developed, which was not too often, Lewis was usually McEnroe's match. Where McEnroe was vastly superior, however, was on serve and return of serve. In 12 service games he conceded only nine

WIMBLEDON '83, which had only one brief interruption by rain, attracted a record attendance of 363,639. The previous best figures, set in 1981 when Wimbledon ended after 12 days compared with this year's 13 — was 358,250.

points, one a double fault, and apart from one ace and a handful of service winners, McEnroe was able to return, usually with interest, everything the New Zealander threw at him.

Lewis held his opening service game to 15 and the crowd wetted their lips in anticipation. In the event their confidence and hopes were misplaced. "After that," said Lewis, "there was absolutely nothing I could do to halt the run of play." A run of 12 consecutive points, many taken with brilliant winners, took McEnroe to 3-1 and after a second break in the fifth game, the American was a set ahead after 26 minutes.

The pattern was similar in the second, despite the fact that Lewis made 70 per cent of his first serves, and as McEnroe neared his goal he was well nigh word perfect. Another scaring burst, this time 13 points on the run, took him to 4-1 in the third and the end came with a gently kissed backhand volley which Lewis had no hope of reaching.

McEnroe, with the title he previously won in 1981 back in his possession, raised his arms in salute, shook hands with first his opponent, then

the umpire, then walked back to his chair to zip away his rackets in his bag as though he had done no more than finish a satisfactory day's work at the office.

Assessing his own performance, McEnroe said he could not recall having played better in a grand slam final. "I was clear favourite and people expected me to win a one-sided match. And that's how I wanted it. As long as I kept my game together it was always going to be tough to beat me."

As to the future he must have pleased many — admirers as well as critics — when he agreed that, if he could harness his emotions, he could play still better. "I'm the sort of person who needs to get involved in what I'm doing. I can't act like Bjorn and expect to be ready for every point. Everyone has his own way of getting psyched up for points."

1983   The Guardian

1983   John McEnroe
beat Chris Lewis
6–2 6–2 6–2

1984   John McEnroe
beat Jimmy Connors
6–1 6–1 6–2

In 1983 and 1984 the winners in each of the five senior Wimbledon finals were the same both years. **John McEnroe** was the men's champion during this time and his domination of the singles was so emphatic that he lost only ten games in the six sets he won in the two consecutive finals.

His semi-final matches were, however, much closer. In 1983 he met the Czechoslovakian Ivan

Lendl who had added fire to their meeting by saying that if officials did not discipline the volatile American he would take it into his own hands. Their match was of the highest quality with McEnroe winning 7–6 6–4 6–4.

In the other half of the draw Jimmy Connors was surprisingly beaten in the fourth round on the seeds' 'graveyard' number two court. His conqueror was Kevin

YOU WEREN'T IN IT, JIMBO!

Magic Mac's title stroll

WIMBLEDON '84

JOHN McENROE, the man they love to hate, yesterday joined the list of Wimbledon " greats."

The 25-year-old left-handed world No. 1 crushed fellow American Jimmy Connors 6-1, 6-1, 6-2 to clinch his second successive Wimbledon title.

It was the prince and the pauper as odds-on favourite McEnroe lived up to his billing in sizzling style.

Mac the Magc has now picked up the title three times since almost turning Wimbledon on its head seven years ago after qualifying and reaching the semi-final only to be beaten by Connors.

But his fiery temper and controversy dogged him until this year when he promsed: "I'll let my tennis do all the talking this time. I just want to get in and get out with the title—without any problems."

In the event McEnroe was "Mr Perfection," battling his way through seven singles matches and six doubles without a warning and rarely a hint of trouble.

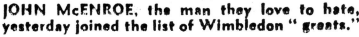

Shaking

Connors, the world No. 3, and the man who defeated him in the final two years ago, was left shaking his head in disbelief after five successive defeats at the hands of the master.

McEnroe was so much in control that it was almost as embar-

By HUGH JAMIESON

rassing for Connors as it was for unseeded Chris Lewis in last year's final.

The champ added: "I think Chris would have liked this one.

"A lot of people said that I wouldn't be able to play like that against Connors or Lendl but I proved them wrong.

"It's a good feeling to play well and keep my cool. I was determined to play it that way this time and I hope I can continue to do so but it's something I can't guarantee."

Connors never had a look-in as McEnroe reduced him to just 13 points in the opening set, 12 in the next and 14 in the last.

It was sheer humiliation for Connors ten years after he had handed out the same treatment as a cocky kid to Australian Ken Rosewall.

He was taken apart as McEnroe moved in with a deadly serve and a battery of shots that ranged from explosive ground strokes to butterfly drop shots.

And as McEnroe finished him off he said:: "I just came here to try and be the best tennis player I can. Hopefully they will see that.

Honour

"I think actions speak for themselves and it's an honour for me to be in the same category as my idols Rod Laver and Bjorn Borg."

Connors would not have stood for these indignities a couple of years ago.

But Jimbo had to admit: "I did not get a chance to jump on any of the returns. All the last fortnight I have been seeing the ball as big as a basketball, but not this time."

The length and width of McEnroe's shots from the baseline were also a major factor. Connors had few chances to get to the net but, above all, it was McEnroe's service that ruled this battle of left handers.

Chances

He hit ten aces in three short sets and against a man of Connors' agility that is a very high number.

When it was over, with Connors' sixth double fault in the final game of the match, McEnroe took the trophy and performed the nearest thing to a lap of honour of the centre court that the old place has ever seen.

He was also seen to smile. This was the year McEnroe raised his gaze from the ground

1984   The Sun

Curren who served thirty-three aces in a four-sets victory 6–3 6–7 6–3 7–6. Curren, born in Durban, South Africa but a naturalized American, reached the semi-final where he received a shock himself losing 7–6 4–6 6–7 7–6 6–8 to Chris Lewis. The 26-year-old New Zealander therefore became the first unseeded player since Wilhelm Bungert in 1967 to reach the final. Despite putting up a great fight, he was no match for McEnroe.

In 1984 McEnroe was confronted by another non-seeded player – this time in the semi-finals. Pat Cash, a 19-year-old from Melbourne, showed exciting promise as he reached the last four and he gave McEnroe a few surprises in their first singles meeting before losing 3–6 6–7 4–6 to the holder.

Connors beat Lendl in the other semi-final to set up a repeat of the 1982 final. It was Connors' sixth final and his worst, as he was crushed in three sets by a rampant McEnroe who thus gained revenge for his defeat two years earlier.

In addition to this singles success McEnroe teamed up with his friend Peter Fleming to win the doubles two years running. This made a satisfying four doubles championship wins for the American duo in six years.

Wunderbar Boris

Report by MALCOLM FOLLEY

Boy Becker blasts Curren and tears up the record book

AT 5.26 yesterday afternoon, Boris Becker threw his arms aloft, tossed back his head and released a scream that pierced the Wimbledon air. At that precise moment, Becker's life changed forever. So, too, had the world's greatest tennis championship.

Becker, 17 years and 228 days old, had fearlessly, gloriously, overwhelmed Kevin Curren 6-3, 6-7, 7-6, 6-4 in three hours 18 minutes that enabled him to rewrite 108 years of Wimbledon history. Wilfred Baddeley was 19 years and five months in 1891 when he became the youngest male winner of Wimbledon. Beside Becker, he appears almost a veteran.

The preposterously cool teenager from Leimen, West Germany, established two other records, becoming the first unseeded player to triumph since the system was introduced 58 years ago and the first German to win the men's singles.

Incredibly, Leonardi Lavalle the Mexican who won the junior boys' title on No. 1 court, is four months older than the German. It is safe to assume that other records will be imperilled by Becker before he grows much older.

Nerveless

On this same Centre Court, Curren had destroyed defending champion John McEnroe and No. 3 seed Jimmy Connors for a total loss of 13 games with some masterful serving. Yesterday, Curren's service barely bruised Becker.

For the past fortnight, we have watched with increasing admiration as the German teenager has dismantled reputation after reputation. His list of victims included three seeds before Curren, Joakim Nystrom, Tim Mayotte, and Anders Jarryd.

In each round, Becker answered questions about the depths of his temperament, but, surely, we thought, even this apparently nerveless young man would feel something in the Final. If he did, he successfully hid the fact from Curren and the 15,000 startled spectators who gathered round this famous tennis battleground.

BORIS THE GREAT! The new champion in full flight at Wimbledon yesterday. Picture: MONTY FRESCO

For the past 18 months two men have worked diligently grooming Becker for stardom. Yesterday afternoon his manager, Ion Tiriac, chain-smoked his way through the match, while his coach, Gunther Bosch, peered intently into the sunlight, watching closely for any signs that anything could be going wrong.

'Game, set, match and Guinness Book of Records to Becker!'

Control

Of course, nothing did. Tiriac, who last year agreed to pay Becker's parents 250,000 dollars a year for the next four years, in return for controlling their son's career, told me last night : 'I didn't know the kid could play a final like today. I don't believe he realises what he's done, honest-to-God, I don't. But all through this tournament when he needed a point, he came up with it.

'Every time he was under stress, in a difficult position, he was able to lift himself up and produce something, if not magic, certainly higher than his normal level.'

At times, Becker's demonstration of aggression on court, when he pumps his arms in salute at a majestic shot, or coldly stares down his opponent, has caused some eyebrows to be raised. But he argued last night: 'I'm going on the court to win and fight while I can, nothing more.'

Tiriac said: 'I am amazed about talk of his aggression. The kid is a human being, not a saint, but tennis players on court are two fighters, one is a winner, and the other, unfortunately, is the loser. The kid gets himself up with his actions, but I don't think he overdoes it.'

Becker's nerveless opening left Curren swiftly fighting a rearguard action. The teenager's return of service disarmed him almost as much as his own uncertain start. Becker was oblivious to his surroundings or the enormity of the occasion while his opponent was old enough and experienced enough to be truly affected by playing the biggest match of his life.

Curren's hang-dog look seemed only to magnify his misery, and the loss of his opening service game was the only break Becker needed to clinch the first set.

But the South African-born No. 8 seed, who recently adopted American citizenship to avoid political obstacles on the tennis circuit, doggedly took a foothold when he levelled the match at one set all, after trailing 4-2, in the tie-break.

Becker has a habit of blowing on his fingers between points, as if his racket is hot—which is precisely what it has been at Wimbledon for the past fortnight.

Ovation

The teenager's only worry centred, briefly, on the low bounce offered by the worn areas around the service boxes. There was a brief crisis for Becker when he lost his service, delivered at a breathtaking 150 mph, for the first time to trail 4-3 in the third set. His response was magnificent. He broke back with a brave, backhand cross-court pass that landed just inside the baseline.

From that moment, Becker never looked back and while he outgunned Curren by 21 aces against the American's 19, the real secret of his success was his unerring ability to play the important points better, and his magnificent returning of a much-feared service.

Boris Becker. His energy, determination and exhilaration are obvious in these two photographs of the final match

---

1985   Boris Becker
beat Kevin Curren
6–3 6–7 7–6 6–4

With John McEnroe threatening to dominate the singles in the same way as Bjorn Borg had done, the ninety-ninth men's Wimbledon Championship looked a foregone conclusion. The champion arrived in London amid his usual controversy. This time he left his girlfriend – the actress Tatum O'Neal – at home to avoid the pressure of publicity. He soon grabbed the headlines himself by complaining as early as the third round about playing on an outside court – the first time he had been asked to do so since losing on number two in 1979.

In fact he came through this match in straight sets but was then sensationally dethroned in the quarter-finals by Kevin Curren. The hard-serving, number eight seed Curren won 6–2 6–2 6–4 and then kept up his unbelievable form by beating Jimmy Connors 6–2 6–2

6–1 in the semi-final.

Curren's final place was well earned; he must have felt confident about winning the title with both Ivan Lendl and Mats Wilander – the second and fourth seeds – having lost in the other half of the draw. However, these games had opened the path for **Boris Becker**, the world's number twenty ranked player. The brilliant West German defied his teenage years by powerfully reaching the semi-finals: a meeting with Sweden's Anders Jarryd. The match was spread over two days because of rain and, following a noon start, Becker became the seventh unseeded player to reach a Wimbledon men's singles final.

Unlike his predecessors, however, Becker won the title. By beating Curren he also became the youngest-ever champion at the age of 17 years 228 days, beating Wilfred Baddeley's record that had stood since 1891.

In 1877 Spencer Gore had received the 25-guinea Challenge Cup. Becker lifted the cup 108 years later and collected a cheque for

£130,000. In addition he received £25,000 from Ebel for wearing a watch, £100,000 from Puma for using their racket and shoes, £85,000 from Ellesse for sweating into their clothing and £38,000 from BASF electronics for advertising their logo on his sleeve. These amounts will no doubt increase.

How the championships have changed since 1877! The profit from 1985 realized £5¼ million; compare this with Wimbledon's first profit of £10. But it is not all about earnings. The Wimbledon fortnight continues year after year and its success can be put down to the British public's love of sporting excellence and love of being surprised – qualities that are provided in abundance in this hugely enjoyable competitive spectacle.

1986 is a special year. The hundredth men's singles final provides a good excuse for reminiscing about the great players Wimbledon has seen, and for looking forward to the greats that are to come.

Championship Roll

MEN'S SINGLES

	CHAMPION	RUNNER UP		CHAMPION	RUNNER UP
1877	S.W. Gore	W.C. Marshall	1929	H. Cochet	J. Borotra
1878	P.F. Hadow	S.W. Gore	1930	W.T. Tilden	W.L. Allison
1879	J.T. Hartley	V.St L. Goold	1931	S.B. Wood	F.X. Shields
1880	J.T. Hartley	H.F. Lawford	1932	H.E. Vines	H.W. Austin
1881	W. Renshaw	J.T. Hartley	1933	J.H. Crawford	H.E. Vines
1882	W. Renshaw	E. Renshaw	1934	F.J. Perry	J.H. Crawford
1883	W. Renshaw	E. Renshaw	1935	F.J. Perry	G. von Cramm
1884	W. Renshaw	H.F. Lawford	1936	F.J. Perry	G. von Cramm
1885	W. Renshaw	H.F. Lawford	1937	J.D. Budge	G. von Cramm
1886	W. Renshaw	H.F. Lawford	1938	J.D. Budge	H.W. Austin
1887	H.F. Lawford	E. Renshaw	1939	R.L. Riggs	E.T. Cooke
1888	E. Renshaw	H.F. Lawford			
1889	W. Renshaw	E. Renshaw	1940-45 *Not held*		
1890	W.J. Hamilton	W. Renshaw	1946	Y. Petra	G.E. Brown
1891	W. Baddeley	J. Pim	1947	J.A. Kramer	T. Brown
1892	W. Baddeley	J. Pim	1948	R. Falkenburg	J.E. Bromwich
1893	J. Pim	W. Baddeley	1949	F.R. Schroeder	J. Drobny
1894	J. Pim	W. Baddeley	1950	J.E. Patty	F.A. Sedgman
1895	W. Baddeley	W.V. Eaves	1951	R. Savitt	K. McGregor
1896	H.S. Mahony	W. Baddeley	1952	F.A. Sedgman	J. Drobny
1897	R.F. Doherty	H.S. Mahony	1953	E.V. Seixas	K. Nielsen
1898	R.F. Doherty	H.L. Doherty	1954	J. Drobny	K.R. Rosewall
1899	R.F. Doherty	A.W. Gore	1955	M.A. Trabert	K. Nielsen
1900	R.F. Doherty	S.H. Smith	1956	L.A. Hoad	K.R. Rosewall
1901	A.W. Gore	R.F. Doherty	1957	L.A. Hoad	A.J. Cooper
1902	H.L. Doherty	A.W. Gore	1958	A.J. Cooper	N.A. Fraser
1903	H.L. Doherty	F.L. Riseley	1959	A. Olmedo	R.G. Laver
1904	H.L. Doherty	F.L. Riseley	1960	N.A. Fraser	R.G. Laver
1905	H.L. Doherty	N.E. Brookes	1961	R.G. Laver	C.R. McKinley
1906	H.L. Doherty	F.L. Riseley	1962	R.G. Laver	M.F. Mulligan
1907	N.E. Brookes	A.W. Gore	1963	C.R. McKinley	F.S. Stolle
1908	A.W. Gore	H. Roper Barrett	1964	R.S. Emerson	F.S. Stolle
1909	A.W. Gore	M.J.G. Ritchie	1965	R.S. Emerson	F.S. Stolle
1910	A.F. Wilding	A.W. Gore	1966	M. Santana	R.D. Ralston
1911	A.F. Wilding	H. Roper Barrett	1967	J.D. Newcombe	W.P. Bungert
1912	A.F. Wilding	A.W. Gore	1968	R.G. Laver	A.D. Roche
1913	A.F. Wilding	M.E. McLoughlin	1969	R.G. Laver	J.D. Newcombe
1914	N.E. Brookes	A.F. Wilding	1970	J.D. Newcombe	K.R. Rosewall
			1971	J.D. Newcombe	S.R. Smith
1915-18 *Not held*			1972	S.R. Smith	I. Nastase
			1973	J. Kodes	A. Metreveli
1919	G.L. Patterson	N.E. Brookes	1974	J.S. Connors	K.R. Rosewall
1920	W.T. Tilden	G.L. Patterson	1975	A.R. Ashe	J.S. Connors
1921	W.T. Tilden	B.I.C. Norton	1976	B. Borg	I. Nastase
			1977	B. Borg	J.S. Connors
(Challenge Round abolished)			1978	B. Borg	J.S. Connors
			1979	B. Borg	R. Tanner
1922	G.L. Patterson	R. Lycett	1980	B. Borg	J.P. McEnroe
1923	W.M. Johnston	F.T. Hunter	1981	J.P. McEnroe	B. Borg
1924	J. Borotra	R. Lacoste	1982	J.S. Connors	J.P. McEnroe
1925	R. Lacoste	J. Borotra	1983	J.P. McEnroe	C.J. Lewis
1926	J. Borotra	Howard Kinsey	1984	J.P. McEnroe	J.S. Connors
1927	H. Cochet	J. Borotra	1985	B. Becker	K. Curren
1928	R. Lacoste	H. Cochet			